MW01156529

The Event

Studies in Continental Thought

Martin Heidegger

The Event

Translated by
Richard Rojcewicz

Indiana University Press
Bloomington and Indianapolis

This book is a publication of

Indiana University Press
601 North Morton Street
Bloomington, Indiana 47404-3797 USA

iupress.indiana.edu

Telephone orders 800-842-6796
Fax orders 812-855-7931

Published in German as Martin Heidegger, *Gesamtausgabe* 71: *Das Ereignis*.
Edited by Friedrich-Wilhelm v. Herrmann

♾The paper used in this publication meets the minimum requirements of the American National Standard for Information Sciences—Permanence of Paper for Printed Library Materials, ANSI Z39.48-1992.

Manufactured in the United States of America

Library of Congress Cataloging-in-Publication Data

Heidegger, Martin, 1889–1976.
[Ereignis. English]
The event / Martin Heidegger ; translated by Richard Rojcewicz.
pages cm. — (Studies in continental thought)
Translated from German.
ISBN 978-0-253-00686-8 (cloth : alk. paper) — ISBN 978-0-253-00696-7 (electronic book) 1. Events (Philosophy) 2. Ontology. I. Rojcewicz, Richard, translator. II. Title.
B3279.H48E7413 2013
111—dc23

2012029109

1 2 3 4 5 18 17 16 15 14 13

CONTENTS

B. Δόξα

C. Anaximander

D. Western thinking
Reflexion
Da-seyn

E. Under way toward the first beginning
The preparation for the thinking of beyng in its historicality
So as to remain on the bridge

F. The first beginning

IV. The twisting free

V. The event

The vocabulary of its essence

VI. The event

VII. The event and the human being

B. Da-seyn
Time-space
Da-sein and "reflexion"
Steadfastness and disposition

C. Disposition and Da-sein
The pain of the question-worthiness of beyng

IX. The other beginning

X. Directives to the event

A. The enduring of the difference (distinction)
Experience as the pain "of" the departure

B. The thinking of the history of beyng
The enduring of the difference (distinction)
The care of the abyss
The timber trail
Thinking and the word

C. Toward a first elucidation of the basic words "Truth" (With regard to: The saying of the first beginning) The "essence" and the "essential occurrence" History and historiality

a. The "essence" and the "essential occurrence"

b. History

XI. The thinking of the history of beyng (Thinking and poetizing)

A. The experience of that which is worthy of questioning The leap The confrontation The clarification of action The knowledge of thinking

D. Thinking and knowing
Thinking and poetizing

E. Poetizing and thinking

F. The poet and the thinker

Translator's Introduction

This is a translation of Martin Heidegger's *Das Ereignis.* The German original was composed in 1941–42 and was published posthumously in 2009 as volume 71 of the author's *Gesamtausgabe* ("Complete Edition"). The book is the sixth in a series of seven reflections inaugurated by the decisive *Contributions to Philosophy (Of the Event).* At the heart of all these reflections is what Heidegger calls "the event," and the title of the present volume thus indicates its close connection to *Contributions* and its centrality to Heidegger's path of thinking.

As with the other members of the series, the current volume fits within the third division of the *Gesamtausgabe:* "Unpublished treatises: addresses—ponderings." The operative words here are "unpublished" and "ponderings." This is not a polished treatise, composed with didactic intent. It is a private pondering, never intended for publication. Thus, with regard to form, the book is replete with the partial sentences and cryptic passages that could be expected when thinkers write for themselves. Moreover, as to content, the pondering stems from a view of pondering or thinking radically at odds with the traditional understanding of these as representation in concepts. For Heidegger, our ordinary calculative, grasping (conceptual) way of thinking actually leads to thoughtlessness. Accordingly, "Today thinking must think in a startling way so as to jolt humans for the very first time into the passion of thinking" (§274). We are here privileged to look over Heidegger's shoulder as he takes up his pen in this startling way, although—in view of both form and content—no one should expect the going to be easy.

My general strategy in translating this book was the same as that employed with regard to *Contributions:* to capture in English the effect the original would have on a native speaker of German. Therefore I made no attempt to resolve the grammatical peculiarities, nor did I impose on Heidegger's terminology the extraordinary sense the ordinary words (such as "event") do eventually assume. This translation is meant to hold that sense open to readers and to invite them into the task of disclosure, but it is ultimately incumbent on the reader himself or herself to decide what that sense is.

I have kept my interpolations to a minimum, and these are always placed within brackets. Braces ({}) are reserved for remarks by the editor. I have compiled German–English and English–German glossaries for the central vocabulary of the book. Heidegger does appeal here not infrequently to Greek terms, but he almost invariably provides his own translation in the text, so I did not think a glossary of these terms necessary. As a final aid to anyone desiring to read this English version closely in conjunction with the original, the running heads indicate the *Gesamtausgabe* pagination.

Richard Rojcewicz

Forewords

καὶ τίς πρὸς ἀνδρὸς μὴ βλέποντος ἄρκεσις;
ὅς᾽ ἂν λέγωμεν πάνθ᾽ ὁρῶντα λέξομεν.

And what, from a man who cannot look, is the warrant?
Whatever we might say, we see in all that we say.
—Sophocles, *Oedipus at Colonus*, vv. 73–74

ἄρκεσις "warrant"—what he offers on a solid basis.

βλέπειν "to look"—to have a view of beings, of things and incidents. In all such matters, this man is lost. He is blind with respect to beings.

ὁρᾶν "to see"—to have an eye for "being"—destiny—the truth of beings. This seeing is the sight of the pain of experience. The capacity to suffer, up to the affliction of the complete concealment of going away.

*

This "presentation" does not describe and report; it is neither "system" nor "aphorisms." Only apparently is it a "presentation." It is an attempt at a replying word, a grounding word; the saying of the endurance; but merely a timber trail off the beaten path.

Everything since *Contributions to Philosophy (Of the Event)* to be transformed in this saying.

*

The destiny of beyng[1] *devolves upon the thinkers*

Each of the basic words says the same, the event. Their sequence is determined out of the essence of the endurance, to whose steadfastness the saying is perhaps consigned at times.

The basic words are traces which, in an unsurveyable circle around the event, lead into a domain that is beyond all nearness and is therefore unknown to every immediate representation.

Every word replies to the claim of the *turning:* that the truth of beyng essentially occurs in the beyng of truth.

---

1. Archaic form of "being" to render *das Seyn*, archaic form of *das Sein*.—Trans.

The ring of the turn indicates the twisting free of the inceptuality.

The thinking of the history of beyng grounds the abyssal ground by holding steadfast in the trueness of the beginning and thus transforming the word.

*

The dispensation of beyng in the event toward the beginning.
The junction is at once structure and compliance.
The conjuncture of beyng is the one and the other out of the junction of the beginning.

*

Not only throughout all the world
but through all of beyng
in the event
toward the beginning
but never in the beginning
thoughtfully compliantly
to think compliantly—to endure the distinction in the departure.

The presentation moves back and forth, follows the turning, and exists in the reverberation of resonance and consonance.

*

In regard to *Contributions to Philosophy (Of the Event)*

1. The presentation is in places too didactic.
2. The thinking follows the dependence (justified only didactically) on the differentiation between the "basic question" and the "guiding question" within the "question of being." This latter question is still grasped more in the style of metaphysics rather than thought in the fashion of the already conceived history of being.
3. Accordingly, even the "beginning" is still grasped as something carried out by thinkers and not in its essential unity with the event.
4. By the same token, the event still does not receive the purely inceptual essence of the abyss in which are prepared the arrival of beings and the decision regarding divinity and humanity.
   The thought of the last[2] god is still unthinkable.
5. Da-sein is indeed thought essentially out of the event, but nevertheless too unilaterally in relation to the human being.
6. The human being still not thought historially enough.

2. sometime

I. The first beginning

A. The first beginning
ΑΛΗΘΕΙΑ

cf. *The History of Beyng* {GA69}
cf. *The Overcoming of Metaphysics* {GA67}
cf. *Meditation* {GA66}
cf. *Contributions to Philosophy [Of the Event]* {GA65}
cf. Lecture on truth 1930: *On the Essence of Truth* {GA80}
cf. *Being and Time* {GA2}

cf. lecture courses:
Winter semester 1931–32: *On the Essence of Truth. Plato's Cave Allegory and Theatetus* {GA34}
Summer semester 1932: *The Beginning of Western Philosophy (Anaximander and Parmenides)* {GA35}
Winter semester 1934–35: *Hölderlin's Hymns "Germanien" and "Der Rhein"* {GA39}
Summer semester 1935: *Introduction to Metaphysics* {GA40}
Summer semester 1936: *Schelling: On the Essence of Human Freedom (1809)* {GA42}
Winter semester 1937–38: *Truth. Basic questions of Philosophy: Selected "Problems" of "Logic"* {GA45}

1. The first beginning

Ἀλήθεια essentially occurs as the beginning.
Trueness is the truth of being.
Truth is "the goddess," θεά.
Her house is well rounded, not closed, never (trembling) dissembling heart but, instead, disclosing illumination of everything. Ἀλήθεια is in the first beginning the concealed—*trueness:* the concealing preser-

vation of the cleared-open, the bestowal of the rising up, the permitting of presence. *Truth is the essence of being.*

*

Beings		*Ἀλήθεια*	(first beginning)
Being	—*Truth*		
Truth	—Being		
	Turn	*Trueness*	(other beginning)
	Event		
	Beginning		
	Distinction		
	Endurance		

"Being" already "is" in the disentanglement (and indeed essentially occurs in the indiscernible disentanglement). *The twisting free of being.*

Of course it will at first be difficult to renounce beyng out of the twisting free and at the same time to experience truth as something that "is more fully" than any cognitive interpretation of its essence allows.

2. Ἀλήθεια—ἰδέα

Disconcealment: when and where does it exist and happen? Can we ask such a question if we know that Ἀλήθεια is being itself? But ἔστιν γὰρ εἶναι. Certainly; this implies, however, that being itself essentially occurs in an originary way throughout time-place, although being cannot be pinned down by indicating a position therein.

Yet does not the question become ever unavoidable: how would ἀλήθεια be taken up and preserved? Surely it is unavoidable, but this taking up (originating essential occurrence of the human being as νοῦς) is not in the first place the grounding of Ἀλήθεια, which essentially occurs only in its proper inceptuality, i.e., only inceptually. Therefore the experience of the inceptual is decisive, and so are, moreover, the renunciation of an explanation and the localization in a place. All this merely raises questions, because we think in terms of beings and are little able to match up to being, which we, following the designation, at the same time take and seek as an "object."

But is the ἰδέα, apparentness, not then the same as ἀλήθεια? Yes and no. In it still the essence of the emergent but at the same time the inclusion of onlooking, whereby the ἰδέα itself becomes that *at which* a directing is directed. This, however, does not at once introduce anything of the "subject" and the subjective. What is essential here is only that unconcealedness comes under the yoke of the ἰδέα, i.e., the act of onlooking, whereby the onlooking does nevertheless not posit and create the ἰδέα but, instead, perceives it.

Yet this indeed seems to have been said already, in the dictum of Parmenides which refers to νοεῖν in its belonging to being. Is εἶναι not here already νοούμενον, thus ἰδέα? Precisely not; precisely that step lies far off. Instead, νοεῖν and εἶναι are named in their belonging to ἀλήθεια. And this is essentially different from the coupling of ἀλήθεια and νοῦς under the yoke of the ἰδέα.

But the ἰδέα as ἀγαθόν moves into the domain of making possible and thus of explaining—conditioning—producing—αἴτιον; αἴτιον is ἀρχή. Yet ἀρχή is not inceptually αἴτιον.

With this step toward the ἀγαθόν, being turns into a being, into the highest being of such a kind that it causes being—not into the being which is inceptually.

These are not the same: the being in the highest sense (the highest being) and that which, as pure being, is never a being and yet precisely for that reason remains the pure essential occurrence and inceptually and uniquely *"is"*—more inceptually than that ἔστιν of the εἶναι in Parmenides.

But then, and before all else, we must consider: Ἀλήθεια is the disconcealment of concealment and occurs intrinsically in the abyssal and the enigmatic. And that is not simply a barrier placed in the way of human understanding; on the contrary, the abyssal character is the essential occurrence itself—the act of beginning.

Indeed the question of the relation to Ἀλήθεια and to the beginning still remains—undetermined in the first beginning, and in the other beginning: Da-sein.

3. Errancy

is the extreme distorted essence of truth.

4. Ἀλήθεια (Plato)

In the Pseudo-platonic ὅροι (definitions):
413c6f.
Ἀλήθεια ἕξις ἐν καταφάσει καὶ ἀποφάσει· ἐπιστήμη ἀληθῶν.
Unconcealedness—comportment in affirming and denying. *"Knowledge" of* what is unconcealed.
413c4f.

Πίστις ὑπόληψις ὀρθὴ τοῦ οὕτως ἔχειν ὡς αὐτῷ φαίνεται· βεβαιότης ἤθους.
Belief, the correct anticipation that something actually is as it shows itself to someone. Stability of attitude.

5. ἕν out of οὐσία

i.e., out of the ground and as the ground.
What sort of "unity"?
Cf. Kant, unity of standing together, *Critique of Pure Reason,* B §16.
"together"—παρά.
"stand"—στάσις.
standing—
"con-stant"—ἀεί.

6. Truth and being for the Greeks (Said and unsaid)

(cf. s. s. 42, p. 34f.)[1]
The experience of being as φύσις does not contradict the thinking based on the unsaid and the *concealed.*
But οὐσία—here also already the start of the destruction of ἀλήθεια.

7. ἀ-λήθεια

In ἀλήθεια the essence of Hellenism is preserved. How should this preservation not also eventuate in the essence of the truth which such a people was allowed to experience? ἀλήθεια—the unconcealed—says that what is true is not the truth; truth as truth also, and precisely, includes the concealed or, rather, the concealment of the concealed, a concealment that allows only a certain measure of disconcealment to emerge into truth.

Here is hidden a determination of inceptual thinking, namely, that it is from the beginning prepared to acknowledge the irreconcilable and the self-excluding, in which this thinking surmises the unity of these as the ground, yet without being able to experience this in a questioning. (the essence of the ἕν!)

1. *Hölderlins Hymne "Der Ister."* Freiburg lecture course, summer semester 1942. {GA53, p. 130ff.}

In this dual essence of ἀλήθεια are to be sheltered the ὄν and μὴ ὄν and their relation; here is the ground for the ἕν—πάντα (Heraclitus B 50), the ἁρμονία ἀφανής (B 54), τὸ ἀντίξουν συμφέρον (B 8), and the σημαίνειν (B 93). All these are now thought mostly in the modern sense, in terms of consciousness, i.e., dialectically, and are thereby also misinterpreted.

8. Ἀλήθεια and "space and time"
Space and spatial representation and thought
(cf. e.g., the essence of the remembrance of *the past*)

It is said that we use spatial representations in all our thought, even with regard to the "spiritual," non-spatial domain.

In truth, we do not use the spatial, but we do not recognize only the so-called merely spatial as a darkening and deterioration of the cleared open realm—i.e., of the ecstatic character of the truth of beyng, a character that can never be grasped either through ordinary time or through the banal representation of space.

In truth, this ignorance of the essence of space and time is of course already very old and almost inceptual, for the essential occurrence of truth in its beginning had to remain ungrounded. Therefore, even in the process of explaining, place and time came into the forefront, and ever since the advent of modern metaphysics "nature" was completely detached from φύσις and was transformed into the objectivity of a mode of representation or into the so-called "biological" in the mode of representation of the equally vague and confused lived experience of the stream of life.

The unbounded twaddle of this way of representation is inadequate to the inceptual experience of beyng.

9. Ἀλήθεια and the first beginning (φύσις)

What essentially occurs in the first beginning, what is more inceptual in it, is ἀλήθεια,

Anaximander :ταὐτά—ἄπειρον

Heraclitus :φιλεῖν *κρύπτεσθαι:* this occurs more essentially than φύσις itself.

τὸ μὴ δῦνόν ποτε

Parmenides :Ἀλήθεια τὸ γὰρ αὐτό

δόξα—φύσις

And precisely this, the fact that Ἀλήθεια is the beginning, and thus the essential occurrence of being and the *most strange*, for "truth" was reinterpreted long ago (since Plato, but, through the lack of grounding in the first beginning, given as advancement).

Therefore recollection must attempt to find immediately in φύσις the first basis for the inceptuality of being and to extract φύσις once and for all from the previous misinterpretation. But here resides the danger, that φύσις for its part is now posited as the beginning and ἀλήθεια merely attributed to it. But it is Ἀλήθεια itself that is *more inceptual*.

As soon as the interpretation of φύσις is for once unfolded sufficiently, as soon as the essence of "truth" is (for the first time) brought beyond *adaequatio* back to unconcealedness as the essential occurrence of beings, as soon as φύσις and ἀλήθεια are loosened from the fetters of metaphysics, and, above all, as soon as the inceptuality of the beginning and its historicality are grasped, we could then venture to name Ἀλήθεια as the inceptual essence of the first beginning.

The result is then again the necessity of thinking φύσις on the essential ground of Ἀλήθεια in the sense of an already determined ἀλήθεια, i.e., of δόξα in the *essential sense* of appearing, *coming forth*.

Φύσις then becomes the essential origin of the ἰδέα; at the same time, however, since the saying of the essence of being has been relinquished to the ἰδέα, φύσις turns into the determination of a still nearer domain, one that is more constant and yet is changing: "nature."

10. ἀ-λήθεια

(its concealed essential occurrence is: concealment as (event))

(cf. On the beginning)

All too completely have we forgotten up to now that in ἀλήθεια the λανθάνειν, the *concealing*, is *"positive."* The α- appears to bring into the open and to make meditation on the λανθάνειν superfluous.

Thus it is in the first beginning and indeed by necessity. Why? Because the emergence, the disconcealment, *first gives the open realm*, and this latter *first* gives the excess—nevertheless φύσις. Heraclitus (cf. on Aristotle's Physics, B 1). *ἀ-λήθεια not other than being: instead, the inceptuality of the beginning.*

11. In the first beginning

Unconcealedness is experienced (φύσις).
Concealment is experienced (φύσις).

Φύσις the emerging regress, as holding constant, into presence ("being" as becoming).
The essential occurrence of φύσις, however, is ἀλήθεια.

But unconcealedness and concealment are not interrogated in their ground.

They essentially occur as the first, as ἀρχή.

Therefore the unconcealed itself must come to priority and with it that which presses forth in the domain of perception.

The unconcealed *in* perceivedness (Parmenides: ταὐτόν), the unconcealed in its visibility (ἰδέα), visibility as constancy of presence (ἐνέργεια).

At the same time: priority of beings themselves in the shift to αἰτία.

Thereby: ἀλήθεια left behind in oblivion.

12. Truth and the true

The true—means that which in each case is experienced and grounded in the unrecognized essence of the true, i.e., in the essence of truth; it is always *the same* inasmuch as it constitutes the relation to "beings" and allows tarrying in them.

Truth, on the other hand, the essential occurrence of the true, is at times, even if seldom enough, in each case different. And this being-different arises out of the riches of beyng itself.

13. Unconcealedness

is wrested from a concealment and concealedness by way of struggle. Must there be a struggle? (cf. Heraclitus: πόλεμος). According to the type and the originality in which the concealment and its belonging to beyng are questioned, and thus in which beyng itself is questioned, and according to the inceptuality of the disposition and consignment in beyng, out of which the questioning first arises, the *un*-concealedness and the essence of the "un" can also be thought.

The "un" is indeed the sign of the type of inceptual appropriation of the clearing of beyng and of the consequent interpretation and conceptual formulation.

The mere introduction of the term "unconcealedness" does not accomplish anything; attempts to think thereby "in the Greek manner" do not at all suffice to gain what is essential.

14. φύσις—ἀλήθεια—beyng

With Plato's interpretation of being as ἰδέα, the essence of ἀλήθεια is brought into undecidedness; but that, too, is a decision. Indeed it is even the decision that should be accorded the most extensive bearing in the entire course of the "history" of "truth" up to now.

Through this decision on the undecidedness—here, it immediately means undecidability—of the henceforth unavailable essential beginning of the essence of truth, there arises an "epoch" in the history of being. Being conceals its essence after its emergence in the first beginning; the concealment lets come into being—i.e., now, into "power"—the abandonment of beings by being in the form of beingness as machination. The "ἀγαθόν," the "good," "is" its essence: the "bad."

15. Ἀ-λήθεια and the open

The concept of the "open," in the context of the history of beyng, is a determination of the begun beginning, i.e., a determination of disconcealment. The open (along with its openness) is an essential character of being and can be experienced only in inceptual knowledge. Inasmuch as only historical humans dwell in a relation to the being of beings, only their perceiving, i.e., the perception taken over by humans, reaches into disconcealment. Only humans perceive an open realm. Unless the strict relation between ἀλήθεια and openness is maintained, the essence of the open, as that essence is understood within the history of beyng, can never be thought with essential legitimacy. Only in interrogating the essential occurrence of beyng does thinking attain the concept of the "open" as thus determined.

Only where this openness obtains is there "world" as structure of the steadfastly grounded open realm (truth) of beings.

A *being* is a *possible* object, something standing over and against (ἀντί), only because it stands in the open domain of being. Precisely where there is an "over and against," something more originary occurs essentially, the clearing *of the "in between."* And precisely this open domain is denied to plant, animal, and everything that merely lives. To be sure, this has happened only where beings have become objects, because at the same time the being of beings is no longer appreciated in its essence but, instead, is taken to be purely decided: precisely as the certain, what is bent back to in "reflexion," and, thus fastened down, the secured. This lack of appreciation of being is, in the mode of the oblivion of being, a proper mode of the truth of beings, a mode that all the more testifies to the essential occurrence of being, i.e., to the disconcealment of the open.

The human being—metaphysically determined—is *animal rationale,* and *ratio* is reflexive: *the human being the one "turned around"* and thus precisely turned toward beings, whereby these can only be objects.

But this "reflected one" is the modern human being. And the turning around derives from the essential occurrence and history of being itself. But the turned around in this turning around is never the essence of the mere "animal"—on the contrary, the turned around is the belonging to the beginning, and this belonging is appropriated only out of the inceptuality. Here, however, disconcealment essentially occurs as the beginning. And animality of every sort is forever excluded from all this.

(An appalling misinterpretation of *Being and Time* [*Sein und Zeit*] takes place when it is subject to the usual historiological comparison, e.g., by connecting it with Rilke's "Eighth Elegy." That elegy testifies in the strongest way to the sheer modernity of this poet, just as "The Angel" indicates his basic position in metaphysics. The human being is for Rilke "inwardness," the confined subject, the inner space in which everything is supposed to be transformed.

Moreover, his impossible interpretation of animality. What is sheer confinement in the lack of an understanding of being is taken by Rilke as the essential; what is outside of openness and closedness he takes as the open. Confinement in the surroundings he takes as a view into the open. Impossibilities and psychoanalytic thinking.)

16. Truth and beyng
(History)

How is truth unconcealedness? (cf. ΑΛΗΘΕΙΑ)[2] Because belonging to being, and being is presence as emergence.

But how is unconcealedness disconcealment? Because it belongs to the clearing, and the clearing names the more inceptual essence of beyng: the appropriating event.

How then is disconcealment history? Because the clearing of beyng fulfills the essence of history, and history arises out of the appropriating event and as such decides the essence of truth in each case and, with this decision, sustains a "time" and grounds "epochs" which essentially occur more hiddenly and are separated qua ages of "world"-history.

2. {Published in GA73}

How is history the essential occurrence of beyng? Because history first separates world and earth and lets emerge that which once gave its name to the emergence itself, φύσις, but now totters indecisively, without measure or justification, between the claim to be beings as a whole and the disavowal of that claim. (Nature as the "elemental")

17. ΑΛΗΘΕΙΑ

What being is (φύσις) is decided for the Greeks by the fact that unconcealedness belongs to being.

To be is to *emerge into the unconcealed,* and the emergent is the originating essential occurrence of the unconcealed.

Therefore visibility
therefore ἰδέα
therefore οὐσία *presence*
therefore ἐντελέχεια.

18. "Truth" and beyng

Whence, how, and why un-concealedness? Because being is φύσις and *therein* ἀλήθεια. (Conversely, what does it say about beyng that ἀλήθεια belongs to φύσις?)

Then whence, how, and why concealedness prior? What eventuates here? *Prior* to the fact that this or that being "is." Why φύσις? *Whether* such questioning appropriate?

Why do we remain inside of errancy and outside of that which should be asked here, as long as we consider only the beingness of the highest being and take as already decided the essence of the human being and the essence of truth?

Because in that way *Da-sein* is never to be known; because Dasein, however, is the first to be appropriated by beyng.

Da-sein bears the abyssal ground.

19. On the question of truth

Truth as *convenientia:* agreement of the representation with the being. How is judgment alone capable of agreement and in that way the "bearer" of truth? What is meant by "judgment"—assertion—proposition (*to address something as something*)? Whence does this arise? How originating out of Da-sein? Representation: presentification of something *as* something.

20. The moment of consolidation

When the ἰδέα consolidates ἀλήθεια. The "against what" for that.

Perhaps ἀλήθεια already drawn toward the ἰδέα—toward the γιγνωσκόμενον.

Cf. *δόξα*!—to show itself as that } in Parmenides
cf. νοεῖν— }
and *Heraclitus*?
From Anaximander nothing; the beginning obscure. Pure intimation of the abyssal character of the inceptuality.

21. ἀλήθεια—ἰδέα

How ἀλήθεια immediately restricted to the ὄν γιγνωσκόμενον and *therefore* then surpassed *by* the *ἰδέα*. ἀγαθόν, incorporated into the ὀρθότης: preliminary stage of representedness.

22. Truth and being

How are we to understand unconcealedness as a character of beings? If it is this, then to be understood only out of beings as such, i.e., out of being.

But do we know being sufficiently? Do we even sufficiently ask about its essence? We ask about beings as beings and help ourselves to an ungrounded decision on being in order to answer the question of beings.

23. ἀγαθόν

1. That which before all else makes all things fit for their presence and constancy, that which before all else is fitting (not at first "*morally,*" although from here the essence of all "morality").
2. What is proper to beings and thus itself is a being for itself—what is present and constant, ὄντως ὄν, the ground that most properly is—case in point—cause: θεῖον, *Deus, creator,* the absolute, the

unconditional; apriori—condition of possibility; "effecting"—participation in it—striving.
3. "Light"—brightness—visibility—*unconcealedness,* in the light, brightness, *eyes*—not *openness-disconcealment.*
4. The *inceptual trace,* i.e., *Parmenides.*

24. How ἀλήθεια

already at the first beginning, in accord with its belonging to φύσις, *leans* toward the side of the γιγνωσκόμενον, although the essential possibility reaches further.

The ταὐτόν of Parmenides, but the over-and-against to δόξα. Here the *appearing*! To be self-showing, to correspond in Plato ψεῦδος [*Sich-zeigen, entsprechen bei Platon* ψεῦδος]. The path to the entrenchment of the ὀρθότης. What lies in this overarching priority accorded to the private and to errancy!?

25. To say simply

1. Heraclitus—ἡ φύσις κρύπτεσθαι; cf. on Aristotle's *Physics* B, 1[3]
   φύσις—λόγος.
   λόγος and the human being.
2. Parmenides— τὸ αὐτὸ γὰρ . . .
   ἀλήθεια as goddess
   νοεῖν—λέγειν: the human being.

(on both: lecture course on Hölderlin[4] and s. s. 35[5])

3. Anaximander—here only the ἐξ—εἰς; everything back to what properly is, freely from what comes later.
4. Unconcealedness—being—beginning.

26. How ἀλήθεια

as unconcealedness *of what is present* is determined by the interpretation of being as οὐσία, i.e., previously as φύσις.

---

3. Vom Wesen und Begriff der φύσις. Aristoteles, *Physik* B 1. {In *Wegmarken,* GA9}

4. *Hölderlins Hymnen "Germanien" und "Der Rhein."* Freiburg lecture course, winter semester 1934–35. {GA39}

5. *Einführung in die Metaphysik.* Freiburg lecture course, summer semester 1935. {GA40}

ἀλήθεια grounded on presencing.

φύσις already in relation to the εἶδος and *experienced only in that way* (νοῦς—νοεῖν). ἀλήθεια already established—*otherwise* the *clearing* "of" the appropriating event. Thus in general the *first beginning*! and *thereby* still *eternal return of the same.*

27. ταὐτόν

(cf. the ταῦτα in the dictum of Anaximander)

as title of the *beginning* which lets arise. The inceptual as unfolding reintegration and thorough essential occurrence (not as identity of the meant, nor as sameness of the object, nor as a belonging together, but instead as the *inceptual,* as what precedes all and yet is not the "apriori").

Unconcealedness—most readily present in beings as things over-and-against—essentially occurring as that wherein the human being also comes to stand.

What is decisive about the beginning, however, does not reside in the fact that the essence of the human being is claimed in the sense of setting free. The essence of freedom derives from the essence of truth. This essence of "freedom," as understood inceptually and in terms of the history of beyng, first goes back behind all metaphysical questions, even those of Schelling. At the same time, it offers the possibility of experiencing inceptually the belonging to beyng and of grasping the essential and thorough penetration of the human being by the *disconcealment*—already grounded as perception in the making free—of the grasp that extends itself in the unconcealed in its own way. From there, it is once and ever again covered over and transformed through ὀρθότης, *re-praesentare,* representation.

28. ταὐτόν

is "correctly" translated as *identity* and sameness, just as ἀλήθεια is correctly "translated" as truth (even if the translation of ἀλήθεια as "unconcealedness" clarifies some issues and removes traditional misinterpretations, yet everything remains just as it was of old).

ταὐτόν—belonging together in one, specifically such that the one, out of its unity (unification), bears the belonging together and allows it to arise. Unification, however, not a subsequent piecing together but, instead, a gathering out of an inceptual gatheredness (λόγος). This gatheredness allows the *ἕν* to become and to be present (catch hold, begin), *constancy* of becoming. *Unconcealedness* (itself present, as it were) belongs to presence. (On the other hand, disconcealment already the *clearing* (event).) The ταὐτόν an ἐξ οὗ: εἰς ὅ, what allows emergence (growth, presence) and passing away (decay, absence) and itself "is" this *rising up* that goes back into itself.

29. How νοῦς—λόγος—ψυχή

come into *opposition* to ὄν and are, so to say, confirmed through an experiencing of present human beings under present things.

How, in the ψυχή (λόγον ἔχον), the relation to being and being itself are misplaced, and everything remains undecided.

The "apriori."

Neither beyng interrogated nor Da-sein experienced.

30. How to come to steadfastness now for the first time

in Da-sein out of beyng? (*Event*) Not something fabricated but, rather, a first inventive saying of the (event) of the abandonment by being (but how abandonment by being without beyng, i.e., without appropriation? Yet how this latter?); as ungrounding of truth. But grounding not "making possible"!

Ἀλήθεια—The essence of truth, not just any "truth" ungrounded; indeed forgotten; and if remembered, immediately mistaken as a question of "essence" in the sense of the indication of inconsequential, general features.

*

That the experience of the history of beyng must be infrequent, almost impossible, and quite without effect (abandonment by being); that therefore every historical experience of the truth of being presents itself in the guise of a "historiological view" which has long since been preoccupied with what is bygone; that in general "philosophy" appears as a succession of opinions of individual persons.

31. One cannot

simply and casually say "unconcealedness" instead of "truth," as if something most essential did not first have to happen in order to justify this name.

As if at issue were only a "better" or even only a "new" version of the concept of truth.

It is always more genuine to "reject" ἀλήθεια as obsolete and impossible; one does not then make a special "essence" out of an unknowable delusion.

32. The ground of the transformation of the essence of truth

The ground of the transformation of the essence of truth, the ground of the inceptual ungrounding of truth, remains concealed to all metaphysics, which never once asks about this ground.

Why must that follow from the essence of metaphysics?

The *ground* (beyng) *of the transformation* determines the essence of the open "history" of truth.

This ground as the beginning.

33. φύσις—ἀλήθεια

(cf. *Besinnung,* 185f.)[6]

Emergence as the going back into itself of the disconcealment of the concealing. Out of concealment, disconcealment. And this as a happening—and indeed the beginning itself. The purest *"the fact that"*! of the beginning.

Being and truth

φύσις ἀλήθεια

The ungrounding of ἀλήθεια—ἀλήθεια is wrested from φύσις, transferred to λόγος, and is unrecognized and forgotten as ground and as domain of clearing.

The grounding of ἀλήθεια as φύσις requires the preservation of the essence of φύσις itself beyond the first beginning.

6. *Besinnung.* {GA66, p. 135–36}

34. φύσις—the emergence that goes back into itself

The character of clearing is transformed into *presence*. And presence steps back behind the things that are present; being becomes ἰδέα.

The character of clearing *never* unfolds its event and intermediaries.

Emergence, on account of what is astonishing about it, immediately becomes *presence*, from which are distinguished coming to be and passing away.

Here what is genuine in the statement that *being* (φύσις), emergent presence, is "becoming."

"Becoming"—but already an ontological concept on the basis of beingness and beings; cf. Aristotle: *from* a "being"—to a "being."

35. Ἀλήθεια → ὁμοίωσις

How unconcealedness becomes assimilation and the latter becomes correctness—by way of essential history.

The *perverted* (the unperverted)
The inappropriate
The unassimilated
The incorrect.

While untruth is grasped as incorrectness, truth becomes correctness.

Whence the thrust of perverting—distorting.
Non-distorting, inasmuch as indeed related precisely in the Greek way to a turning-toward and φαίνεσθαι.

What eventuates here, in such a thrust, with respect to φύσις—ἀλήθεια? (*Presence*!, emergence) Emergent self-concealing, admission of the perverting, *intervention of the representing* (νοεῖν!, λέγειν!).

Heraclitus, frg. 16: τὸ μὴ δῦνόν ποτε πῶς ἄν τις λάθοι;
|
φύσις
(constantly emerging) (to stand in concealment)

Essentially the inner relation of εἶναι—ἕν and λέγειν. λόγος gatheredness as originary gathering as *remaining with oneself*—concealment as *disconcealment*. ἕν *in the manner of presence and of clearing*. Cf. thinking. (Cf. remarks pertaining to "What is Metaphysics?").

Ἀλήθεια—whether there does not remain a historiological retrospect (cf. 38/39. ms. 110f.[7]). Retrogression into the beginning is the leaping ahead on the part of what is coming as it approaches.

But whether we *begin* the *beginning*?

36. Beyng and the human being

Why are we constantly asking about the relation of the human being to being?

Why do we thus question in each case from the point of view of the human being?

Is this approach to the question not still the unsurmountable affirmation of subjectivity?

How is "the human being" taken into question in this question? Why do we not for once ask about *the relation of being to the human being*?

But how can "*we*" ask so decisively on the basis of beyng?

Or is this inversion merely afflicted with the curse of all inversions so as not to liberate into the originary but, rather, ever to ensnare in the merely supervenient?

But how to question otherwise, since indeed *we* are always the questioners—*we*?

Thus here indeed lies the decision—or being in general no longer *out of* the relation to the human being and *as* the relation? But how is that?

How the questioning arises out of a discovery and "merely" unfolds it.

37. The beyngs of beyng

No longer on the basis of representation: beings as such and as a whole, but *historically* in the clearing of the in-between (strife and encounter: the most remote decision).

---

7. *Zur Auslegung von Nietzsches II. Unzeitgemäßer Betrachtung*. Freiburg seminar, winter semester 1938–39. {GA46, p. 99ff.}

38. The first beginning

The first beginning and the inceptuality itself are experienced for the first time in the other beginning. This experience can be presented by paying heed to the dictum (Anaximander, Heraclitus, Parmenides) in which the beginning is brought to words.

This heedfulness has already experienced the disentanglement, out of the essence of which it thinks ἀλήθεια and φύσις.

It is not the case that ἀλήθεια is a "moment" of φύσις, but φύσις is an unconcealedness of disconcealment, which is an (eventful) disentanglement. (The turning in favor of being as beingness; ἀλήθεια to ὁμοίωσις). The disentanglement (as the origin of the advancement) conceals itself in unconcealedness as *disconcealment,* and this latter first integrates itself into the *emergence* (φύσις), specifically such that here already the going back is immediately concealed and the *sheer emergence* settles itself at once into *presence,* possibly into that which never goes down (τὸ μὴ δῦνον, Heraclitus).

Ἀλήθεια is the essence of being, indeed such that ἀλήθεια disentangles itself from the beginning. Following this disentanglement, being disentangles itself from ἀλήθεια, becomes φύσις, and, instead of holding sway inceptually, . . . to itself its ground in relation to νοεῖν—λέγειν (→ ἰδεῖν).

The event-related essence of the human being remains concealed. Why? As first predominance of *beings* as such, the thrust of "beingness." Humans themselves at once establish themselves in the τέχνη τῶν ὄντων. But because they are consigned to being, they must indeed satisfy being. They follow the disentanglement into the advancement and find "themselves" saved in the ἀγαθόν and in the ἰδέα.

39. The experience of the disentanglement in the first beginning (the first and the other beginning)

This *experiencing,* the most remote pain reaching into the extreme remoteness of the nearness of the inceptual, the pain of standing firm in the difference between the first and the other beginning; not the pain of the non-essence of the *first* beginning but, rather, the pain of enduring the departure in the other beginning.

The first beginning (ἀλήθεια) is ungrounded; in emerging, the beginning disentangles itself from its skein, which is itself concealed and which first appears in the experiencing of the other beginning as the unapproachably other.

The first and the other beginning are not two distinct beginnings. They are the *same*—but they are now in the in-between, which opens itself to experience as *bygone*.

By emerging as unconcealedness—disconcealment, the first beginning loosens itself from the skein in the sense that the essential occurrence of the first beginning is not turned toward the inceptuality (downgoing) but, instead, has the character of self-loosening. That is the ground of the advancement toward metaphysics. The beginning first began with the disentanglement, otherwise there would be no ἀλήθεια and thus never the possibility *of preservation*.

40. *τὸ ἕν—τὸ ταὐτόν—ἀλήθεια*

in the character of the emergent disentanglement; this is not a tearing away, because the basic essence (the event) indeed remains that which disposes. Yet this emergent disentanglement is the gathering (λόγος). That from the beginning there eventuates precisely *no grounding*, i.e., precisely disentanglement, shows itself in the fact that only the ἕν emerges and the emerging is determined as a ἕν (ἕν as a *gathering* σύν)—gatheredness—taking back in and one.

Heraclitus: which fragment is said to be the first, all-disposing? Frg. 16: τὸ μὴ δῦνον. (φύσις—ἀλήθεια—λανθάνειν).

To experience the beginning—to say the event. The essence of "thinking" out of beyng as event. With what right does this relation of being and thinking lead the way? Out of the falling toward beings—the human being; *being and thinking.* Cf. more inceptually νοεῖν—εἶναι.

41. The experience of the first beginning

1. What *the first beginning* is; what *the beginning* is; what the other one. The other beginning is the inceptuality of the unbegun (i.e., of the first beginning).
2. What *experience* is.
3. Under what *precondition* this experiencing stands.
4. That all experiencing and non-experience stand under their junction.
5. That we have long reflected on what is named here.
6. To what extent we must consider this to be first and for all: only if there is a thinking which, in the remotest remoteness, corresponds to the essence of the thinking of the first beginning can we expect to experience anything at all. Accumulated erudition does

not help us cross the deciding bridge, one which still needs to be slung. And this bridge building cannot simply be willed and carried out by a human being. Even this preparation for thinking must already be appropriated and must be safeguarded in an experience of the concealed beginning. (The experience of the bygone) Cf. frg. 18 (τὸ ἀνέλπιστον).

7. Therefore still best to begin immediately, of course with the knowledge of the (in itself ordained) provisional character of the attempt, not the hazy or half-hearted, basically sentimental, although at the same time presumptuous, admission of a sheer incapacity; this is not less importunate than the claim to know what has been thought here.

ἀλήθεια—in it disentanglement as disconcealment. How *therein* νοεῖν (νόος): the apprehending belongingness (*predilection*).

(Truth—being——humanity)

↑

Lack of a sense of plight—without the true, without the essence of truth
abandonment by being
the human being

ἀλήθεια is itself already disentanglement out of the ground of being and truth, a ground still concealed.

If being is at all to come into truth, if being is to occur essentially and truth is to occur essentially, then both must first disentangle themselves from the (ground) and thereby venture{?}.

Why then does being immediately step into relation to νοεῖν and λόγος?

42. The first beginning

is not to be reached "in itself," nor is it merely intended historiologically from an arbitrary, later standpoint.

The first beginning is recollected in thinking ahead to the other beginning.

The recollective thinking ahead is the experience of the history of beyng, an experience which itself arises out of the experience of the event as appropriated by the event.

Being itself and its essential occurrence decide here; not "we" and just anyone—we can among ourselves come to an understanding only if we are the experienced ones.

43. For the interpretation

For the *interpretation need to bring in everything* expounded about "metaphysics," beingness, objectivity, "unity," ἕν, reflexion, and negativity.

And specifically with the aim of showing that the first beginning is outside of metaphysics although becoming, at the same time, its impetus.

This relation to metaphysics, however, under the aspect of the history of being, a history which itself is to be experienced out of the inceptuality of the beginning. And this what the word is to answer.

44. Beyng is

Here the "is" is used as an absolute verb [*Zeitwort;* lit., "time-word"]. The word of time, which is how time originarily occurs as the time-space of the Daseyn-related in-between of the turning.

B. Δόξα

45. From ἀλήθεια—φύσις to the ἰδέα over δόξα

ἀλήθεια and δόξα— not as "truth" and falsity
instead
disconcealment and *appearance*— presence in the outward look.

In disconcealment as emergence lies *appearance,* the presence of the outward look, and this suggests remaining in the acceptance of the most proximate in what appears, wandering around in all of it, thus grasping it as individuated, and preserving it (τέχνη—λόγος).

Appearance—what is *more present,* and to it, in the first emergence, everything related—ἕν—gathering.

ἀλήθεια— (in the manner of the event) the claim of humans to their essence, which, like the ungrounded ἀλήθεια, also first unfolds itself only in the first beginning.

46. δόξα—gleam, shine, radiance

Emerging out of itself and yet remaining with itself—continuously radiating out from itself and yet nothing given away or lost. Gleaming—shining not only away from itself and an emergence, but also beckoning back into something dark, concealed, inaccessible.

Shining—the radiance of the self-concealing.

47. τὰ δοκοῦντα

δόξα (*beingness*)? "of beings"

Beings themselves in *their* appearance as themselves. τὸ ἐόν *beings in their beingness* in something other than themselves, an "other" which is such only in the relation to beings *in themselves.*

τὰ δοκοῦντα thus not mere semblance but, in accord with the plural, *also beings* (which in another grounding and on the basis of the certainty of the representation are the objects themselves—in Kant, *"appearances"*); it is just that being, εἶναι, for Parmenides neither objectivity nor conditionality but, instead, ἀλήθεια—ungrounded.

48. The provenance of δόξα

the first beginning

Because in the first beginning beyng and truth are ungrounded in the abyssal ground, because beyng does *not* occur *inceptually* in the mode of the transition, and because what is first in the beginning is emergence, being itself surrenders itself to appearance, δοκεῖν, beings (τὰ δοκοῦντα) are perceived accordingly, and so one δόξα then stands against the others and all their manifoldness against the one, ἕν, of pure seeming itself.

δόξα as occasioning the advancement to the ἰδέα.

To ἀλήθεια belongs the outward look in the *appearance,* which is at once an *appearance* that seems to be such *to me* and then *only* seems to be such. (cf. s. s. 35)[8]

8. *Einführung in die Metaphysik.* {GA40, p. 105ff.}

49. *ἀλήθεια—δόξα*

δοκίμως—in the manner of a seeming that is intrinsically a self-showing (ἀλήθεια—φύσις) and *thereby* (taken for itself on the basis of the respective thing that shows itself) a semblance.

All *beings*, taken for themselves, have this feature. For:

1. as beings, they are present
2. but, as present, they look as if they were merely themselves and almost being itself.

Everything that emerges enters necessarily into the essence *of δόξα*.

Why and how?

δόξα is not simply falsity but, instead, is the everyday *truth*, the necessarily *most proximate* truth.

50. *Parmenides*

δύο γνῶμαι—in each case two and various aspects, these in each case aspects without the ταὐτό—Ἀλήθεια. They in each case constitute only beings, ones versus others and thereby ever again others—alteration.

When we say, *"No being without seeming,"* what does *"being"* mean? Emergence, unconcealedness, self-showing. Only this, as seeming (shining), bestows the possibility of semblance Cf. s. s. 35.[9] *Being —seeming.*

ἄκριτα—undecided, not to be able to distinguish *beings and non-beings*, because not within the difference between *being and beings*, ἀλήθεια and δόξα. δόξα—more inceptually as what comes forth in the most proximate clearing.

κρίσις—the *reckoning that distinguishes*. To distinguish—not formally; instead, according to the truth. Here Ἀλήθεια itself as essence of the ἐόν qua εἶναι. δόξα as essence of the ἐόν qua δοκοῦντα.

Ἀλήθεια—θεά

δόξα βροτῶν—i.e., beings, as they appear, when perceived from themselves by a mortal with no θυμός for Ἀλήθεια (not appropriated and therefore blind to beingness and to what beingness is; whether and how beingness is the *same* as νοεῖν on the ground of Ἀλήθεια).

δίζησις—*seeking*, to search thoroughly for what emerges (Ἀλήθεια). κρίσις and the *ways*. The one who goes along the way—as *sojourn*—in each case with σήματα, with what shows itself (and at the same time conceals itself).

9. *Ibid.*

To what extent does (ungrounded) Ἀλήθεια require a relation to νοεῖν εἶναι, to λέγειν, κρίνειν? Like the relation between Ἀλήθεια and ὁδός—way *to* Ἀλήθεια, ways *in it, "its" way. The essence of the way.* (In connection with the Parmenides interpretation of 1932,[10] the work authored by Otfrid Becker arose, but insufficient because Ἀλήθεια and εἶναι not actually *experienced.*)

Ἀλήθεια and errancy cf. truth-lecture of 1930.[11]

ἀλήθεια —being ⟩ the difference
δόξα —beings ⟩

The moon—not itself luminous—can emerge, but borrowed light. In the same way δόξα: self-showing only under the precedence of ἀλήθεια.

51. δόξα

Ἀλήθεια distinguished against δόξα. How?

But now ἀλήθεια as unconcealedness the essential occurrence of being—presence.

Thus also δόξα as the essence of the δοκοῦντα—presence in what is closest on the basis of beings.

How then νόος? Here the difference between pure νοεῖν, which is the *same* as εἶναι, and human νόος. The latter *vacillating and malleable.*

δόξα is not discussed as to its content; instead, its essence, which pertains to Ἀλήθεια, is determined as a necessary mode of presence.

52. δόξα and τὰ δοκοῦντα

What appears, what comes to presence, but taken precisely as such: as such, i.e., only as it stands *with respect to* humans and their usual apprehending and determining.

ἐοικότα 8, 60—what appears? The appearance itself is not mere seeming, but is a coming to presence, yet in such a way as if it essentially occurred without presence and thus let itself be scattered in the wandering perception of mortals.

δόξα thus becomes a prey of mortals, and they dispose of it, i.e., δόξα βροτεία 8, 51.

---

10. *Der Anfang der abendländischen Philosophie (Anaximander und Parmenides).* Freiburg lecture course, summer semester 1932. {GA35}

11. Vom Wesen der Wahrheit. {In GA80; reworked version in *Wegmarken,* GA9}

Nevertheless, δόξα is not *made* by the human being; instead, it is only *misunderstood* by the human being. It is taken for presence itself, which it also is and yet is not. δόξα not without further ado already something "mortal"-human. *δόξα* is the presence of what comes to presence, the self-abandoning *emergence,* which dominates and penetrates everything present, taken as such.

δόξα is φύσις. (but ἀλήθεια the *essence* of φύσις). *κατὰ δόξαν ἔφυ,* frg. 19.

53. γίνεσθαι—ὄλλυσθαι
(Parmenides 8, 12; 8, 27)

Coming forth and passing away—not possible determinations and essential grounds of presence released for themselves; on the contrary, just the reverse: they are *withheld* through the junction in the essence of presence. In presence, coming forth and passing away are *waxing;* waning then is the coming to presence of δόξα.

γένεσις—ὄλεθρος as *autonomous determinations* are driven off far away *into what comes to presence.*

The falling apart—the dispersal of the gathering, of the unicity of presence.

C. Anaximander

Cf. s. s. 41, pp. 20–32.[12]
Cf. "Der Spruch des Parmenides," June 1940.[13]

54. If the ἄπειρον of Anaximander were ἀλήθεια?

Then πέρας would have to coincide with λήθη. All delimitation (*restriction*) (in the Greek experience: confinement) would then be (a locking up, obstructing: *setting before of confines*) "concealment."

Concealment and concealedness precisely as constraint within confines, on account of which what is present could never place itself purely in the open realm of its presence. πέρας the termination, enclosure, encompassment, confinement, restriction, and specifically

12. *Grundbegriffe.* Freiburg lecture course, summer semester 1941. {GA51, p. 94ff.}
13. Lecture to the Freiburger Kränzschen, June 1940. {In GA80}

with regard to φύσις, entrenchment in the seeming which is individualized in each case and separated out from φύσις.

τὸ ἄπειρον—the repudiation[14] of limits (is starting point and mastery for the respective present thing).

ἀρχή: "starting point"—allows going out, sets free (insofar as it itself is the unobstructed open realm, essentially disconcealment.) Starting point as opening up prevails in advance over the open realm as the domain of presence.

Inceptually the α-; cf. *ἀ-λήθεια*. The "un" (without . . . , against, but not necessarily *negative*!) has the basic character of ἀρχή: starting point, mastery, *setting free*. Only what is open for, and thereby already prevails, can set free.

ἀλήθεια is not sheer openness and nothing else, but is α-, related to λήθη. This latter essentially occurs, but its essential occurrence is named only mediately in the first beginning.

55. The transition

γένεσις and φθορά and ἀλήθεια are characteristic of *what is present*, because this, as something present, is consigned to the essence (beings pertain to being, and what emerges in beings derives from being).

What is present comes to presence in a coming forth and a going away. Even φθορά is γίνεσθαι: coming forth, a kind of φύσις, *emergence—disappearance—going down*. The quintessence of γένεσις as φύσις is transition, the unity of coming forth and passing away, and the latter essentially occurs in the *same*, in *ἀλήθεια*, because ἀλήθεια is conjointly and essentially concealment—withdrawal into concealing. This transition is the presencing which, however, now remains precisely hidden in favor of the *presence* of that which is present, that which is beaten into limits and as such is then pursued and dispelled in change.

The *transition* will not be involved in the entrenchment of what comes to presence. The transition *preserves* the ἄπειρον. Presence is transitionally the gathered-gathering peak of φύσις, i.e., of unconcealedness. Presence *must* be experienced *aletheiologically* and *not* metaphysically in terms of the constant and the objectively present. Then it becomes clear that "being" pervades not the factor of duration of objective presence but, rather, the unique gatheredness of the

14. Reading *Verwehrung* for *Verwahrung* ("preservation"), as occurs in the following pages and also in the parallel passage from *Grundbegriffe* (GA51, §23). —Trans.

emerging-perishing disconcealment. (Cf. the interpretation of what it means to remain)

56. *τὸ πέρας—τὸ ἄπειρον*

τὸ πέρας — the end, the last, the limit, that at which something stops, that whereby something is restricted to what it is. Restriction as enclosure in the current appearance. Restriction as highest and fulfilled exerting force. Restriction in the Greek sense as confinement within boundaries, ones which simultaneously merely let the restricted thing be seen and also delimit it against other ones, and

— conceal it in its belongingness to them. Restriction a sort of concealment, especially if seen in terms of the pure presence of that which comes to presence, rather than in terms of the respective "this" in its individuation.

τὸ ἄπειρον — that which dis-confines, holds off boundaries and restriction, because itself unaware of these as what pure emergence itself is.

Dis-confinement—disconcealment—
the non-*forceful*— the *whence* of *emerging*
the *whither back* and *passing away*
(of presence) (of being)
these themselves *in the plural* ἐξ—εἰς ταῦτα

the essential occurrence of presence
ἀλήθεια

τὸ χρεών the compelling need, the purely and simply necessary, said in relation to the whence and whither of presence and absence.

57. *ἀδικία*

Failing—or allowing a failure—in what is fitting, through preoccupation with the mere appearances of individual things, things which everywhere are released into dispersion, out of which results a manifold that only subsequently gains in each case the appearance of a "unity" in which what appears is at the same time both this and not this.

ἀδικία is non-compliance with unconcealedness; it is persistence in the current appearance of what has come forth (δόξα).

58. In the dictum of Anaximander

the word ἀλήθεια is not uttered, but ἀλήθεια is experienced as the whither of the coming forth and the whence of the passing away. The whither and whence: *presence,* but presence as transition, i.e., as dis-concealment *and* concealment (cf. s. s. 41, p. 32).[15]

Ἀλήθεια is without a beginning to a greater extent than is φύσις.

59. The utterance of being

in the first beginning of Western thinking. The oldest dictum handed down is attributed to *Anaximandros* (c. 610–540). It says:

> ἐξ ὧν δὲ ἡ γένεσις ἐστι τοῖς οὖσι, καὶ τὴν φθορὰν εἰς ταῦτα γίνεσθαι κατὰ τὸ χρεών· διδόναι γὰρ αὐτὰ δίκην καὶ τίσιν ἀλλήλοις τῆς ἀδικίας κατὰ τὴν τοῦ χρόνου τάξιν.

"From out of which, however, the coming forth is to the respective present things there also comes forth the passing away into this (as the same) in accord with compelling need; it, namely each present thing itself (out of itself), gives what is fitting and also allows honor (approval), the one to the other, (all this) out of the twisting free of what is not fitting, in accord with the assignment of the ripening through time."

ἀρχὴ τῶν ὄντων τὸ ἄπειρον

"What provides for anything to come to presence is the repudiation[16] of limits."

Preparation for the interpretation of Anaximander: (briefly mentioned, s. s. 41. Recapitulation 10; the interpretation *ibid.* p. 20ff.).[17]

Language
The past
The matter at issue
History
The relation to the beginning
The steadfastness in being
out of the overcoming of metaphysics.

---

15. *Grundbegriffe.* {GA51, p. 116}

16. Reading *Verwehrung* for *Verwahrung.*—Trans.

17. *Grundbegriffe.* {GA51, p. 94ff.}

Constancy — here fully conceived as persisting in (insisting on) the permanence of presence in the enduring present.
The later determination of beingness in the sense of the ἀεί, continuance, but also in the sense of *aeternitas* as *nunc stans*, is the truth (posited in itself) of beings, which commences with that toward which the inceptually conceived constancy is in strife.

Constancy — does not come into being (presence) from the outside, however; it belongs to the essence of being as what is counter to being and as its distorted essence; for permanence strives throughout everything that comes to presence; why?
And whence at all the distorted essence in the essence? Whence and how essence?

ἄπειρον — in what way the repudiation of limits is preponderant and therein the transition is victorious.
The transition of coming forth into the coming forth of passing away as the extremity of presence.
How in the transition as such all continuance is without essence.

πέρας — limit in the sense of the ending of the transition (and that means the ending of the coming forth and of the passing away).
The ending as the final end, the finality of continuance.

"ἄπειρον" — what is essential to the ἄπειρον does not lie in *immateriality* and thus not in the distinction between the material and the immaterial. That would indeed only be a distinction within beings and in particular a distinction that adheres to the material and proceeds from it. What is decisive is that being is differentiated from beings. And this differentiation is already a consequence of thinking into being.
This inceptuality lies in the ἄπειρον. But later, and indeed immediately, *limit* (πέρας—τέλος) becomes the characteristic determination of beingness. The two are not "contradictory"; more precisely: the desire to uncover a contradiction here, something that, in accord with this interpretation of the ἄπειρον, is suggested by considering the essence of the εἶδος (μορφή), would mean the desire to constrain the concealed history of being into the rules for thinking about formal objects.

But it would be no less erroneous to interpret the ἄπειρον and ταῦτα in the sense of a pre-Platonic Platonism and grasp them as what remains, over and against γένεσις and φθορά. In view of the strangeness of every beginning, it is no wonder that the greatest misinterpretation intrudes precisely at the beginning, and the *material* (or, which is no better, the immaterial) is raised to a "principle."

The unexpressed φύσις. Emergence, transition; disconcealment; reverting back to oneself. Provision, inclusion (gathering, λόγος—unity, ἕν). (*Nowhere* "becoming," and therefore also not "being" in the sense of constancy). Here still no possibility of metaphysics.

*

To what extent it can be presumed that all interpretations of the dictum that are suggestive of anything that comes later are already erroneous, since such an interpretation does not acknowledge the strangeness of the beginning.

*

That here at least the trace of an anthropomorphizing of being, if such should be possible at all. Anthropomorphizing can perhaps befall beings (God, world), but even there it is always to be asked how "the anthropos" is experienced.

The basic faring [Grund-erfahrnis]

"Basis" (cf. Lecture course s. s. 1941) "basic concepts."

The basic faring 1. *Faring* [Fährnis] (projection)
constantly endangering
2. *Experience*
not mere taking cognizance,
instead, making one's own

To what extent the basic faring is disconcealment (being) as repudiation of limits and thus ἀδικία! Beings as *twisted free* in the essence of beyng (ἄπειρον), but nevertheless essentially *dismissed.*

*

How in the dictum is hidden
φύσις-ἀλήθεια?
How the intimation of *the* inceptual, the concealment?

*

How being is *infinitely* distinct from beings and yet not χωρισμός

moreover, not uniformity;
instead?

*

How the words of Anaximander say φύσις in its most concealed essence without naming it.

The dictum of Anaximander

does not express any experience of many or some
but is instead the projection of a single one.

The dictum does not bear out a dominant view.

The dictum does not express something self-evident.

It does not *justify* itself through correspondence with the usual view.

The essence of its truth is strange in every way.

D. Western *thinking*
Reflexion
Da-seyn

60. Thoughtful thinking and the "concept"

The name seems to say that this thinking is an intensified, heightened, "more energetic" thinking, one which takes hold of itself by force and brings itself forward with force, i.e., forceful thinking. Certainly more concentrated, but for that very reason less forceful; indeed in its purity it is without force.

On the contrary, it is ordinary thinking which is *pressing*, calculating, planning, *ingenious, restless*—a matter of *lurking, assaulting, mastering.*

Otherwise with thoughtful thinking (thanking). The diffidence of distinguishing; the diffidence of experiencing the uncanny. Hardly a representation in the sense of a *bringing* before oneself.

In the modern age, through calculative thinking we have long ago become accustomed to seeing in thinking, and demanding from thinking, grip [*Zugriff*], grasp [*Griff*], and concept [*Begriff*], i.e., we understand the "concept" on the basis of a grasping: *conceptus*—no longer ὁρισμός.

We know rigorous thinking only as *conceptual* representation. But its rigor rests in the originariness of imageless *saying* in the compliant word that inheres in the essence of truth.

The invasion of the uncanny in the sudden.

61. Why nothing "comes forth" in "thinking" (as "philosophy")

It is because the thinking of the thinkers thinks only of what has already "come forth" and thus of what constantly occurs by essence *in that which has already come forth,* prior to all results and all productivity. The "coming forth" itself is Ἀλήθεια, being.

"With" this thinking nothing ever comes forth *incidentally,* to which one could then pass "over"; instead, thinking is the preservation of the "coming forth."

Thoughtful thinking does not lurk for the coming forth of a result, because it enters into that from which all coming forth proceeds—Ἀλήθεια.

62. The beginning of Western thinking

This title does at first hardly require extended commentary, since we can easily circumscribe it and thus allow what is meant to present itself ever more clearly. Instead of "The beginning of Western thinking," we could also say: The inception of the philosophy which arose in the West and has been found there ever since. For, "this thinking" = philosophizing—φιλοσοφεῖν. Hence the expression "thinking" obviously names not just any sort of thinking but, instead, the thinking of "the thinkers," the ones also called "philosophers." The Greek word φιλοσοφεῖν is the standard term for those who think in a preeminent sense. The term indicates that sometime in Greek antiquity the standard and the law were given for the essence and historical course of subsequent thoughtful thinking.

Yet of what sort is this that is called "thinking" in an emphatic sense? In what does thoughtful thinking distinguish itself from ordinary thinking? What in general is thinking? We must be clear about all that if we are to experience "the beginning of Western thinking" with any understanding.

But if we now attempt to think back to the start of Western philosophy, then misgivings immediately arise, provided we do not enter into the project with our eyes closed. Going back to the start of Western philosophy, assuming such is at all possible, may certainly yield some use inasmuch as knowledge of the start can show whence and how each of the philosophers has developed. We could thereby calculate, at least approximately, the presuppositions, influences, and developmental conditions of the later and especially of the more recent philosophy.

Yet what would be the point of all that? To collect information *about* the great philosophers—that simply means to reflect on a former way of thinking instead of thinking for oneself out of, and on behalf of, the present time.

But to mark out and adhere to *one* especially striking philosophy out of the previous instances: Plato, Leibniz, Kant, Hegel, Nietzsche, as a mixture of all or some—yet, even so, only a thinking *about thinking*—and *not* itself a thinking; merely flight into historiology—instead of thinking immediately out of, and on behalf of, the present time.

This makes everything clear, such that with a hasty resolve we abandon historiology and at least demand, in case we cannot carry it out ourselves, that thinking arise out of, and on behalf of, the present time and replace historiological discussions of antiquated things.

63. To think about thinking

In preparing to answer this question, we find ourselves unexpectedly in a position that makes us wonder. We are thinking about thinking. Those who live naturally and straightforwardly do think as well, even if it is something pressing that they think about, think over, and think through. We draw help from thinking, like a kind of tool there for us to wield. (Hammer—to clinch the nail; so likewise with thinking and that which we *represent*. That is in order.) But what if we think about thinking; it looks like an attempt to hammer the hammer. That is not in order, at least not as regards one and the same hammer: it is not to be hammered with itself.

If a hammer were hammered, and actually is hammered, that could be only with the help of a second one. If, e.g., the handle has loosened, we hammer it back on so that the hammer is again in proper working condition. To hammer the hammer, to think about thinking—not again and again, but precisely only on occasion, to keep the tool *in good repair.* Hammering as hammering of things. So also thinking of objects. To think about thinking to keep it in good repair. *If thinking is no longer "capable" of thinking,* then putting it back into good condition. (On the contrary, peculiar; if only "about"—namely, such thinking both *twisted* and deranged ("reflexive"), egocentric, to trap unnaturally.) But in our case, not about thinking but, rather, to distinguish various modes and to clarify the essence of the preeminent sort of thinking. To *distinguish* one thinking from another. These at hand, lying before? like hammer, pliers? So indeed here also (psychology of thinking) into the ordinary and philosophical thinking. Here we have already made a distinction. Nevertheless—who tells us that thinking is something thoughtful—*Kant,* e.g.? Certainly; but what is *philosophical,* and what is ordinary? The philosophical is unusual, offers no help, (to have already distinguished. To distinguish!: thinking! not only not lying before, but also not tool, but instead? Faculty and activity (acts of thought), comportment—*"being."*) To think about thinking—not reflexive, *inward*-turning, but thinking out—fantasy.

Thinking—poetizing: the *word*—the same and yet precisely not. Philosophy—Dasein (thinking).

64. The beginning of thinking

1. Beginning as commencement and start.
2. Beginning as *that which* thinking (thanking—poetizing) has to think.
3. What is to be thought as the essential ground of thinking.
4. Thoughtful thinking thinks only the beginning (the true and truth, the *essence* of truth).
5. The beginning itself—what is making a beginning—the law of the beginning, the first beginning—the other beginning.
   The beginning—beginning of emergence—Ἀλήθεια.
   Inceptual thinking (cf. conclusion of 42–3).[18]

65. Philosophy—thinking—being

Under what conditions is "philosophy" a "being" [*ein "Sein"*] in the sense of the essential belonging of the historical human ("Da-sein") to the truth of being?

How does this "being" as thinking not require a "result" (which "comes forth" only afterwards)? (1. because "results" not at all essential; 2. because "being" prior to all productivity.) How is it nevertheless not a mere "existentiell" circling around the human being? ("Existential philosophy" attends to beings and does not make being its own. Nor can it do so, precisely because "existence" no longer *existentia,* let

18. *Parmenides.* Freiburg lecture course, winter semester 1942–43. {GA54, p. 240ff.}

alone being itself in the essence of its truth.) How is *history* here, the essence of *history*, a matter of the event?

66. Tradition out of the essence of historiality

Historiality [*das Geschicht*] is essentially consigning as ordinance (event). In consignment, *tradition* is grounded—only as grounded is it genuine tradition. To what extent are cognitions required here? Cognitions without *remembrance* are null. Consignment—*beginning and remembrance.*

67. History and historiology

Historiology brings us to the point that we, although in essence historical, behave everywhere unhistorically.

How can historiology do that? Because historiology, as belonging to the essence of technology, has its origin in the essential transformation of truth and being.

Historiology—as exploration—calculation about the past, as authorship, as science, as literature, as journalism, as research and archival organization; propaganda as planned *historiologizing*, radio, film. In the sphere of historiology and technology, representation is directed only to institutions, accomplishments, works, productive persons, individuals and masses; directed to civilization, culture, and *politics*—all things made by the human being, nowhere *reality* itself.

Because this lack is felt, one escapes to "*ideology*" and to "ideas," the history of "ideas."

Platonism in historiology—in accord with the metaphysical essence of historiology—is unavoidable; the various forms of banal Platonism; the misfortune of the consideration appropriate to the lack.

E. Under way toward the first beginning

The preparation for the thinking of beyng in its historicality

So as to remain on the bridge

68. Key words with respect to being

Being is the most common of all and the emptiest.
Being is the most understandable and the most banal.
Being is the most reliable and the most uttered.
Being is the most forgotten and the most compelling.
At the same time, however:
Being is the surplus and the uniqueness.
Being is the concealment and the origin.
Being is the abyss and the reticence.
Being is the remembrance and the liberation.

69. To arrive at the domain of the disposition . . .

To arrive at the domain of the disposition
of the word of beyng

To become heedful of the
claim of the dictum of the beginning.
Heedfulness as obedience.

Obedience as forbearance
and magnanimity with respect to the inceptual pain.
The experience of the abyssal ground.

The disposition of the claim disposes the
human being to the steadfastness of the
preservation of the clearing of beyng.

*

Speechlessness, having been attained, most readily conceals the awaiting of the word, i.e., the attentiveness to the event, and this is already the disposedness toward the courage of steadfastness.

Pain holds steadfast in the inceptual difference of the event-related opposition between the departure and the difference. These latter, for their part, essentially occur in each case again in the opposition between the disentangling and the twisting free and are illuminated in their unity. It is as this unity that the turning of Da-sein essentially occurs.

*

Essential questioning stands outside the restlessness of curiosity and does not allow itself to dispute the equanimity in which forbearance with respect to the truth of being is reconciled with magnanimity toward the errancy of the abandonment of beings by being so as to be prepared for the diffidence which opens the human being to the claim of the inceptual.

*

By attending to the simplicity of beyng, we experience the claim of the event and, in such experience, hear the word from which arises the language whose "use" belongs under the law of the beginning.

70. The transition

The destiny of beyng transits over to the thinkers. Their saying, in enduring the transition, must often speak in the mode of denial. Yet their denying language does not by any means remain on the level of the negative and the reactive. (Refusal of the departure.) Their denial is determined by the riches of being, i.e., by the difference as the departing inceptuality.

Moreover, this negating is not in any way the negativity of absolute dialectic.

It is a "no" that cannot be sublated, but the impossibility of sublation is a sign of the inceptual transition.

The transition, which the thinkers "follow," itself follows as the course of the overcoming which arises out of the twisting free of beyng. Attentiveness to the transition is the enduring of the difference into the departure; it is the abyssal ground of the beginning.

*

The transition

(*Transition and overcoming twisting free*)

follows the overcoming of metaphysics. The overcoming, in the realm of the history of beyng, is essentially a twisting free.

The overcoming twists metaphysics into the wreath of the turning. *This* twisting first brings metaphysics into the honor of its concealed essence. The twisting free is reverence for the dignity of beyng. This reverence eventuates in the nobility of beyng and is all that the thinker follows and abides by.

Here the "overcoming" does not in the least possess the pejorative sense of forcing down, beating down, the sense of removal or curtailment. It is not the triumph of better insight and greater cleverness but, instead, is an event of beyng itself.

71. The collapse of Ἀλήθεια out of the global mountain range; the beginning of the destiny of being.[19]

Ἀλήθεια—Perhaps the unconcealedness of what is present belongs in the mountain range of the difference. There are still no paths available for pondering this surmise in a fitting way.

All history, and the destiny of beyng as well, must remain behind here. Thinking stands at the foot of the global mountain range.

From this range Ἀλήθεια once collapsed suddenly, and in Ἀλήθεια is concealed: destiny, which is the destiny of beyng.

There rules in the global mountain range nothing of passing time and therefore also nothing of eternity (of timeless time).

The mountain range is the locale in whose guise the essence of time eventuates out of the worldly nearness. The nearing of the nearness, dispropriating into the difference, eventuates as the lighting and sounding of the event in the veiling of light, in the quieting of sound. Lighting discloses; sounding gathers. Lighting and sounding illuminate, and resound, throughout the fourfold in the global mountain range; they are the resonance.

In collapsing, Ἀλήθεια takes along the gleaming of the light: the emerging that essentially occurs in Ἀλήθεια and the clearing (brought

19. {Excerpt out of bundle VII (annotations), from pp. 164–70}

forth in this way) of the unconcealed: φύσις. In collapsing out of the mountain range, Ἀλήθεια takes along the breath of the sounding, the sheltering gatheredness of the unconcealed: λόγος.

In collapsing, Ἀλήθεια is that which it takes along and, in bringing along, brings hither into unconcealedness and forth into what is present, which *therefore* is what first matters.

Φύσις and Λόγος essentially occur hiddenly in the lighting and sounding of the global mountain range, and it is as this that the difference appropriates and the event dispropriates.

In the bringing forth of the collapse, Ἀλήθεια is gathered into the sending [*Schicken*] and is the destiny [*Ge-schick*], the assignment, Μοῖρα, in which Ἀλήθεια is retained and gathered, cleared and sheltered. Φύσις, Λόγος, Μοῖρα collapse as Ἀλήθεια out of Ἀλήθεια into the Ἕν, which itself essentially occurs in a concealed way, according to the modes of Ἀλήθεια, and in such an essence takes hold.

This until the Ἕν, remaining forgotten in its essential provenance out of Ἀλήθεια but at the same time purely and simply coming to presence as arisen lighting and gathered destiny, is itself apprehended (Δόξα) as something present and is gathered on the basis of apprehension and perception (νοεῖν), i.e., numbered, and so is made subject to the σύνθεσις which employs διαίρεσις. Thus the bringing forth (the essential occurrence of Ἀλήθεια) arrives at the domain of placing over to and of placing before oneself in νοεῖν. This essential occurrence of unification, as the most alive, is entrusted to ζωή and ψυχή; the latter, as νοῦς, becomes the native place of Λόγος.

The entire essence of Ἀλήθεια is distorted. The ἰδέα usurps the position of the lighting. The outward look of the lighting stamps that which comes to presence, demands the μορφή, and provides lodging to the ὕλη. The apparatus of metaphysics is complete.

Incipit comoedia. Ἀλήθεια is forgotten. But everything lives on this forgotten forgottenness. In the prologue of the machination of the framework (*creatio*), the mere masks are converted into the persons. Personality is created. What is alive can be represented only as person. Blind screaming for the personal Thou counts as the ultimate in thoughtfulness. The paths of thinking have been abandoned long ago—admittedly in such a way that this *wild flight in the face of* thinking (i.e., in the face of the withstanding of the belongingness to the essentially occurring essence, to the provenance of Ἀλήθεια) appears to be the *victory* of thinking and therefore at the lowest stage of the decline is not afraid to present thinking as a believing.

For a long time thinking has no longer been thinking.

Thinking counts as philosophical belief.

There are supposed to be people who believe something like that. Who will deliver us from this deliverance?

At the same time, it is surprising that the human being, who is concerned with philosophical belief, also discovers atomic energy, for it *is* in fact the same human being who, out of the same forgottenness of beyng, nourishes the roots of the power of beyng.

Ἀλήθεια collapses out of the constantly concealed global mountain range and in the collapse becomes the bringing-forth-hither which at once brings the "hither" as clearing ("there") and the "forth" as presence.

In this bringing is gathered the staying which belongs to presence, i.e., the *tarrying*—as the sojourning of presence in unconcealedness.

Tarrying [Verbringen], thought according to the bringing-forth-hither, names the protracted presencing—out of which essentially occurs the constant presence that is determinative of "being" in metaphysics. This determination includes the positedness of the being of beings (Ποίησις). This positedness is, to be sure, unexperienceable since it is distorted for metaphysics and through metaphysics. Although it is as such unrecognizable, it comes to light inasmuch as being is effected and, in the broadest sense, conditioned: effected by the first cause (*ipsum esse* as *actus purus*), conditioned by the conditions of necessity and universality (*esse* as objective reality), and, finally, conditioned as having become dialectical—in the coupling of both modes of grounding.

The doctrine of the transcendentals, which relates to ὄν and ἕν, ἕτερον, ἀγαθόν, ἀληθές, καλόν, and which is clarified in terms of *creatio*, points back to this conditionality, i.e., to the effectedness and lodging of being.

To be pondered: how is there the bringing-forth-hither *in* the collapse of Ἀλήθεια out of the forgottenness of the global mountain range?

How does the collapse take hold, hiddenly, in Ποίησις, which itself remains concealed?

How does the forgottenness distort Ποίησις everywhere, throughout metaphysics, and in a most complete way in the framework? How does this distortion correspond to the forgottenness? How does the distorting remain accordingly—as forgetting—the essential provenance of the framework?

All this is nevertheless to be thought apart from destiny and out of the nearness of the mountain range.

Here resides the essential dimension for the provenance of causality (four αἰτίαι and the ἀρχαί) and of its articulation.

Lightning can suddenly illuminate distant peaks of a mountain range. Thus it is unnecessary to scale those peaks and shine a light on them out of their dark nearness; that is effectuated by the historiological description of what is handed down as the history of philosophy.

What remains essential is whether a thinking is enough of a tree so as to call down onto itself a flash of lightning that confers such illumination.

To understand a thinker means to stand face to face with his thought upon a "most separated peak," it means to be a peak oneself, it means to endure the silence and the light of the mountain range. Will we ever understand this understanding? Or is it definitively lost?

F. The first beginning

Cf. On the beginning[20]

Recollection of the first beginning

72. *The time is coming*

since only seldom may one know of the beginning of Western history, out of which an essence of truth has been decided and the West has been predetermined in its limits.

73. *Truth and cognition*

"Thinking"

In the first beginning: νοεῖν—λέγειν, gathering apprehension in and with the unconcealed (not at all "*intuition*"; this latter only since νοῦς and νοεῖν have become ἰδεῖν with regard to φύσις as ἰδέα; also not "thinking," for that is representation in the sense of the delivery to oneself of something as something, whereby the "as something" is the *conceptum* of a *concipere* as *percipere. Capere:* grasp, capture, seize, hunt down.) Apprehending as belongingness to what emerges. Out of it and with it, arising and setting. Anaximander.

20. *Über den Anfang.* {GA 70}

At the extreme end of metaphysics	: thinking—consciousness in the certainty of unconditional knowledge and of the authority of the guarantee.
In the other beginning	: Forbearing steadfastness in the clearing of the appropriating event. Clearing as protection—sheltering of *truth.*

Metaphysical thinking out of *representation—repraesentare,* out of conception *con-ceptus; per-cipere—capere; seizing*—snatching to *oneself*—conveying to—securing. *Certainty*—adequation.

"Thinking," in the first beginning, as gathered apprehension of what emerges.

74. On the presentation of the first beginning

I. Immediately taking up the series Anaximander—Heraclitus—Parmenides each of these for himself.
II. Each already different—also in implicitly thinking ahead and in reference to metaphysics.
III. How especially the first beginning in its inceptuality.
IV. The fact that here beginning and something unavoidable—
thence ground of history
thence the coming
thence the other beginning
thence the enduring.
And only out of this nexus beginning ↔ beginning
To say what is essential for the interpretation, so that this latter itself becomes experienceable as history and every semblance of methodology falls away.
V. The intimation of beyng.

Nowhere historiological presentations. Solely recollecting everything and thus a reticent steadfastness, even if only preparatory.

On the interpretation of the first beginning

The respective interpretations of Anaximander, Heraclitus, and Parmenides lead so far that ἀλήθεια ever resounds: first in the recollection of content, then comes the genuine step to Ἀλήθεια as the inceptuality of the beginning. And so intimation of the essential occurrence of "being." (Being as emergence—not twisted free. Consequently the disentanglement, which arises out of not yet appropriated, although concealed, twisting free.)

To show, in the respective interpretations, that not only the being of beings, but already the essential occurrence of being itself; yet . . . not such that the beginning itself proceeds inceptually back into itself, but immediately proceeds forward into what has emerged and therein stabilizes itself. Why?

Being and truth diverge; more precisely: truth, in its inceptual essence, is still not cleared toward the truth of being.

75. The essence of being in the first beginning

reveals itself, i.e., at the same time, essentially occurs inceptually, in emerging, advancing. Only if the basic traits of the inceptuality come to be recollected constantly, above all in their inceptual unity, can the first beginning be surmised.

Being is the *beginning.*

The beginning is *disconcealment toward unconcealedness* (ΑΛΗΘΕΙΑ). Disconcealment is the *emerging* that goes back into itself, because disconcealment possesses the concealment out of which it emerges.
Emergence is φύσις.
Emergence is *presence* (οὐσία). To presence pertain:
the nearness—παρά
the view—visibility ἰδέα
the disburdening—against μὴ ὄν
the magic—καλόν.

Presence consists in *constancy* and is then permanence (ἀεί).

Presence is then the *essential occurrence in the work and as work,* wherein is gathered the presentness of rest and motion: ἐνέργεια; ἐντελέχεια. Co-position: ἐνέχεια τὸ τέλος.

Every emerged determination of being can in a certain way stand for the beginning, and all of them can be especially attributed to the beginning. And yet they do not exhaust it, because it itself, as the first beginning, must take over the advancement.

Nevertheless, the beginning remains embedded in concealment, but one which itself remains concealed and thus is completely lacking in presence and so must be replaced by "truth" as ὁμοίωσις and as disfigurement of the cognizing human being.

Being ἰδέα—ἐνέργεια is simply beings. And beings provide the measure for being, whereby the previous manifestness of beings has fallen into thoughtlessness and questionlessness.

76. Recollection into the first beginning

stands trapped in the semblance that here something historiologically far remote and hardly accessible could be attained immediately, through a leap over all previous history.

What is to be recollected, as the opinion goes, is additionally a past that is present at hand and ungraspable only in its remnants.

But what is to be recollected is nothing past; instead, it is the essential occurrence of what is coming—being itself in its truth.

We do not need to flee from ourselves, but we also must not vindicate ourselves to "us" ourselves as ones who simply wander around arbitrarily and stay well informed. On the contrary, we need to become aware of the changing essential relation of self-projecting being to the *essence* of the human being. And required *for that* is "only" steadfastness in what is overly close.

77. φύσις and the first beginning

Within this presentation of the first beginning, a presentation that is inceptual (i.e., dealing with the history of beyng), to what extent must being indeed receive precisely the name of φύσις, although φύσις does not express the essence of the *truth* of beyng as that essence is thought in the other beginning?

Using the name φύσις here is necessary to the extent that φύσις, correctly grasped, points to emergence and thereby intimates ἀλήθεια and also to the extent that φύσις at the same time is in this determination sufficient to unsettle immediately the previous misinterpretation of the beginning as a philosophy of nature.

Yet the correctly grasped essence of φύσις is in the end not strong enough to allow a surmising of the knowledge of the beginning in its inceptuality.

The inceptual question of φύσις is neither philosophy of nature *nor* metaphysics. The former starts with Aristotle, the latter with Plato. Both the former and the latter characterize the start of "philosophy."

78. What does not yet begin in the first beginning

Beyng as event

φύσις : emergence; the emergent striking of roots and thus the giving of a stance to what stands constant (as tarrying, but *not* permanent) in standing out into the emergent open domain. Emergence therefore: presence and constancy. Constancy—to what extent the distorted essence of presence?

φύσις: says then at the same time φύσει ὄν—beings of such a kind.

But more inceptual in φύσις is already *concealment;* ἀλήθεια essentially occurs as the transformation and coming forth of concealment. Concealment grounded in concealedness.

But still more inceptual in concealedness is sheltering, which is not a subsequent retrieval but, instead, the originarily proper preservation. Sheltering is the enshrouding (protection) that preserves the emergence: the most proper essence of the beginning, its indestructible act of beginning, i.e., its going back into itself. This inceptuality, experienced—from the perspective of beings—as withholding, is the preservation of the opulence of the beginning in its pure self-donation.

Unconcealedness is then *one* mode of the disconcealment of concealment, inasmuch as for concealment, and out of it, concealedness (λήθη) appears as its most proximate essence and is determined as φύσις.

More inceptual, however, is disconcealment, if it at the same time allows sheltering to occur essentially into the beginning and if it is itself the appropriating event.

But how is one supposed to think the essential fullness of that which we later call the event of appropriation?

The more inceptual essence of φύσις, the other beginning, which at the same time takes back into itself metaphysics, i.e., the history of the arisen "truth" of beings.

79. The first beginning and its inceptuality

The first beginning
is the act of beginning in the sense of the disconcealing of disconcealment, but thus the emergence into the constancy of disconcealment in unconcealedness, but thus the appearing forth of the latter in the act of appearing, but thus the pressing forth of appearing as appearance, but thus the subjugation of unconcealedness, but thus the relinquishment of the inceptuality of the beginning, but thus the abandonment of the beginning to the advancement, but thus the commencement of the truth of being as the beingness of beings, but thus the priority of beings themselves as that which in the proper sense is present *prior* to presence.

There is no "dialectic" here at all, neither that of being nor even that of the thinking about being.

Essentially occurring here is the beginning of the first beginning and nothing besides this act of beginning.

Recollection into this is already appropriation.

80. The first beginning as Ἀλήθεια

Disconcealment is τὸ αὐτό of νοεῖν and εἶναι. This implies that being already comes to an essential occurrence which thrusts presencing (in the sense of disconcealment) into presence and so into *constancy.* Here the εἶναι is already determined by the ἕν, and the latter is grounded beforehand in τὸ αὐτό, although containing the impulse to rule completely in its own proper limits, to set everything on the *uniqueness of presence* as the uniqueness of the one (τὸ νῦν), and to keep all σήματα gathered together on that basis.

Here, too, still a repudiation of limits, inasmuch as the respective appearances of what is precisely present and absent never satisfy being but, instead, are already its appearing, an appearing which to be sure makes itself available to a grasp through the decay that, for its part, is grounded in the human being.

In the first beginning, being is indeed of the same essence and yet is already history, and must already be history, and is also the inceptuality of the advancement established in the ἰδέα as the essence of ἀλήθεια.

Disconcealment shows the relation to concealment (Heraclitus), and therefore being is indeed already distinguished through the ἕν. What essentially occur even more, however, are the gathering of λόγος and, in the gathering and for it, the counter-turning. This latter is the inceptual self-containment of ἀλήθεια, and ἀλήθεια nowhere already releases δόξα in the proper sense. And here is the ground for the essence of the character of πόλεμος and ἔρις in being and in ἀλήθεια. This character does of course equally show the impulse toward constancy, but now first of all in autonomy.

Here, too, the preserving of the limit as the essential occurrence of being, but still more inceptually than with Parmenides.

Anaximander still says the first beginning. Being is the repudiation[21] *of the limit, the provision of disconcealment.*

(But never is a "doctrine" intended here in the sense of an opinion; instead, the beginning itself, being, truth, which is recollected and hence must be recollected in enduring the beginning itself through a thinking ahead into the event.)

---

21. Reading *Verwehrung* for *Verwahrung.*—Trans.

81. In the first beginning

there essentially occurs being as emergence. The saying of being is the *"dictum."* Here "dictum" does not simply mean "adage," nor simply "statement" as individual proposition; it means the gathering and naming of the inceptual, and the inceptual endures and decides in concealment.

It is only of secondary significance that these "dicta" have come down to us as fragments.

"Dictum" does also not mean "maxim" and must not mislead us into searching for rules of life here. Dictum is judgment in the sense of sentencing to thought, to the interrogation of being.

The "dictum" therefore embraces a manifold of propositions. And the mode of saying is hardly made clear.

82. The thinkers of the first beginning

Anaximander, Heraclitus, Parmenides cannot be called pre-Socratics or pre-Platonics, because in that way they are precisely not thought of as the ones who carry out the beginning but, instead, are understood in terms of Socrates—Plato.

By the same token, Plato is not simply a fully developed Parmenides, nor Aristotle the completion of Heraclitus. The inceptual thinkers are not the preliminary stages of the supposed pinnacles (highest stage and completion in Plato—Aristotle), nor are the later thinkers merely ones who have forsaken the beginning.

Quite to the contrary, there is advancement here, but Plato indeed stands entirely, as does Heraclitus, within the necessity of the history of being. When inceptual thinking becomes historical by necessity, however, the beginning *occurs more essentially* than any advancement does. But here exaltation has as little place as disparagement: for never can any one of these thinkers be taken as a model to be emulated or even repeated.

83. The first beginning

It is apparently a sheer accident that the first beginning has been handed down *in fragments;* in truth, however, it is a necessity, for only in that way does the beginning appear as something to be striven for in its inceptuality and never something to be possessed.

Are we not in this way making a virtue of our plight? No—for we are by no means in a position to experience and take seriously even this plight, the one of the beginning and of inceptual thinking.

Yet that which for the handing down of the first beginning is already a necessity is for the preparation of the other beginning afortiori something inaccessible and therefore never knowingly first something fabricated: the fragmentary character—the fragments not as the remainders of a previous whole but, instead, as intimations of a subsequent unity.

84. The interpretation of the first beginning

is recollection into the past and requires a regress to remote times. How are we supposed to be able to assure ourselves of what is essential in these respective ages if we are not blindly satisfied with making the bygone "time" "close to the present" through a zealous and unexamined interpretation of the representation which just happens to be current?

Appeal is made to the demand that, above all, "what is contemporary" to the inceptual era and to the later one must be heeded correctly and the proper shade of "color" must be used everywhere. In the "history of the concept," the word usages of the time must especially be heeded and sufficiently determined; thereby a barrier is immediately set up against hasty modernizings.

This obvious advice forgets what is essential. For

1. in each case that which is "contemporary" with what is to be interpreted does itself first require an interpretation out of the totality of the respective era. Why should what is contemporary be more understandable and, so to speak, of itself less needful of an interpretation than that which, like the beginning, also and afortiori belongs to that "time"? But how could what is "contemporary" be interpreted in advance? It is no easier here to avoid the danger of hasty modernizing. Moreover, the appeal to what is contemporary as an interpretative aid still contains its own quite proper difficulty. For

2. it is by no means assured in advance that what is contemporary possesses, or could possess, to a preeminent degree a fitting understanding of that which eventuates to its era as essential. Exactly the opposite is the case. Thus one could at most appeal to what is contemporary in order to recognize, through the opposite, that which has been mistaken by what is contemporary. But, for that, what is contemporary would have to be grasped first of all *as* in fact the opposite of the mistaken, and, for that, this latter itself must first be recognized. And so

we are standing precisely where the appeal to what is contemporary as an interpretative aid was to take us. It helps not at all. This appeal merely confuses, and it magnifies the semblance that the adducing of a great variety of incidentals and circumstantialities makes the interpretation "more concrete" and therefore "more real" and therefore "more true." The expending of the historiological merely obstructs the simplicity of history. To say nothing of the fact that often, with the inclusion of what is contemporary, a *special* game is still played by thoughtless "modernizings" and "truisms."

Thus there remains as the only recourse
the leap of recollection into the first beginning. Yet this leap is not a mere renunciation of the ordinary, not a mere appeal to what is posited precisely in meditation. The leap has its own historicality, one determined out of the belongingness of thinking to being and one still in bondage to the confrontation among the beginnings. The leap succeeds once out of much effort. And it is also then never something "in itself."

85. In regard to the interpretation of the first beginning "Myth" and "philosophy"

To explain "philosophy" from myth is erroneous for several reasons.

1. Inceptual thinking, which is to be "explained," is not yet "philosophy"; the latter only since Plato.
2. Thinking as the thinking of being is intrinsically and essentially a beginning and cannot itself be an "heir" of "myth."
3. Inceptual thinking cannot at all be "explained." It must in each case only be begun; those who think it must think inceptually.
4. The mixing in of historiology blocks every path into the first beginning and foists on us the opinion that one could know what "myth" and "philosophy" are so as to deduce them from each other and make everything "understandable."

86. The interpretative recollection

The unique, but all-decisive, presupposition of every recollection into the first beginning of Western thinking; that a thinking began there, i.e., that *being* was thought: that being appropriates thinking, that truth essentially occurs.

The simplicity of this presupposition does nevertheless require long meditation and preparation in order to be equal to its execution.

87. Procedure

Various interpretative claims and ways. In each case, pre-having—preconception. We cannot "posit in itself" the dictum and its content.

Therefore 1. which presuppositions? Those as inceptual as possible, as decisive as possible, as full of presupposition as possible—what is highest, so that ultimately the lack consists not in the too much of presuppositions, but in the essentially too little of them.

2. To master {?} the highest presuppositions as such, so that they are essential for us in the same.
Beginning—metaphysics—end.

3. Alienation

Thus pure arbitrariness, unconcerned with the historiological, as regards what is to be investigated and to be brought together out of what is investigated? No; quite to the contrary, historical indication ← φύσις—ἰδέα—ἐντελέχεια.

A. the lack in what is too small of the projective breadth.

B. the claim: *not* toward correctness.

C. restriction, but not to an empty possibility and usefulness; instead, *essentiality.* Turning back to the beginning. Not displacement therein, but in the turning to the remotion into the most proper remoteness, *alienation.*

D. this, however, again the decisive.

E. the interpretation not as "artifice"; instead, "history" (essential occurrence of the truth of being: grounding of being).

What is evident—natural—anthropomorphism. "Windelband"; only to translate in order to know everything—| if not (being and truth) the most worthy of questioning!

1. what the human being is and how the human being is
2. whether anthropomorphism
3. how so—then indeed beings themselves *given* in advance, in order to be subjugated to this placing in advance. Wherefore precisely according to these human relations; δίκη—τίσις—whether there are such.

88. The obvious objection

the interpretative recollection

Anaximander can indeed not have thought what we are discussing here.

To be sure, he did *not* think it *in this way*, with the same explicitness and the same terminology. Yet that is not because the interpretation imposes something extraneous and thus demands *too much* of the dictum. On the contrary, it is because every interpretation attains *too little* of that which is inceptually disconcealed in inceptual knowledge.

The interpretation is in fact unsuitable—not because it attributes to the beginning too much, but because it attributes too little, always something too un-inceptual, to the beginning.

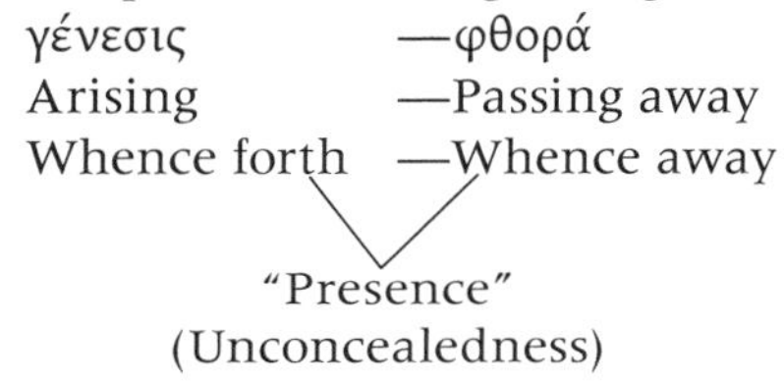

89. Anaximander and Heraclitus

The same as τὸ χρεών
τὸ χρεών as χρόνος
The same as ἀρχή
ἀρχή as τὸ ἄπειρον
τὸ χρεών as ἀδικία

Preservation as the beginning
The beginning as concealment.
How here at first φύσις and ἀλήθεια "concealed."
↓
Heraclitus

90. Anaximander and Parmenides

If, however, being is the repudiation[22] of the limit, i.e., of constancy in permanence, then being indeed has its *extreme distorted essence* in the ἀεί. Then nothing which would be permanent can be a being. And everything permanent (steadfastly enduring) is merely semblance—the distorted essence of being (being as emergence in going back).

τὸ γὰρ αὐτό—! What content does this dictum now receive? And what does the ἕν of Parmenides say? Was it not always merely misinterpreted

22. Reading *Verwehrung* for *Verwahrung*.—Trans.

Platonically, instead of being grasped out of the ταὐτόν of the ἀρχή of Anaximander?

91. Heraclitus and Parmenides

What now for Anaximander is λανθάνειν as the essential occurrence of being?

Why not said, not sayable, and not to be said?

Why? only a matter of thoughtful saying or of being itself?

The most inceptual concealment, whose extreme form of letting go into the brutality of beings?

How the "α" in the entire beginning

ἄ- πειρον	ἕν—ταὐτόν	
ἀ- δικία	λόγος	(not an identity, whether
ἀ- λήθεια	φύσις	formal-logical or
		ontological-dialectical)

Being and beings—the difference?? The abyss between being and beings.

G. The first beginning

92. The first beginning
ἀλήθεια

as the first emergence of the departing essence of being qua event-related beginning. What is first—it rests on the fact that in general the "clearing" emerges as disconcealment. But at the same time the essence is concealed and receives its determination from beings and from the uniqueness of being.

The uniqueness is grasped out of the gathering (forerunner of the κοινόν) in relation to the permanent—not out of the breadth of the event.

What is first with regard to emergence is both its "that it is" and the concealedness of the essence. Out of the concealedness arises the unmediated character of the unquestionableness of ἀλήθεια, and through the concealedness the unmediated character refers {?} to the ἕν and ὄν as εἶναι and is chained to the distinction between ὄν and μὴ ὄν.

In this μή, the uniqueness of being is brought to a disconcealing, although its ground cannot be experienced inceptually.

The μὴ ὄν—what never could or can "be" a being, i.e., emerge as a being.

The shadow that everywhere follows beings?

The shadow the first illumination of being itself? Why then inceptually already the *not*? Why does this become so preeminent that it places itself, so to speak, beside the ὄν? What is involved in this "not"?

93. To show the first (beginning)

and so illuminate the relation to what is inceptual.

This showing thinks for the first beginning, in that it illuminates the truth of being; out of this truth, the beginning occurs more inceptually now and in the future.

The first beginning requires the other one; otherwise it would not be the first. Indeed this requiring is not a lack; on the contrary, it is the unexhausted riches of what is first, which uniquely encompasses the preliminary character of the beginning.

94. The concealed ineffability of the first beginning

eventuates in the experience of *the fact that beyng is*. The event-related "fact that" is illuminated first as ἀλήθεια. In the pure "fact that" is the inceptual event. To experience this means to endure, without support or foothold in beings, the fact that being is illuminated in its abyssal remoteness, that a clearing essentially occurs; and it means to be without an utterance.

The pain of the inceptual separateness
the horror of the abyss
the bliss of the departure.

The inceptual pain is the original unity of horror and bliss; not a compound out of both. (On the "fact that" and the later distinction between the "that something is" and the "what something is," cf. *Aus der Geschichte des Seyns*. II. Projection[23])

23. *Aus der Geschichte des Seyns*. In *Nietzsche II*. {GA6.2, p. 417–18}

95. The first beginning

The human being exists as intrigued by "being." The human being exists as having come to terms with beings. The human being exists as predisposed toward being. (everything out of ἀλήθεια as the "same")

96. The first beginning

appears, in its inceptuality, primarily in the transition to the other beginning. The transition is experienced in the experience of the demise of metaphysics. But that eventuates only in knowledge of the historical essence of metaphysics.

97. Not all thinkers at the start

of Western thinking are inceptual thinkers.

We do not know whether the inceptual thinkers we recognize are the only ones at the start.

98. The first beginning

The disentanglement out of the still unexperienceable turning.

ἀλήθεια "is" φύσις, in which the concealment is itself concealed, such that pure emergence appears and such that the emergence seems to be pure presence.

In ἀλήθεια, as thus essentially occurring, there resides necessarily the *outward look* (δοκεῖν) of presence, and the δοκοῦντα are beings and specifically in each case in the presence of the δοκοῦντα, i.e., *separated, individuated.*

δόξα is the most proximate appearance of φύσις—ἀλήθεια.

In emergence ἀλήθεια—φύσις, a being appears (δοκεῖ).

Beings themselves are taken as what is self-showing.

Over δόξα, being (φύσις) becomes ἰδέα. Because now being is apprehended only on the basis of beings, and no longer, as in the beginning, are beings apprehended on the basis of being.

In the first beginning, which must once emerge, the inceptuality remains concealed, and thus the truth (of being) is here related (in a concealed way) to the concealed and is the unconcealedness of emergence, i.e., unconcealedness as emergence. Therein essentially occurs already the letting go of semblance, appearance, and seeming, especially since emergence, if apprehended for itself, is encountered in such a way that the apprehending must be pure letting-appear.

99. The first beginning

Start immediately with the comments on the dicta.
Anaximander (cf. s. s. 41, concluding part)[24]
Parmenides (cf. s. s. 32 and later s. s. 36)[25]
Heraclitus (cf. s. s. 36 and ff.)[26]
In addition, the preparation of the entire ms. 40–41.[27]
Say what is essential, in the semblance of sheer conjecture.

ἀλήθεια—φύσις—ἕν
λόγος—νοεῖν

Cf. *the comments on Anaximander, Parmenides, Heraclitus* 1941.[28]
Cf. *ms. on the first beginning*[29]
The ἕν as the seemingly most empty and most general out of the essential fullness and uniqueness of ἀλήθεια; respectively different in Anaximander, Parmenides, and Heraclitus and yet unitary in the same.

H. The advancement of the first beginning into the start of metaphysics

Constancy

100. Ἀλήθεια → ὀρθότης

An elucidation of the essence of ἀλήθεια—ὁμοίωσις (ἰδέα) under the guidance of Aristotle's dictum (in the *Poetics*) that ποίησις is φιλοσοφώτερον ἱστορίας.
φιλοσοφία—σοφία—ὄν—ἕν— ἀγαθόν—θεῖον
ἰδέα—οὐσία—ἀλήθεια

24. *Grundbegriffe.* {GA51, p. 94ff.}
25. *Der Anfang der abendländischen Philosophie (Anaximander und Parmenides)* {GA35}. *Einführung in die Metaphysik* {GA40, §§36, 43, 50, 53}.
26. *Einführung in die Metaphysik.* {GA40, p. 13ff.}
27. {Here in GA71}
28. {Here in GA71 (I. The first beginning)}
29. {Here in GA71}

ποίησις—τέχνη—εἶδος—δύναμις
ἱστορία—αἴσθησις

101. The advancement out of the first beginning

must take its emergence out of the first beginning without this beginning being the cause of the advancement.

The advancement is the emergence of constancy as the genuine mode of the presence already transferred to appearance.

The directedness toward constancy resides in the way disconcealment remains in itself unpreserved by the essence of concealment as also by the essence of the transition.

Anaximander thinks more inceptually than Heraclitus and Parmenides.

Heraclitus already says τὸ μὴ δῦνόν ποτε,
Parmenides says ἕν
each a way of directing the advancement to the ἀεί.

102. Presence, constancy, rigidity

Constancy in something entrenched is in each case in itself a marking off, limitation, separation, tearing away out of the essentially occurring presence.

Therein resides the possibility of beings prior to being. But therein also resides the possibility of a stiffening into what stands for itself and thus stands apart and stands rigid. This rigidity [*das Abständige*] produces the possibility of objects [*das Gegenständige*].

Thus, in the advancement out of the beginning, there is predelineated the basic structure of the truth of beings in the metaphysical sense.

103. φύσις—ἰδέα

(τέχνη)
(δόξα)

The essential origin of being as ἰδέα resides in φύσις, whose inceptual essence finds its determination in the (admittedly ungrounded, and thus at once uninterpreted) ἀλήθεια.

The arising of τέχνη is essential for the possibility of being as ἰδέα. That means unconcealedness, i.e., the presence of what becomes present, is brought into that apprehension which makes it possible to hold fast to what is proximally present and even to set it forth and produce it. τέχνη is the mode in which the apprehension that pertains to εἶναι (presence) makes itself constant and thereby stamps ἀλήθεια in a corresponding way. Involved here is the fact that presence (φύσις, ἐόν, εἶναι) disconceals itself in the most proximate "view" and that this most proximally present outlook (δόξα) becomes that which is held fast. Thus presence forms the character of appearing self-manifestation (visibility) and then even exhausts itself in it.

II. The resonating

A. The resonating

Vista

104. The resonating

The resonating of the beginning (hidden in its inceptuality;
the first and the other beginning
are concealed)
Modernity and the West
Modernity; metaphysics as episode
The consummation of metaphysics; the *passing by*
The episode; the first and the other beginning
The abandonment by being; beinglessness
The abandonment by being; the devastation
Devastation and erosion
The bondage of nihilating and of passing away

105. The resonating

is the first and most proximate indication of the other beginning. It indicates accordingly the transition from the first to the other beginning; it indicates this transition as a mode of inceptuality; but the inceptuality is at the same time counter to the advancement of the first beginning into metaphysics.

The resonating indicates metaphysics as the episode constituted by the dominance of beings and of their truth.

The resonating indicates the overcoming of metaphysics, an overcoming that eventuates out of the twisting free of the disentangling.

In terms of the history of beyng, metaphysics is to be experienced as an episode. The time-space of the duration of metaphysics and that of its demise as "worldview" must not muddle its distorted essence as understood within the history of beyng.

The resonating indicates the passing by.

The resonating is the first indication of the history of beyng and, within that, the first indication of the essence of history as *historiality.*

The devastation under an errant star in the age of the demise of metaphysics is not to be overcome through a mere "shift" in "representing" and "becoming." It itself finds its end in the demise.

106. The resonating

of the transition of history into its more inceptual essence, i.e., into historiality, which allows the truth of beyng to occur essentially in the beyng of truth and allows this turning to begin as the appropriation of the twisting free in the clearing of Da-seyn.

History is not merely in transit to another age *within* the *previous* time-space of metaphysics; on the contrary, time-space itself is becoming other, inasmuch as it is only now being illuminated in its essence as Da-sein.

History and historiality.

107. The history of beyng

does not know any succession; the dispensing of the history of beyng is inceptual and is back into the beginning. The experience of the disentangling and of the advancement to metaphysics is not the experience of a sequence of stages. Such things are found only by historiological calculation, which has already set everything on explanation, and this explanation also already determines the "out of which" and the manner of the derivation. Historiology cannot ever think the inceptual. Above all, the history of beyng "is" constantly the beginning. And the beginning is ever and always in everything that presents itself to us proximally, in being made known, like an elapsing phase.

Even in the abandonment of beings by beyng, since beings alone seem to reign in the manner of power and actuality, such that the whole of being is, so to speak, sucked up and tolerated only as pretense and useful fiction, there still eventuates to nonbeings a truth, which is thus the truth of beyng. The turning essentially occurs. The semblant talk of "being itself," a talk which indeed knows only beings, must in fact still confirm the history of beyng. Historiality is constantly of the appropriating event.

108. The resonating

In the resonating, a clarification must already be prepared regarding that which otherwise are called beings; in what breadth they are thought; how at any time in them beingness already essentially occurs; how an intimation of beyng can thereby be experienced.

(Cf. the manifold characterizations in *The Overcoming of Metaphysics* {GA67}, *The History of Beyng* {GA69}, *The Saying* {GA74}, *On the Beginning* {GA70}; cf. *Contributions to Philosophy (Of the Event)* {GA65} and *Meditation* {GA66}.)

Why must speaking be at first defensive here?

1. Beings do not constitute the "appearance" and the "expression" of being; but neither does the converse hold.
2. Beyng has no "medium" of transparency; the clearing, in which beyng essentially occurs, is its proper essence.
3. Beyng is also not the reflected radiance of beings.
4. Beyng is utterly not a piece of beings or their nucleus.
5. Beyng is not the objectivity of representation, as that objectivity bears on beings.

109. The first resonating is that of the passing by

The resonating, as that "of" beyng, is the resonating of the history of beyng. But that history is dispensation into the structure of the beginning; the dispensation of beyng in the event toward the beginning.

The resonating of the catching hold (entanglement) of the beginning up to the open realm of the history of Western mankind.

beyng (i.e., the conjuncture of beyng) and
the human being (i.e., historically Western mankind).

The resonant consonance of the dispensation of beyng.

Abandonment by being (———) Downgoing
Demise in disintegration | The inceptuality of integration
The passing by
The event "of" the passing by.

*

The *resonating* is resonating *of* beyng and thereby of the differentiation and, with that, of the overcoming, which is itself only what is most proximate of the twisting free.

(The resonating fits into the pain of experience.) The resonating is the most proximate displacement into steadfastness in the between.

The resonating renounces all marks and measures that in any way aim at securing and binding.

The resonating is that of being; its soundless voice and its imageless conjuncture become perceptible. Wherein? In the first experience of the lack of a sense of plight.

The pain of the lack of a sense of plight as knowledge of the plight. In this plight what is illuminated first of all is the question-worthiness of being in the ungrounded disposition of the differentiation.

The lack of a sense of plight —the passing by—the West
passing each other by:
the abandonment of beings by being
the twisting free of beyng into the beginning.

110. The resonating

The resonating of the departure

of the appropriating event in the word of the utterance of the enduring. That a soundless tuning arrives in a still-undetermined domain of the confused age, such that we pay attention to beings and being, yet without noticing that the truth arrives in beyng. For this latter is, in the most proximate resonating, the inconspicuous and the overlooked. But the task in all the describing, explaining, and pursuing of beings is to recognize the imperceptible gleam of the enigma. The dazzle of this gleam appears with the lessening of the blindness that is rooted in the forgottenness of being.

The dazzling, from the simplicity of the simple, pertains to the proximity of the in-between, in which the remoteness is illuminated, into which an arrival of the essence of truth occurs. This destiny sends out, in the resonating, the first trace of beyng.

You may hunt down all beings, but nowhere will the trace of being show itself; for you will constantly be wandering about only where the nearness is already overhasty, the nearness in which beyng confers itself to the endurance.

You may rearrange all beings; you will constantly be arranging only arrangements and will never find the open place in which the incursion of beyng eventuates.

B. The signs of the transition
The passing by
The in-between of the history of beyng

111. Signs of being in the age of the consummation of metaphysics

Even in the age of the abandonment by being, when the will to willing pursues uniquely the priority of beings, and being is forgotten, being nevertheless remains in the essential nearness that is sheltered toward the clearing of its relation to humans. This nearness arises out of the mysterious essential occurrence of being, and that occurrence, experienced in terms of the event, reveals itself as the dispropriation. The nearness of being is in this way unavoidable. The nearness must therefore also still appear in the abandonment by being and must manifest itself in the veiling. This appearance eventuates in the signs. The inevitable shows itself in the signs of the incalculable. But the latter shows itself in the compelled craving for totality, which is a sign that calculation is supposed to resolve itself without remainder. Therein it is shown that calculation steers the relation toward beings alone. Because the nearness of being can nevertheless not be driven away in remainderless calculation but can only be confirmed, the calculating about beings must then also reckon with being. This happens in such a way that the calculative understanding is forced to the expedient of claiming that being is something merely invented in thought. The calculative understanding cannot notice how close it comes to the nearness of being with this degrading of being into something "abstract." If we adhere to beings, according to this sort of calculation aimed at the "concrete," wherein all useful things have intersected, then being is merely the invention of a thinking which does not reckon with beings. Whether nevertheless this inventive thinking produces being merely as a formation of nullity, or whether being gives to thinking this last guarantee to think it indeed still within this disappraisal, and whether the mere inventive thinking already thinks out of the relation of being to thought and only in that way can think—these matters are still open to question.

The global cry for wheat and gasoline does not arise primarily from a shortage of these items. It is uttered everywhere on earth. Nor is it a catchphrase for a "materialism." It is evidence of the bond to being, with being now appearing, admittedly, only as the will to willing. Nor are wheat and gasoline the purpose of bustling about and arranging. They present only the forefront of the configuration of the conditions which the will to willing must pose to itself with a view to the unconditional enabling of its dominance. The will to willing, which wrings that cry from the most modern human being, is the most spiritual form of the "spirit"; for spirit is "consciousness," and consciousness is self-consciousness. Self-consciousness arises out of the priority of the truth of beings in the sense of certainty, to whose essential requirements belongs the first one, namely, to be self-certain, i.e., self-secure. But certainty is the assurance of the correctness of representation, which, as *perceptio,* is grounded in *idea* and therein testifies to its provenance out of being, whereas being has delivered itself into beingness in the mode of the ἰδέα.[1] The will to willing is pure and unconditional "spirit." But "spirit," identically to the ἰδέα, whose essential history it consummates, is already the advancement from the still-unilluminated truth of being. Being, which, as beingness, has been abandoned to metaphysics, is everywhere the spirit itself; accordingly, there is no "spiritual" being, as if there would also be a spiritless beingness.

The global cry for wheat and gasoline, incited by what is unrecognizably inevitable, must now drown out the joyful grief of the future of the poetic word "bread and wine."

In the domain of the most modern humanity, a sign of the abandonment of beings by being, a sign of the transition contained in this abandonment, namely, the transition between the first to the other beginning, is the intertwining of the obsession with beings and the indifference toward being.

Those who are indifferent make it appear at times that they are the serene ones. Indifference seems like a weapon of the strength the superior person enjoys. But in truth this indifference is not an original ground of a stable attitude; instead, it is the extreme consequence of an unrecognizable instability arising out of the breakdown of an essential trait of the historical human being. That is the imagination, which can allow the signs of being to show themselves with respect to beings, although indeed being could never be derived from beings as one of the pieces or parts of their inventory. The imagination of this essential type must obviously break down, if barred to it is the open realm in whose guise being has illuminated itself. The barring of the open realm takes place here as a darkening which comes over beings because calculation, with its supposed universal validity, secures itself against the graciousness and sublimity of things and brings to extinction the stargazing of bestowed hours. The darkening

1. degeneration {Marginal remark in typescript}

of beings is the consequence of the straying into errancy as into the definitive distorted essence of truth.

112. The errancy of the errant star as the in-between of the passing by

To say errancy: unconditional Godlessness
unlimited order (technology—historiology)
the will to goallessness[2]
the will to willing
the unsuspecting rejection of the essence of truth
the devastation
and nevertheless, indeed only because,
pure lack of a sense of plight
forgottenness of the errancy
erecting of the surrounding world
the human being as the satellite of the devastation
and as the "guarantor" of the truthlessness[3]

113. The essence of truth in the passing by

Certainty as assurance of the unconditional presentification of arranging and
the cautiousness of the preservation of the dignity of beyng.
In the former, a calculating in goallessness
In the latter, an enduring of the differentiation into the departure that goes down.

114. The unavoidable

Metaphysics and
the truth of being

is being, insofar as the bustling about with beings under the dominance of metaphysics strives, without knowledge, to avoid being, which is unrecognized in its truth, in order not to be disturbed by

2. "humanity" and liberation of the proletariat only pretexts for the unsuspecting will to willing {Marginal remark in typescript}
3. "degeneration" {Marginal remark in typescript}

being and by its question-worthiness in the establishment of assurance in beings. In appearance, the averting of the unavoidable succeeds in the unstoppable expansion of the domain of calculating and arranging, an expansion out to all beings. But the whole of the calculable is not the sum total of the calculated nor even the product of what is without remainder, as posited in calculation by way of anticipation. The whole of the calculable is the incalculable itself, even when this latter is thought only with respect to the original whole of the calculable. The compulsion toward totality is the law of the inevitability of what is unavoidable. The expansion of the unavoidable into the manifold signs of its advent is only one of the forms in which it illuminates its already appropriated nearness in the whole. The fact that calculation thinks in terms of succession means that what it has not yet grasped, or what escapes it, is pursued in steps and as occasion offers. The unavoidable, however, has already eventuated. It cannot be explained from circumstances and incidents. The removal of these can never drive away the unavoidable. The pursuit of assurance in deliverable beings suppresses unknown being and furthers indeed, contrary to knowledge and will, that which is rebellious against the will to willing. The erecting of order in beings does specifically avert unknown being and, contrary to knowledge and will, brings into consideration the signs of the nearness of being. At times, when the conditionless dominance of the will to willing compels its executors to act against themselves, in that they unveil the signs of that which is unavoidable, by the very fact that they cover over these signs, there must then be prepared in the essence of being itself the shift whereby the concealed event abandons the dispropriation of beings from the truth of being and releases the consignment into the grounding of the truth of being. This event-related shift in being, whereby being twists itself free into the beginning, is the historical origin of the transition from the first to the other beginning. This transition shows itself first in the configuration of the overcoming of the episode in the history of being, and it is as this episode that the essence of metaphysics becomes evident. What is unavoidable constitutes the sign of the event.

115. The demise of metaphysics; the transition

The demise of metaphysics is not a particular incident, on the heels of which the transition to the other beginning then follows. Quite to the contrary, the beginning eventuates inceptually, and this eventuation *is* the overcoming of metaphysics, and this overcoming is the transition. The demise and the transition pass each other by; according to the law of the releasing of being into its extreme distorted essence (i.e., into the will to willing), beyng lets the distorted essence go on. Beyng overcomes the dominance of the distorted essence not by "engaging" with it and overpowering it but, rather, by releasing the distorted essence into its demise. The abyssal sort of overcoming is the releasing of that which is to be overcome into the fanaticism of its distorted essence, wherein it is engulfed. This releasing is to be experienced in knowledge of the fissure of the passing by, in which the will to willing and the event do not and cannot turn to each other. But this releasing is nothing "negative"; instead, it belongs to the dispropriation characteristic of all metaphysics since the start. And this dispropriation is proper to the event.

116. The passing by[4]

In the two historical currents, there pass each other by: the demise and the downgoing.

Who sees the constellation of such a passing by?

And where do those stand who see and experience?

The demise is only the cloud-made shadow of being and has its own necessity.

117. The passing by

The time of the thinking
of the history of beyng

The passing each other by of the abandonment of beings by being and the twisting free of beyng into the beginning. The time-space of this passing by as an event of the history of beyng is appropriated in the event of the beginning.

The constellation of the passing by

The clearing of this con-stellation (unlucky star—to star [*zu Stern*]). What is its "between"? The self-preparing inhabited place—Da-seyn.

Out of this "between," the *"in-between"* is determined, and that determines the *now* and what is current in the history of beyng.

The lack of a sense of plight.

The claim to reordering is the immediate boundary of the modern with respect to what is new and newest; i.e., it is the thinking of the will to willing, a thinking which seeks a decisive consummation.

4. in*sufficiently* thought {Marginal remark in typescript}

118. The passing by

of the unlucky star	(of the disintegration of machinational demise)
and	
of the fore-star	(of the downgoing into the inceptuality of the integration in the event)
	experienced on
the errant star	of the earth which, straying between planetary devastation and the concealment of the beginning, bears the in-between, which is the abyss.

119. The passing by

of the commencement of the essential unfolding of modernity (the three previous centuries were merely transitional preparation), and *of the beginning of the West.*

The respectively different time-spaces of the things that pass by.

The inhabited place of the constellation.

The passing by is the conjuncture of the transition.

120. The resonating

Passing by and episode

In the age of the consummation of metaphysics, there arises an appearance of exhaustion, because now, out of the will to willing, creation and the creative are expressly ruled out as principles and are transferred into planning. But since all creation can do nothing against the will to willing as the being of beings, and since creation has already delivered itself up to this will as a matter of instrumentality and contrivance, and since in general the creative—a prejudice of modernity—never attains what is essential to beyng, exhaustion must therefore be felt as a mysterious menace and, accordingly, the will to willing must be affirmed all the more, so as to suppress every sign of failure, up to the collapse of the distorted essence. The duration of the dominance of such a will, which in quantifiable time is longer than any historical span (which is unmeasurable), effects the passing by of each other of the devastation and the twisting free, specifically such that neither can "know" of the other. Or, in the experience of the history of beyng, is there not indeed a knowing in which the passing by is in fact experienced?

121. The overcoming of metaphysics

(The passing by, steadfastness in it)

Although, with respect to the event, the overcoming is historical in the twisting free, and although the releasing of metaphysics into its demise gives metaphysics itself over to its own distorted essence, out of which it can no longer raise itself (since to this distorted essence there pertains dominance of the will to willing, i.e., the fanaticism of the ensnaring into the unknowable demise), so historical humans, even in the transition, according to the relation of beyng to their essence, must be steadfast in the overcoming. Indeed humans cannot start this overcoming and cannot bring it about, and yet they are a party to it.

Humans could immediately be concerned with breaking the will to willing. That would mean, however, wanting to master beyng itself and to direct it. No being, not even that being (namely, the human being) which draws its historical essence from the relation of beyng to itself, can ever effect and determine being. Instead, the historical human being must correspond to beyng. Beyng itself and its respective truth are to be appropriated only out of beyng, inceptually. To the releasing of being into its demise, there corresponds steadfastly the tranquility of patience, which experiences the passing by, already knows the twisting free, listens only to the resonating of the beginning, and prepares the word for the voice of the beginning.

C. Modernity and the West

(Cf. On the beginning {GA70}; the inventive thinking of the beginning)

122. The demise of metaphysics; the transition to the first beginning

That the history of beyng here diverts cannot be accounted for by any "diversion" in the sense of inversion or reversion, not even the one into the first beginning, apart from the fact that that one, if it is not to remain mere historiological presentification, must itself come out of what is inceptual. But that can then only be the other beginning. The diverting eventuates, in this unique time-space of the history of beyng, only as the beginning. By that is to be measured how far every historiological reckoning of situations—even planetary, universal situations—is removed from the course of history and from what this course demands essentially of the future human being.

In the transition to the other beginning, the first beginning appears for the first time in its inceptuality. (Cf. above, I. The first beginning)

123. God-lessness experienced in terms of the history of beyng
Hölderlin—the destiny of the thinking of the history of beyng

Of what sort is the God-lessness of the modern age, such that only if aware of the history of beyng can a thinking of the twisting free of beyng into the beginning experience the truth of this blockage of every time-space of a divine realm and be grounded in the enduring of such experience, with the result that the appropriated habitation of the foreignness in beyng can be consigned to humans in their essence (toward Da-sein)?

This God-lessness is not simply the loss of the Christian God. On the contrary, this God is still everywhere—and indeed without churchdom—and is invoked in the most unrecognizable configurations and in changing forms of genuine and non-genuine belief. God-lessness, experienced as a matter of the history of beyng, arises in a fleeing from the plight of the lack of a sense of plight, a fleeing destined by the abandonment of beings by being (i.e., destined by the power of the will to willing). The age of the will to willing is without plight, because being, as an ordinance of appropriation into the truth of being, is unexperienceable, and thereby so is the twisting free into the beginning, and thus also the essential grounding of the human being, a grounding that can be determined only out of the truth of being.

This lack of a sense of plight, however, is in concealment the highest plight, if the forgottenness of being, derived from the abandonment by being, does indeed pass over what is most in plight: the experience of beyng over and against all fabricating and arranging of beings in the guise of their beingness, wherein "facts," "actualities," and "dynamisms" are presented as beings.

God-lessness is the blockage of the time-space of an appearance of a divine realm; the gods of this realm have not yet been decided. This God-lessness does not stem merely from human disbelief or from moral incapacity. This God-lessness is appropriated history within the history of beyng itself.

Insofar now as the thinking of the history of beyng, after its first, insufficiently self-understood attempt (in *Being and Time*), saw itself thrown into God-lessness, then, as can be said after the fact, a naming of the divine and of the super-divine had to become destiny so that historically there could be a support on which a thoughtful confrontation might preserve the inceptuality of its questioning. Accordingly, this support itself, which thereby never becomes a mere means to an end, might be clarified in *its* own poetic history. For it came to light, not only as a consequence of the crude, anthropological-existentiell, theological misunderstanding and misuse of *Being and Time,* that this questioning still had to be powerless in order to resist, from its own resources, the urge toward "metaphysics." This powerlessness went so far that such thinking, despite the inner determination of its questioning of the truth of being, tried to make itself intelligible to itself still within the broadest sphere of "metaphysics."

In this moment of the casting off of the last misinterpretations occasioned by metaphysics, i.e., in the moment of the first, extreme question-worthiness of beyng itself and of its truth (truth-lecture 1929–30), Hölderlin's words became destiny, words already known previously along with those of other poets. From the outside, this then appears to be the flight of thinking into the certitude of poetry. But this is thought in a metaphysical-Christian way, provided it is genuinely thought at all.

Everything now falls upon "the gods." By referring to the poet we are indeed compelled, in accord with his words, to speak about the "gods." Yet here, as everywhere, we must know that our speaking can only be an attentive heeding to the domain of the not yet experienced truth (sacredness) of this poetry.

We can neither judge about the "gods" from the standpoint of Christianity and its monotheism (accepted as true) nor can we, by engaging with the myths, make usable for ourselves the earlier "mythology" like a medicament against the enormity of technology. In that way, we are remaining completely within metaphysics and indeed within one we do not experience or endure. And we are bringing ourselves away from the genuine plight of the course and into the pure inhabited place of the inceptual God-lessness.

124. The consummation of modernity[5]

is the age of the *demise of metaphysics.*

5. Cf. The twisting free of metaphysics {in GA67}; *The history of beyng* {GA69}.

In terms of the history of being, the appearance of metaphysics in its consummation has three aspects, ones which in themselves unitarily determine the same:
the dominance of world-view (world-picture—arrangement—values)
technology (the planning of calculation)
historiology (the calculation of planning).[6]

From every side, and under an errant star, there proceeds the precipitation of all powers into the will to willing which, establishing itself in itself, has the "goal" of arranging the arrangements. This is a "goal" which, essentially thwarted by the setting of goals, is never allowed. Thereby the will is thrown back on itself and so constantly creates for itself the possibility of willing itself and nothing else.

Here eventuates the complete dispropriation of beings by being, in such a way that being is forgotten and is at once replaced by beings.

The demise of metaphysics into worldview is, with respect to the history of beyng, the event of the abandonment by being. Technology is technology of historiology; historiology is historiology of technology. These labels do not here refer to factical "appearances" of "culture" as understood in metaphysics; instead, they mean the concealed essential configurations of the truth of beings, beings which have entrenched themselves in beingness in the sense of actuality ("life") and objectivity.

The precipitation of "powers" in the will to willing results from a concealed unanimity in the essence; this belonging-together is the ground for the acuteness and the passion of the discord which grants validity only to the reciprocal nihilation; for, in the will to nihilation lives the will of the uniqueness of the one essence, of the will to willing. The devastation, under an errant star, has its unified ground in the concordance of all powers in the same will. Hence the technological steering of the "history" that still remains (a steering which has dissolved itself into a mere arranging of life processes in service to the will to willing) is guided by the principle of the fastest imitating and quantitative surpassing. Nowhere is there transformation, meditation, reconfiguration, but only the single overreaching in more and more devices and implements of the will. The presupposition of this unhistorical history is the renunciation of what is proper, the lack of desire to know an origin and a destiny; hence the running after the "comparative degree" which secures what is "technologically better" and

6. *Machination* as the essence of the will to willing and at the same time as the distorted essence of Φύσις—τέχνη, Ζωή—λέγειν. Certainty—will to willing and thus power in the form of *morality.* {Marginal remark in typescript}

"historiologically" (in instruction and proficiency) faster (cf. the demise of metaphysics in the will to willing).

125. The passing by

(The will to willing)

The irresistibility of the metaphysical essence of technology now incorporates the human being, calculated as "the most important raw material." The universally unmistakable consistency of the progression testifies that the *will to willing* has become the actuality of the actual.

We must pursue this process with the befitting coldness of experts but must also realize that inceptually already something else has begun, for which we must admittedly never try to find a place in the previous world.

We are standing in the con-stellation of the passing by of the errant star with respect to the earth.

Erosion and devastation.

The function of sheer nihilating and passing away.

126. The time of the thinking of the history of beyng
The passing by

This time is determined out of the history of beyng and is experienced in the thinking of beyng; this experience alone recognizes that now is the time of thoughtful questioning.

This time is determined by the fact that the extreme abandonment by being, as dominance of the will to willing, is passing by in the resonating of the twisting free of beyng into the other beginning, a resonating which itself is passing by in that devastation.

The passing by is the highest constellation of the abandonment by being and the twisting free of being. In the time-space of this con-stellation, there eventuates the history of the start of the genuine West.

In the age of the passing by, the extreme lack of a sense of plight and the purest plight are therefore unknowingly and simultaneously next to each other. The full and longest devastation and the simple grounding and founding of thinkers and poets. The unconditional arranging of purely and simply delivered objectivities of the planet and of its atmosphere and the questioning, as a matter of destiny, of the free experience of what is non-holy and non-native.

In the meantime, however, there still totters the desire to go back to something earlier that is precisely still spoken of. Also tottering is the overhasty planning of "reversals" and alterations. The hoping for an escape and the flight into something hardly yet established. The reckoning up of both and the tired sliding of everything.

This mediation in the age of the passing by is at its strongest, and it surmises neither the truth and necessity of the devastation nor the question-worthiness and freedom of the grounding. It is without nearness to the nearest and without remoteness to the remotest. It totters from the placeless to the timeless and from the latter to the former. *It* is what first introduces confusion into everything.

127. The will to willing

The West

The highest danger for the advent of the West is concealed in the fact that the Germans are succumbing to the modern spirit, in that they are abetting it along with its unrestricted capacity for organizing and arranging into the most vacuous unconditionality and are threatening to become the victorious vanquished, without this "spirit," i.e., the "truth" of being as the will to willing, thereby changing even in the least.

If the will to willing, in its inmost core, also wills that it could and should know nothing of its essence and destiny, and if, under the semblance of a legitimate struggle against that which is falsely taken as "knowledge," i.e., against the intellect, the lack of will to know the true and the truth is raised up to a basic trait of the genuine comportment toward reality, then the danger arises that every danger is denied and only extrinsic dangers of "outer" existence are thrust into the scenario.

The will to willing requires anthropology, because only anthropology constrains the human being to what is human; more precisely, this metaphysical event accomplishes the dominion. For, to see the human being humanly (humanistically, humanely, anthropologically) and even all-too-humanly ("psychologically") means to experience nothing of the human being. Humans remain in the compulsion of this view, even if they still patch on to "happenstance" a "fate."

128. The errancy of machination

(the will to willing)

The will to willing pursues the establishment of unconditional certainty in arrangements, and what is meant is that this would have to be accomplished first, in order subsequently to build on it the rest ("culture"—spirit—and also what lacks culture and spirit). It is not that machination never comes to this goal, which is its doom, but that machination in general misappraises itself in the essence of truth and believes it can at first pursue beings in order then to bring forward being (which machination does of course not grasp). The will to willing establishes the extreme forgottenness of being by still keeping open the prospect of being (while mistaking its essence) but in such a way that before all else everything is already driven to perversity.

129. The essence of "modernity"

The age which is eager for the new as the new and which reckons on the new for the human being's own self-reckoning.

Modernity [*die Neuzeit*] is not simply the "new time" [*die "neue Zeit"*] following in the wake of an obsolete one, whereby the series is discerned and divided up by some indefinite observer and appraiser. In its consummated start: the new order.

Accordingly, the newest age is also not simply the one that has been planned and is precisely now just dawning; on the contrary, it is one which purely and simply, without any possibility of increase, has in essence "liberated" the calculation of the newest in each case, the possibility of order, into the principle of its own calculation.

Belonging together essentially with this "tendency" of the age is "technology"; for technology is the essential ground, form of completion, and goal of modernity; the basic kind of innovation.

"Technology" is here understood metaphysically, however.

Modernity, to the degree that it presses forward into the newest and into what is "authentic" of its essence, must reject, and bring into oblivion, that which belongs to the West.

130. Modernity and the West

To await the evening[7] as the going down in which the inceptuality of the beginning essentially occurs is to have a relation to what is coming. But this coming is the beginning. This relation does not pertain to the "new" in the sense of the innovative. It pertains instead to the

7. The word for "West" in German is *das Abendland* and literally means the "land of the evening." The English word "West," from the Latin *vesper,* means the same.—Trans.

"old," assuming the old is not equated with what was earlier, is now past, and is still in some way retained and handed down.

Assuming that the old is conceived as the inceptual. The having-been of what is coming.

131. "The West" and "Europe"

The West, as a concept of the history of beyng, has nothing to do with "Europe," as a concept of modernity. What is European is the preliminary form of the planetary. The new order that is Europe constitutes an anticipation of planetary dominance, which of course can no longer be an imperialism, since emperors are impossible in the essential domain of machination.

What is European and planetary is the ending and completion. The West is the beginning.

Neither can know the other (cf. The passing by). What is European can surmise and know nothing of the West. The latter can no longer admit Europe and the planetary as beings. But it also does not strike out against the planetary; instead, it has inceptually already and simply passed it by.

Europe, considered in terms of continents, belongs to Asia.

Eurasia—to it belongs Russia as well as Japan.

132. The West and Europe

The "West," experienced in terms of the history of beyng, is the land of the evening, and the evening prepares the night out of which the day of the more inceptual beginning already eventuates.

"Europe" is the historiological-technological, i.e., planetary, concept that includes and integrates the "evening" and the morning, as West and East, out of its appointment as consummation of the essence of modernity, an essence which in the meanwhile dominates the Western hemisphere (America) in the same unequivocalness as the East of Russian Bolshevism. Europe is the consummation of both. Europe is the unconditional and calculative order for actualizing the downgoing of the West. The name for the fact that this "downgoing" is not simply allowed but is urged on and made secure as the unconditional devastation.

133. Abandonment by being; the West

The danger of stubborn presumptuousness and the danger of over-hasty retreat are nevertheless pressing, because they correspond to each other. In both cases, the way out leads into beings, which, now as the calculated, now as the handed down, place themselves in power over and against being.[8] In both cases, the unknown forgottenness of beyng pushes on. That is the sort of concealment of the abandonment of beings by being which can expand untrammeled only in such concealment.

The age of the hardly surmised forsakenness is other than the age of the abandonment by being. Here is already the transition—a first recollection of the past, a first admonishment toward what essentially occurs, the admittedly still unknown essential occurrence of the truth of beyng.

The recollective admonishment issues from the resonating of beyng and is itself tidings of history and determination of its occidental essence.

The West attains now for the first time the basic traits of its historical truth: the land of the evening. The evening is the end of the workday as the eve of the holiday, the completion of the day of the first beginning, the advent of the twilight and start of the night as the transition to the other day of the other beginning. The other beginning is nevertheless only the genuine inceptuality of the *one*. The evening is the advent of the time leading to the dawn of the festival. The West is the land of the other beginning, a land that takes its first delimitation out of such an advent.

(The "West" is understood otherwise by Spengler, for example, and taken to be the demise of Western civilization as "culture." The demise thereby possesses the form of the expansion of this modernity, having come to itself, into the planetary. The "West" perishes in that it settles into its demise as the highest progress.)

The West is the future of history, provided the essence of history is grounded in the event of the truth of beyng.

The West demands not only another chronology but even a change in the relation to history, a change that cannot be attained through an alteration of historiological conceptions of the past or through an establishment of a new present.

---

8. this, written in 1941, holds today in 1948 *all the more* {Marginal remark in typescript}

The historiology of the past and the technology (appertaining to historiology) of the present remain infinitely distinct from the change of history which arises out of the essence of history itself.

The West issues from the night land. The current night is not at all unholy; it is primarily a-holy; therefore world-history proceeds without a "world."

The West must first become the twilight of the "holy night" in which the poets move from land to land. In that way arises a world-time. It sets in without an uproar. The inconspicuousness holds out still in the unobtrusive. Meanwhile, there commences the ending of the demise of modernity. That incident must, according to the essence of this age, bring itself into the scene. Such can succeed only if the start of the demise mistakes itself in an excess of self-certainty, whereby the start pretends to be the beginning of a new time (thus of the newest of what is already new).

The ending in its demise should not be resisted. Yet we must also not abandon to it anything that is preparation for the beginning. We should not impede the demise. We must not claim that the withdrawal into "fatalism" is an "attitude." We cannot hope for anything from progression or regression. The beginning is everything.

134. "The West"

The concept of the West, as understood in the history of beyng, needs to be delimited against the historiological-geographical concept, which remains oriented to the morning and evening in the sense of the Orient and the Occident and thus in a certain way does indeed still refer to the domain of metaphysics and of the history of beyng.

The concept of the West within the history of beyng.

The metaphysical concept. (Platonism)

The historiological concept. (Christianity)

The essence of the West, as understood in the history of beyng, corresponds to an essence of history, an essence which appertains to the event and which concerns the twisting free of beyng.

135. The West

is not thought, with respect to the history of beyng, out of the past "morning land," the East; it is not the "Occident" of the "Orient," nor "the fruit of Hesperia" (Hölderlin, *Brod und Wein,* strophe IX); instead, it is the evening determined out of a forthcoming (not a past) morning and day. Occident and Orient must first undergo devastation out of the planetary. But why is the evening the first resonating of what is coming?

And *how* indeed is the *past* history of the Occident-Orient *inceptually* recollected and handed down?

The West—land of the evening of time, with time understood as the fore-time of that night which is the mother of the day of the more inceptual beginning.[9] We are going toward the evening and are returning home into the indigenousness of its land and its landscape.

This course is disposed by the beginning, whose time no one knows.

The West—*the passing by—the twisting free.*

The truly Western, in the sense of the history of being, eventuates inceptually out of the twisting free.

The twisting free as the return out of the advancement from the disentangling.

The West—*inceptually* experienced
is not "the geographical West"
is not "the Christian"—"Roman"
is not "the European"
is not "the modern."

All of that pertains to the *Occidental.*

To talk of "Western" metaphysics is ambiguous and means: (1) metaphysics insofar as it bears the Occidental and determines the history of the Occident. (2) the same metaphysics insofar as, having been overcome, it is recollected out of the twisting free of beyng and into the *Western* beginning.

136. World-history and the West

World-history can be experienced and thought in relation to the history of beyng only out of the essence of the "world." Otherwise, "world" means no more than earth or cosmos, nature, universe, universal history. This concept of history is determined out of historiology and out of the sphere of that which historiology encompasses; in the concept of universal history are thought all incidents on the entire earth, the latter taken cosmically as a planet. The concept of the planetary is the last stage of historiologizing, which now also appeals to a concept of nature as cosmos.

The newest modernity starts to enter into the planetary state of affairs. Everything is now reckoned planetarily, and, out of such reckoning, each thing is brought first to the calculative position and

9. the *epochal* of the *unification* in the *difference* {Marginal remark in typescript}

thus through the "position" to its historiological, and presumably historical, "place."

The state of affairs stretches over the whole planet, yet it is not the quantitative completion but the essential exclusivity of the historiological in the planetary which indicates that now everything presses on to a historical location of decision, a location this state itself cannot know.

The age of the commencing machination as the time of the abandonment by being is thus at once an age of complete undecidedness. This latter, however, is concealed behind the semblance that everything would now be decided for a new order and as a new order.

In the age of the—from the point of view of the history of beyng—undecidedness of the human and the divine realms to be there, only a few will experience this as something disposing a pure thoughtful joy.

Otherwise, however, the ones will "work themselves out" in machination, the others will "peevishly" immerse themselves in the past, and they all will fight against one another with unequal weapons and outlooks and together will help maintain concomitantly the state of concealed undecidedness.

The age of the newest modernity is, according to the essence of this (subjectivity), undergone by an unconditional consciousness (historiology-technology). This consciousness cannot be removed by a flight into the unconscious, especially since "instinct" likewise has become an appearance of controllable, breedable consciousness.

Even if one could extend (now only "measurements" count) consciousness so far that one could survey everything transpiring on the planet, even then, indeed then especially and fully for the first time, this extensive viewer would be unable to see the single unique reality beyond such extended knowledge of real things. For such a viewer has long since been blinded by predecessors and can see only real things and is therefore blind to beyng. Indeed not only blind to beyng; for in that way this viewer would have been excluded from beyng and debarred from a relation to it. This viewer has forgotten beyng, specifically such that the forgottenness remains swirling in its own abyss.

Only those who originate purely out of the beginning, and are disposed for the inceptual, can here see what is. And what is, what properly and exclusively is true, is *beyng.* Its truth, however, happens in a Western way.

The West cannot be determined in relation to "Europe"; Europe will one day be a single bureau, and those who "work together" will be the employees of their own bureaucracy.

137. Certainty, security, establishment, calculation, and order

Ordering and the will to order are in themselves already the renunciation of question-worthiness and of essential decisions. Ordering presupposes the actual as the given and posits, at the same time, along with the presupposed, the more or less secure sort of order and its guiding aspects of establishment and alignment.

Thinking is terms of order is calculation. Calculating is securing. Securing is the holding fast to something decided. This holding fast is something compelled by decisionlessness.

All calculation adheres to "plans" and prescriptions, which change in each case, according to need, within the parameters of change that are appropriate to the process of securing.

All calculation reckons with "facts" (which are brought forward as unconditional) without ever considering that even the most naked fact is already laden with an interpretation, albeit a very ragged one.

All calculation with facts and in plans does at times abandon ideals and prototypes, which can be rescinded overnight once they have served their purpose.

All this pertains to the correct carrying out of ordering.

138. Devastation

The unconditional establishment of machination and the aligning of mankind to this establishment constitute the installation of the abandonment of beings by being, an abandonment unknowable in itself.

In that way, the erosion of the previous essence of the gods becomes complete. The devastation appears in the form of the swiftest and widest progress in all planning and calculating. The machinational basic form of the devastation is the new order, which can be fully carried out only in a struggle over the supremacy of ordering and of the claims of order.

As soon as the last restraints to the devastation are overcome and "destructions" are recognized as mere temporary passageways, there results for the human will to ordering the chance of a complete calculation of the globe in terms of its "goods" and "values." Finally arrives the prospect of storing up a "potentiality" of powers which can be sufficient, in the most plightless moment of the age of the complete lack of a sense of plight, to deliver up the globe, along with its atmosphere, to an explosive charge.

This blowing up of the globe by the *animal rationale* will be the last act of the new order.

This act is the appearance of the extreme impotence of humanity, by which it is excluded from everything inceptual. Therefore even this "record accomplishment" of the carrying out of the devastation can never have even the smallest effect in relation to the beginning. The latter now remains completely untouched in its inceptuality. Meanwhile, the appropriation of Da-sein has taken place. The appropriation does not need to be announced and reported.

The ground of the West lies in the inceptuality of the beginning.

139. The inceptuality of the beginning; beyng

How indeed in the truth of historical humans, and in their word (language), *beyng essentially occurs*—even if already for a long time there has been an overcoming of being and a twisting free of beyng.

Must the inceptuality, as a declining one, necessarily remain in such remoteness, even to the point of steadfastness? Yes.

And must it not become known that this remoteness from inceptuality and from Da-sein is appropriated as the abyssal nearness?

Eventuating here is not the abandonment of beings by being but, instead, the *ceding of beings to inceptual beyng.*

*

Beyng (in inceptuality) appropriated to Da-sein?

Steadfastness in the clearing.

Obedience to the appropriation. Appropriation as appropriative event (inceptuality): beyng and the human being.

Patience for the light out of indigence within "beings." The graciousness (the gentle care) of what is noble, which is disposed out of the consonance of world and earth and is more inceptual than mere consonance.

Steadfastness—the question presses: what should we "do"? What is at stake? *Da-sein.* The weaning (negation!) from producing and making, out of the appropriation into Da-sein.

The most proximate course.

Inceptuality of the beginning—steadfastness as reception of the inceptual—steadfastness as questioning—questioning as hearing of obedience—thinking as the "there."

Once again the boldest liberation toward the advent in the garden of the noblest mildness of pure recollection of unique intimacy.

D. Metaphysics The episode between the first beginning and the other beginning The transition (its signs)

140. Metaphysics

is, in terms of the history of beyng, the *episode* of the dominance of beings over beyng such that beyng releases itself into the beingness of beings and accommodates itself to the abandonment of beings by being.

Thus are prepared the beinglessness of beings and the possibility of the other beginning.

The beinglessness in the age of the demise of metaphysics is essentially other than the one preceding the first beginning of the history of beyng.

The episode is the history of the essential occurrence of being as ἰδέα, ἐνέργεια, *actus, perceptio,* actuality, representation; these essential forms are gathered together in the will to willing.

The episode is between the first and the other beginning. Via this episode, the inceptuality of the beginning achieves a first resonating.

141. "Metaphysics"

Distinguish:

1. the essence of metaphysics as that essence is understood in terms of the event (i.e., in terms of the history of beyng): the episode of the essential occurrence of the truth of beyng between the first and the other beginning. The advancement from the former into the priority of beingness (i.e., the priority of beings) toward the abandonment by being. The investigation of self-relinquishing beings in the bridging time between the disentanglement toward beingness and the twisting free of beyng.
2. the "thinking" that remains in metaphysics:
   Anthropology in the sphere of the unconditional priority of "technology," in the sense of the calculative planning of the order for

the consumption of beings, ultimately corresponds to the essence of metaphysics in its completion. The using up of beings in service to the securing of the possibility of order is the last thwarting of a truth of being.

3. metaphysical thinking "about" metaphysics; "metaphysics" of metaphysics.
4. the confrontation, from the point of view of the history of beyng, with inceptual thinking; in this confrontation the previous distinctions step forth, and metaphysics is experienced in its necessity.

142. Beginning and advancement

Uniqueness and dispersal

Variety

Calculation

The obstructing of the beginning as the arising of calculation; λόγος becomes *ratio*. Reason and "order."

143. Metaphysics and beyng

Yet metaphysics would not be metaphysics, i.e., the truth of beings as such, if it did not essentially occur out of beyng, since indeed even beingness remains on the basis of the essence of beyng. That is why in metaphysics, provided we become ever more experienced, there are indeed resonances of the beginning everywhere. But they are reinterpreted and appear as what rests in itself—the absolute, the unconditional,[10] the "origin," and the principle—and thus by themselves prevent the beginning from being questioned otherwise than in their measure and their sense.

Even in the forgottenness of being in metaphysics, whereby metaphysics can never experience the truth of beyng and, in that truth, beyng itself, there still essentially occurs the essence of being as that essence occurs in the first beginning.

144. How and in what sense

does the distorted essence belong to beyng? (From beyng as *beginning*). The distorted essence not the "negative," the "occurrence of

10. supreme cause, first ground {Marginal remark in typescript}

negativity" essentially in the (event), but also not in the sense of the previous sublation in the absolute, such that, as in Hegel, negativity is mere semblance and can never become a *serious* disposition.

145. Metaphysics

"Logic"
"System" "Aphorism"

It is according to these standards that we judge the thinking of thinkers. If the thinking does not meet the standards, we assign it to "art" and "poetry" or to confusion and arbitrariness. In all this we never wonder whether or not the standard of thinking is actually derived from that which is to be thought.

And if that is beyng?

And if that can be said only in the pain of the experience of the event?

146. The demise of metaphysics in the will to willing

The preliminary stage of the will to willing is the "will to power." The will to willing is the will that wills itself. What does the will will? Willing. What is that? The bringing before oneself of what can be represented. And that is the totality of objects; objects are beings within the truth of certainty, i.e., within the delivery to oneself of something established. Pure calculative objectification determines the being of beings as objectivity. Yet insofar as this objectification is the will to willing, being itself possesses the essence of willing. The will to willing is that which underlies itself as the ground of itself; i.e., it is the subject. Calculative objectification can uncover for itself only ordering as a goal (intention), an ordering that secures the progression of the objectification only as the basis for "more" willing, i.e., for ever less of that which does not undergo objectification and could emerge out of itself. The dominance of the will to willing, however, does in no way bring being itself into the truth; it deals only with beings, posited as what is supposed to require objectification, i.e., as "value." In the highest stretching up of this being [*Sein*], beings come into the abandonment by being.

At its highest stage, the will to willing is the unconditional unwillingness for truth, inasmuch as the will to willing does not want to experience the essence of truth, i.e., here, cannot admit of this essence, since the will adheres to representation and thus indeed claims unknowingly, and at the same time disavows, the unconcealedness of beings and the clearing of being. Thought more inceptually, the will to willing abhors every appropriation, every truth, and every carefulness.

Objectification as the self-willing of the will is the unconditional actualizing of the actual and thus is actuality itself. Accordingly, objectivity (objectness) and "actuality" coalesce.

The abandonment by being asserts itself in manifold forms: as the emergence in what is objective (technology—historiology), specifically such that, in the object, what is encountered in the sense of appropriation is precisely not the being in *its being;* as the dissolution of everything into effective "life," where objectivity has seemingly disappeared and everything is mixed into everything (neither beings nor being, but mere goading and lived experiences).

The difference is utterly unexperienceable.

147. "Essence" and "being"[11]

Metaphysics thinks the essence as *essentia* and thinks this latter as *quidditas,* i.e., οὐσία as beingness.

The first and the second οὐσία.

Why does the whatness (τί) gain priority over the ὅτι?

In truth, the whatness is only a stilling of the ὅτι, of the still ungraspable (and already, as φύσις, renounced) "that it is" of the (event).

Because the "that it is" remains, so to speak, concealed in its truth, it appears as *factum brutum* and something which is not open to further interrogation and which is seized upon by explanation through causality, wherein the intention of the "that it is" already announces itself as *effectivity.*

Here in general the priority of the ἰδέα is essentially occurring; *"existentia"* becomes the name for something indispensable although unknowable.

148. The end of metaphysics; "world-picture"

Calculated historiologically, the history of metaphysics extends through two millennia. Experienced historically, as the history of the truth of beings, it is the way from the realm of the "cave allegory" to the "world-picture." Were it not for the former, the latter would not be.

11. Cf. On the history of the concept of existence. {In GA80}

In the "world-picture," the "world" has become the plan of self-instituting. What is plain and level in the prevailing calculation determines what is visible. The "planning" within the plan predelineates the possibilities of the world. The "cave" is the genuine world, the one and only world, but is now illuminated by the "light" of planning. The upper region is composed of the "Ideas," which are mere values, as changing, empty, and intrinsically unstable forms and conditions of planning, the means of securing all of the making sure of the unrestricted capacity to be planned.

In the essence of beings as a whole, as that essence is understood in terms of world-picture, the relation to the domain of the cave allegory can no longer be immediately recognized. And yet it is the same world. To be sure, the modern essence of beings, the world as "picture," is not merely the "reversal" of the first, Platonic, "world"; the distinction between the supersensible and sensible "worlds" is, under sublation of both, incorporated into the pure securing and producing of everything.

149. The consummation of metaphysics[12]

1. Amplification of unconditional subjectivity (amplification of the spirit).
2. The reversal of unconditional subjectivity (reversal of the spirit).
3. The leveling into complete (amplified, reversed) subjectity [*Subjektität*]—the leveling of actuality as machination.
4. Machination is, in terms of the history of beyng, the abandonment of beings by being.
5. The abandonment of beings by being is inceptually the failure of the truth of beyng.
6. This failure is a forerunner of the downgoing, and the downgoing is always, before all else, genuinely occurring in the beginning.
7. The downgoing of the saying is the reticent stillness of the protective graciousness.

150. Steadfastness within the beginning

The two intrinsically unitary *turns* in
the transition to the other beginning.
From humanity (and "anthropology") to Da-sein.

12. Cf. On the history of the concept of existence. {In GA80}

From beingness (and metaphysics) to beyng.

This turn, however, must out of itself already contain the essential character.

This turn is never merely the change of an "attitude," whereby in every case the one who changes remains the same in essence and preserves this self-sameness.

The turn [*Wendung*] here is self-devotion [*Sichverwenden*] to another essence.

The turn is dedication [*Zuwendung*] to the relation of beyng to the human being.

All comportment and intention is then already always mere application [*Anwendung*] of the turn and is a devoting of it to steadfastness in beyng.

151. "Being"

is always understood by me out of its difference to nothingness, specifically such that nothingness and the difference itself are grasped out of the essence of being. And all this is thought only in order to ascertain, by questioning, the ground of the essence of being, this ground understood as the truth of beyng.

Since Hegel's "dialectic" remains wholly within metaphysics, it is insufficient for this questioning; nor may we appeal here to Hegel's concept of being or to his interpretation of negativity, an interpretation in terms of consciousness.

Being, as differentiated from nothingness, is thought more originally than all becoming; all becoming is being. But "being" need not—metaphysically, from Plato to Nietzsche—signify "rest" in the sense of rigidity. Beyond that, there is a rest which first bears the usual difference between becoming ("life") and being.

152. "Order" and the forgottenness of being

The essential character, now in demise, of the last mode of *metaphysical truth* is certainty as the security of the making secure of the fund of beings (which are determined unconditionally and in advance as objects).

To this truth of beings there corresponds thinking in the sense of ordering. The unconditional mode of order aims at the ordering of ordering. Ordering means in this case the planned distribution into sections (sectors); within these themselves everything must be surveyable for an instituting which makes everything ready for any arbitrary utilization in service to the will to willing ("culture" taken consistently as a "sector"). The ordering of orders is "new," i.e., in accord with modernity [*Neuzeit*], and is therefore the "new order." In the "world" of order, everything is already decided. The inner presupposition of the ordering of ordering is the unconditional lack of goals; the ordered stoppage of the questioning of truth: the unconditional forgottenness of being. The world here becomes a "picture." And "picture" means the view that at once presents the whole plan, the controllability of the institutions. To be "in the picture" = to be informed, to be well versed, to be present where the "action" is. "New order," "new values," are necessarily the consequences of the unconditional demise of metaphysics.

153. The end of metaphysics; reflection

The way of the thinking of beyng.

At the end of metaphysics, truth, as the securing of the fund of the effective and the effecting, is thrust into the ultimate height of consciousness. What, before that, occurred immediately, "outside" of consciousness and unavailable to objectification, namely, "race" and "character," "instinct" and "deed," now becomes what especially has to serve as a means of equipping and ordering and must be "rationalized" through "legislation," etc. Here the task is to recognize that the consummation of metaphysics cannot be halted. At the same time, however, there arises for the transition a necessity to experience, indeed not "reflexion," but its essential truth, *thoughtful questioning* itself, as the essential occurrence of the truth of beyng, rather than (versus reflexion and its misinterpretation as intellect) merely appealing to the "unconscious" and the "organic." Yet all concern over disposition also still belongs here if such concern makes the dispositions into objects or even only attempts to grasp their more original essence—instead of disposing in thought and by way of thought and not discussing the disposing power of disposition.

154. The last remnants of the demise of "philosophy" in the age of the consummation of metaphysics

are cramped together in the forms of "ontology" and "anthropology." *Being and Time* supposedly has to do with both, but its "ontology" is said to be insufficient and its "anthropology" one-sided. If only it could have been recognized that the book does not "do" either "ontology" or "anthropology" and that "fundamental ontology" can only mean getting at the ground of ontology and thereby at the same time steering clear of anthropology.

If only the simple attempt had been made to think what is thought there, namely, the truth of being or even only to follow the way to such thinking.

If only care could have been taken to be satisfied with the provisional character of this thinking, instead of raising it up, beyond all measure, to claims which it itself does not make and cannot make.

If only, for the moment, the essence of the ground, as that essence is thought there, could have been accepted.

155. Forgottenness of being

In the age of the forgottenness of being, the human being is at once the forgotten and the forgetful.

The human being is forgetful not only as no longer thinking of being but also as unable to ponder being in its truth.

The human being is forgetful in such a way because this being is not admitted into the recollection of being and, as the preserver of the truth of being, is repulsed from being itself and remains entirely abandoned to beings themselves and to their supremacy. The *supremacy* of beings means that beings themselves are in power and that being is the will to power.

The "will to power" is the last veiling of the "will to willing" wherein actuality and objectivity find themselves as the ground of this veiling.

156. Being as machination[13]

If being has terminated in machination, it loses not only every balanced distribution of weight but also all weight whatsoever. It can now no longer be asked whither, in the essential occurrence of being, the weights are tending and shifting.

To be utterly without weight and empty of weight is a distinctive mark of the unconditionality of power.

Power does not rest on something else and does not have in this its heaviness, i.e., any weight at all; instead, it essentially occurs in the

13. (com-posing [*Ge-Stell*]) {Marginal remark in typescript}

unconditional empowerment of itself. The unconditionality of the will to power is not a consequence of "nihilism"; on the contrary, the will to power has the unconditionality of its essence and thereby nihilism as consequences. Nihilism, however, signifies altogether nothing for the will to power. Nihilism is "nothing" the will to power could dwell on or get worked up over. The nothingness of the utter nullity of being, inasmuch as being is released into its unconditional distorted essence.

157. Being as the non-sensory

This interpretation provides a mark and yet is merely averting and metaphysical and relates being to the appropriate apprehension and representation.

Does the mark offer anything to be marked? The fact that we must not seek beings as the source of being; moreover, that even beings are indeed never the "sensory."

The *mark* provides a hint into what is closest to us, closest by remaining the highest and most remote.

(In the same way that a more remote, higher mountain is nearer to us and is nearness, versus that which we hold in our hands, the obvious and banal.)

Cf. the dicta about beyng, s. s. 1941 {*Grundbegriffe* GA51}.

Cf. Kant's assertion that being is not a "real predicate" [*"reales Prädikat"*].

"Reality" (Intensity of the sensed as such; effectiveness of the effective).

Reality— as *affirmativeness*
as "matter at issue"
(Is being a "predicate" at all, i.e., determinable on the basis of predication as such?)

158. Metaphysics: Kant and Schelling—Hegel

Kant remains mired *in* metaphysics; that means he does not at all ask the question of being.

The furthest he reaches is the distinction of all objects whatever into phenomena and noumena; being as being-in-itself and as "appearance."

1. Being?? How is that understood here in advance? *Objectivity*—but in what sense? And how grounded?
2. The distinction itself is not grounded, because its ground is groundless.

Kant does not ask about the truth of being but only about the *being* of beings and that by way of asking about the objectivity of the objects of experience.

This holds completely and unconditionally for Hegel and Schelling.

*

The strict determinateness of metaphysical thinking at the stage of consummation: Hegel—(Nietzsche)
and the apparent indeterminateness of the other beginning, because here essentially another *disposition.*
The inceptual and not the *unfolded*—
The inceptual and its *one-fold* (downgoing).

*

Ignorance is the *origin* of "willing," an origin such that the *will* becomes the essence of actuality.

Ignorance in the form of the claim to *knowledge and insight* (representation).

Inceptual ignorance—patience—forbearance; thanking.

159. Truth as certainty

(ἀλήθεια and the clearing of being)

i.e., 1. demonstrable in intuition
2. valid for everyone

Therefore "true" knowledge only as "appearance."

Kant's concept of knowledge as "appearance" is determined from the essence of truth as *certainty.*

But is that the essence of truth? According to what do we decide truly about the essence of truth? What is here, and how questioned?

160. Biological "life" (Nietzsche)

Where beings are the actual, and actuality is "the will to power," there "life" becomes the impulse that merely presses after the pressure which overwhelms the impulse.

Everything is measured by the quantum of pressured impulse.

Therefore art is essentially a "stimulant" of "life"—goad, stirring up of the impulses. Everything must be calculated toward exciting this goad and maintaining the excitation.

Everything is related "causally," effected by the pressing impulses. All "life" is appraised only with respect to the cultivation of the capacity for impulses. The animal is indeed not a "machine" and yet is more fateful than this, the cultivatable, calculable, excitable, merely stimulating pressure of bodily life.

Everything is worldless and dislocated from the earth.

161. Metaphysics

The concealed truth of metaphysics can be grasped only in inceptual thinking, never metaphysically.

Only in light of this thinking is it possible to illuminate what genuinely lies in metaphysics.

162. The demise of metaphysics

The γιγαντομαχία περὶ τῆς οὐσίας is now fought by the dwarfs of "ontology" and by the henchmen of "anthropology."

If thinking has passed over into erudition, feeds on the results of the sciences, and counts on the approval of the sciences, it has arrived at its emptiest distorted essence. Even those who are thoughtless will then recognize how inessential it is.

163. The saying

Attending to being (beginning).
Attending to beings (*beingness*)
what is without beginning.
Attending to history qua destiny and beginning.
Attending to history qua happenstance.
"Technology" as the basic truth of history qua happenstance.

E. The will to willing

164. "Being" in metaphysics

In terms of history of beyng, beingness proceeds into its distorted essence. This proceeding, as a releasement of being into truthlessness, is determined by the disentanglement.

Actuality (*actualitas* of the *actus purus*) enters into the essence of *vis,* i.e., exertional representing, i.e., willing, a willing that keeps itself concealed as the will to willing and appears at first as reason, spirit, will to love, denial of the will, and the like, and appears ultimately as the will to power.

The will to willing, as the basic trait of being, determines being as machination. What satisfies machination is only unconditional will to order; i.e., the ordering is ordered. That is the goal of planetary devastation.

The consumption of raw material and the deployment of humans as the most important raw material ("human resources") are merely consequences of the devastation as the extreme securing of the unrestricted possibility of the will to willing.

What does it mean to be faithful to one's own essence, if this essence is calculation and the hunger for power?

The will to willing arrogates all things as tools for its own benefit, especially the metaphysical ideals and their morality: "honor," "sacrifice," "loyalty," "teamwork."

In the domain of human formation, *fanaticism* corresponds to the essence of the will to willing.

The will of the claim to know (and to dominate and not release) everything conditional as unconditional.

Fanaticism as the last way out of the perplexity in the stretching up into the emptiness of willing.

The will to willing
engagement; activism—
anonymity—irresponsibility—degradation of humans and destruction of their bearing; the extreme unbridling of all arbitrariness in the semblance of order.

165. The will to willing

(Spengler)

This extreme essence of beingness within the history of metaphysics can be experienced only when the transition to the other beginning has already eventuated. Yet, prior to that, there can already be indicated, mediately, how this essence essentially occurs, since it provokes and determines the consistent interpretation of Nietzsche's metaphysics in various respects. Two notable forms for us are Spengler's *Untergang des Abandlandes* [*Decline of the West*] and Ernst Jünger's *Der Arbeiter* [*The Worker*] and his treatise *Über den Schmerz* [*Beyond Pain*].

What makes Spengler's aesthetic-physiognomic culture-soul interpretation an offshoot of Nietzsche's metaphysics and the genuine precursor of all "worldviews" of the twentieth century?

The "idea" of "expression."

Spengler recognizes that "art and philosophy" "have become irrevocably past" (II. Bd. 585). Yet he does not see that "philosophy" means for him only "metaphysics" and not the thinking of beyng. He does not see that his physiognomics is only the latest scion of precisely this "irrevocable past" and so is the *plu*perfect, on which no past is conferred. Spengler always thinks in terms of that dichotomy which resides essentially in the will to power and which was given clear recognition by Nietzsche: the transfigurative, willful becoming ("time") and the fixing and securing of content (space). The crudeness, groundlessness, and superficiality of Spengler's depth considerations are simply covered over for a while by the material, the historiologically collected illustrations and portrayals of "cultures." The epigonal character of his "philosophy" corresponds to the lack of measure in his dogmatics, which is full of claims, and to the emptiness in questioning and in issues genuinely worthy of question.

The talk of the "streaming of existence" and the "currents of life" is a mark of the radiating outward of the will to power. Cf. Spengler's table of dichotomies.

166. The will to willing

is the genuine unconditional consummation of the "will to power." The will to power is still suspended in unconceived "actualizing." The actuality of the actual has not yet receded into the pure essence of subjectity.

The I-think is the *I-will;* for the I-think, as I-combine, is self-positing-to—it is securing, self-willing.

(The age of unconditional thoughtlessness)

III. The difference

167. Beyng

On the beginning

is groundless and therefore does not know any "why." Beyng is, in that it is pure appropriating event.

As the abyssal ground, however, beyng is the beginning of all consignment of beings to their essence.

For here prevails the deep mystery that everything, resting in itself, harbors incontestable strangeness and becomes the call which inceptually calls forth the rarity of self-belonging.

168. Introduction

Exclude for once mere description, which always takes refuge only in "beings," forbid mere reports, which are given over only to the past, desist from plans and calculations, which are attached only to the immediate future—and then still try to think and speak. Then to you it is as if there were nothing. Yet then to you would be what is: beyng.

We seldom accede to that universally extensive renunciation of beings and of their offering us a basis for representation and opinion. And if we are granted this, we scarcely find our way in the initially assailing emptiness, because the renounced claims and pre-opinions always still want to have our ear, since we too easily supply ourselves with an implicit justification of the ever-sought excuse by way of the opinion that this renunciation is an "abstraction" (although it remains unclear what this term is supposed to mean). In fact the renunciation is already the consequence of a submissiveness we now carefully allow to prevail in us without correctly experiencing that this submissiveness arises from a consignment to beyng, a consignment that has eventuated inceptually, i.e., as something inceptual.

What purely and simply is not nothing is a being. Nothingness itself, however, is being.

What is beingless is other than being (to which nothingness appertains). Non-beings are other than what is beingless.

Beyng (Essential occurrence of truth)—The difference:
Being
Nothingness
Beings
What is beingless
Non-beings
Da-seyn

Only in the twisting free of beyng into the turning of the event does the experience of beyng become true.

Whence the difference between true and untrue? (ἀλήθεια—δόξα; ὄν—μὴ ὄν) Out of *the difference* itself.

In the emptiness of the renunciation, the nobility of indigence can be experienced through the experience of the event and specifically of the event of the inceptual dispropriation—*the withholding.*

169. The difference
(Outline)

A. *First of all to point into the difference and specifically on the basis of the differentiation.*
   1. the first indication of the differentiation.
   2. the differentiation as the ungrounded ground and arena of metaphysics and of its world-play.
   3. This indication already goes beyond metaphysics.

B. *The exhibition of the difference as departure.*
   4. The difference as self-differentiating (event).
   5. Beinglessness and the event of withholding; the inceptual dispropriation.
   6. The difference and the differentiation.
   7. The difference and the distinctions; and the *"as"*
      a. of the human being to beyng
      b. of the human being to beings
      c. within beings—the regions.

   (κρίνειν, the ᾗ, *qua,* as, διαίρεσις-σύνθεσις: ἕν, διαλέγεσθαι—the negativity of Hegel)

C. *The difference and the twisting free of beyng.*
   8. The difference and the downgoing.
   9. The downgoing and the departure.
   10. The departure and the abyss.
   11. The abyssal ground and the more inceptual beginning.

12. The inceptuality of the event and the enduring of the difference.

D. *Enduring as suffering. Its suffering is the experience of departure.*

13. The essence of experience.
14. Event and experience.
15. The experience of the history of beyng—this experience as the essence of inceptual thinking.

E. *The differentiation and metaphysics.*

16. The differentiation of the τί ἐστιν and the ὅτι ἔστιν. The priority of οὐσία: the relation of whatness and thatness. Cf. On the history of the concept of existence {in GA80}.
17. The indeterminateness of the differentiation of beingness and beings in the vacillation of speech, which now designates beings as "being," "that which is," and now designates "being" as merely beings themselves.
18. The differentiation and the apriori—the question of possibility, the sensory—the supersensory, the hither side and the thither side; "transcendence" (Cf. The twisting free of metaphysics, ms. p. 19ff. {in GA67, p. 24ff.})

F. *The essence of the difference.*

19. The difference is a matter of the event (the resonating of the turning).
20. The difference and Da-seyn (the in-between).
21. Da-seyn and the appropriation of the human being.
22. The distinctiveness of the human being as the historiality of the history of beyng.
23. The difference and the opening up of the levels of beings (in each case, historial); at first the human being simply follows concomitantly under beings; *animal—rationale.*
24. The "ontological difference" [*Differenz*] in *Being and Time* as the first reference to the difference [*Unterschied*] as such. The thrown projection of being; i.e., the *appropriation* into the truth of beyng.
25. The dispropriation and the abandonment of beings by being.

G. *The difference and the first beginning.*

εἶναι and τὰ ὄντα

ἀλήθεια—τὰ δοκοῦντα

How in this way the difference is experienced, although remaining ungrounded. The double danger facing us: that we either misinterpret the difference metaphysically or "subjectivize" it in terms of modes of representation!!

170. The difference and nothingness

The inceptual nothingness is the purely bestowing clearing as the event of the turning. In this nothingness, the refusal essentially occurs as the basic trait of the abyss.

Out of this nothingness and its negativity, i.e., its refusing, i.e., its inceptuality, the "not" and the "no" are determined in the difference. Yet inasmuch as nothingness is beyng, beyng is essentially the difference as the inceptually concealed and refused departure.

171. The difference and the event

In the difference and out of it, being never "comes to" beings as a "predicate," nor is being in relation to beings something to which they are "entitled" and their state of affairs. On the contrary, in the difference beings rather "come to" being, i.e., they "approach" being in that they come forth—toward—being in the clearing. Beings *arise* from beyng.

Being, however, ises[1] as the appropriating event. Being is not always. It itself brings time-space in the clearing and thus first grants the possibility of determination, explicitly on the basis of beings, according to the now and then.

"Constancy" and "moment" already belong *in* the appropriation of the difference and so cannot be utilized to determine the event.

172. The difference

(the differentiation and metaphysics)

which first allows beings to arise as beings, and separates them to themselves, is the ground of all separations in which beings can first "be" these respective individuals.

The separations and the things separated make possible something other than the usual "differentiating," on the basis of which we characterize thinking as a "representing."

The difference does not separate being as the supersensory world from beings as the sensory world; on the contrary, all things, the sensory, non-sensory, supersensory, are beings and different from being.

1. *Istet*: third-person singular form of the coined verb *isten*, "to is."—Trans.

Metaphysics does not know the difference, because it indeed uses and must use the difference, inasmuch as metaphysics deals with ὂν ᾗ ὄν, yet immediately misinterprets the difference in what is differentiated from beings, insofar as metaphysics explains even "being" immediately on the basis of beings and the highest being.

On the other hand, in the first beginning the difference purely emerges in emergence (φύσις), is indeed experienced (Parmenides), but is not grounded. This inceptual lack of grounding is, however, more inceptual than all groundings since Plato, ones that lose beforehand what is to be grounded and postulate as the ground (the highest being amid beings) something that is already a consequence and is never the abyssal ground.

173. The difference

(on the use of the word)

The differentiation of beings and being (ground).
The difference of (*genitivus subiectivus*) being with respect to beings.
Beyng as the difference—essentially occurring as the departure.
The twisting free of the difference into the departure.
The difference is the resonating of the departure and is how the latter should be thought.
The thinking of beyng as the enduring of the differentiation.
"The differentiation" is ambiguous:

1. seen from the viewpoint of metaphysics, it is the blind carrying out of the representation of beingness as what is universal to beings, thought on the basis of beings. Thus the differentiation is the representational presentification of an objectively present (!) difference.
2. understood in terms of the history of beyng, it is the obedience to the pure difference, an obedience which protects for this difference the twisting free into the departure and achieves this only through steadfastness in the difference itself and in its essential occurrence (which is a matter of the event and, at first, a matter of the turning).

To that extent—and thought in the respective distinct dimensions—we can say: enduring of the difference and enduring of the differentiation. The first denomination pays heed to the fact that the enduring is appropriated; the second, to the fact that the enduring, as appropriated, follows the difference while "differentiating."

The difference, as beyng itself, appropriates the differentiation in which at any time obedience[2] is involved.

174. The difference and the "understanding of being"

If the difference of being and beings is taken in terms of the representationally understood "differentiation," as its object, and if "beings" are understood as the actual, and the actual as the sensuously perceived, then being immediately appears as the non-actual, which, since it is not completely nothing, is assigned as *ens rationis* to "mere" thinking and representing as an "object." In this way, being is a mere "thought" or only a "concept," the concept of the non-actual. And it is then also not correctly understood what this non-actuality is still supposed to be "in its difference" from the actual; it is relegated to "philosophy."

If, on the basis of this usual opinion, the understanding of being is "explained," then being is the object of the understanding; it exists merely in the "understanding"—something thought. And since indeed "thinking" is taken to be the activity of the "subject," and the subject remains distinguished from objects and the objective, being is something merely "subjective." If need be, this explanation of being as a product of the understanding can still be joined to Kant's idealism, according to which the categories are indeed concepts of the understanding and all objectivity is the "subjective" apriori of objects. But "understanding" is projection, and projecting is something thrown and is admitted into the clearing of beyng on the basis of beyng.

*

The difference as the essential occurrence of beyng itself, which differentiates *itself* and in that way lets beings arise in emergence. The differentiation is inceptually the difference. In what way the differentiation remains concealed in the first beginning and, in the advancement to metaphysics, completely hides and is masked in the dominance of logic and ontology and their "truth," in relation to the outward look of beings themselves. In what way the differentiation first comes to light and essentially occurs in the "ontological difference " (*Being and Time*), insofar as this difference is thought out of the experience of the truth of being.

2. (suffering) {Marginal remark in typescript}

175. The differentiation[3]

of being and beings. (With a view toward beings, dominated by them, we constantly say and name being: the "is" and the word in general.) When we designate these, it seems we are relating to two pregiven "objects." A third, perhaps a consciousness and representation of these, seems to differentiate them and must thereby claim a "regard." Why this is so, or even only that it is so, seems not to trouble us. We even believe ourselves justified in dismissing this differentiation or at least in neglecting it as the emptiest "product" of an unproductive abstraction. And ultimately it can without any difficulty be made clear to anyone that nothing can be represented with respect to this differentiation and what is differentiated in it. The differentiated elements are themselves without any place or soil, unless an empty activity of human understanding is claimed on their behalf.

Yet being differentiates itself from beings. Being does the differentiating and "is" the difference. We ourselves do not first make the differentiation. Instead, we follow it, and this following first gives us understanding in general. We can follow only insofar as we sojourn in this differentiation.

The differentiation is the inhabited place of our essence, an inhabited place indeed concealed from us.

But *how* does it eventuate that being itself differentiates itself? (that is the appropriating event itself)[4].[5] Is there a universal understanding, a world-reason? We, "we," can "think" of the differentiating only as an activity of the understanding, so long as we merely stare at ourselves—without actually knowing the horizon (that of the metaphysical human being)—and explain beings as produced things.

Without having experienced the truth of beyng as event, we will be unable to know the difference and, thereby, the differentiation. For so long it will be alien to us that "being" differentiates itself; since being is to us only an empty concept and is itself the product of a differentiating; but this—once again let it be admitted to us, who are of the opinion—is our doing.

The difference, in which the differentiation essentially occurs, is the departure as the downgoing of the event into the beginning.

---

3. Cf. summer semester 41, especially recapitulation, pp. 7–8 {*Grundbegriffe*, GA51, p. 41ff.}

4. (not: being and then the event "with" it, but being itself the event and only this) {Marginal remark in typescript}

5. Not to ask "how," but to experience the "that it is" in its essence. {Marginal remark in typescript}

In the difference is the resonating of the twisting free, and the twisting free eventuates inceptually as consonance.

To *think* being means to endure the differentiation in questioning it and to experience the differentiation as the inceptual distinction of the departure—*pain* as the essence of the difference.

176. The differentiation and the difference

The term "differentiation" calls attention first of all to what lies at the basis of all metaphysics, in that metaphysics makes use of it everywhere inasmuch as metaphysics thinks the beingness of beings, i.e., beings *as* beings. In advance, unobserved, unconsidered, and thus unquestioned and ungrounded, the differentiation of beings and being essentially occurs in metaphysics. And if metaphysics does not invent things, but only comes upon them, then it testifies in its own way that indeed *the difference* between being and beings is what is essential in the differentiation. Yet at the start of metaphysics, notwithstanding the fact that now and then in its history the difference could become questionable as such, what is differentiated within the structure of the differentiation is at the same time indeed determined thus: being in terms of the ἰδέα, κοινόν, γένος: ἕν; and "beings" in terms of what is properly not a being inasmuch as it does not essentially occur as pure beingness: the μὴ ὄν. Beingness is the πρότερον τῇ φύσει and is what makes beings possible; to be sure, beingness, because constantly thought on the basis of beings as present-produced (εἶδος-τέχνη), must also be interrogated with regard to its αἰτία, and an ἐπέκεινα τῆς οὐσίας must be conceived.

Insofar as the differentiation is expressly said, thinking has already gone through metaphysics to its ground and is no longer metaphysical. Admittedly, at first everything remains indeterminate; indeed there arises the appearance that the differentiation itself and the differentiated even allow themselves to be made into objects of representation, whereby the differentiating is assigned to the familiar way of thinking (representation), and being, along with the beings differentiated from it, is objectified into a relation. As a consequence of this representation, which can attach itself immediately to the making prominent of the differentiation, it can then be asked further: if being and beings are here differentiated, in what respect are they different and in what do they agree? The second part of the question is necessary, for otherwise being and beings could not be brought together for the sake of setting off one *against* the other. If we once pursue this objectification and the differentiation and in turn the differentiated and interrogate within them the essential structure of the differentiation, then the one "side" of the differentiation, namely beings, might indeed be exhibited at any time. On the other hand, in attempting to represent being as the "object" differentiated from beings, we immediately fall into the void. The differentiated elements of the differentiation show themselves as entirely heterogeneous, whereby we still admit that indeed the familiar side itself—beings—cannot be represented without a representation of being, which precisely means that what, strictly taken, belongs on the side of the unrepresentable has also already turned up unavoidably on the side of what is familiar. Thus it comes to light that the differentiation at the same time again appears entirely on the one side—the side of beings—and that the differentiation sought at the outset is not at all a pure one and never can be such. For, a being, as a being, is indeed something extant and a being [*Sein*]; it is never the beingless. If the objectification of the differentiated in the differentiation does not succeed—and the preceding shows that it must necessarily fail every time—then the differentiated of the differentiation cannot at all be thought in such a way. Or the thinking of the difference must be other than metaphysical-logical thinking, i.e., objectifying representation; that another thinking is required here and that metaphysical thinking is insufficient; for the differentiation must indeed be named and be known as such, although it immediately also requires the carefulness which heeds the experience in which what is said in the differentiation can be experienced. The attempt to objectify and explain the differentiation with the methods of metaphysical thinking and of the question of possibility will at once fail and must then experience that it can do nothing because, on the side of the familiar, both sides of the differentiation have already and immediately appeared. Nevertheless, supposing that this attempt does not adhere obstinately to logic and to logical thinking, it can experience that indeed the differentiated must rather be thought on the basis of beyng. But this includes a requirement to look away from beings, to avoid objectification, and to experience being itself. Here the attempt reaches the limits of its capacity and must indeed acknowledge beyng itself, no matter how indeterminate and ungraspable may be the occurrence of beyng. Non-representable being is not an empty word-sound, if indeed beings as such remain perceptible and understandable even to a metaphysically determined apprehension. (Cf. The twisting free of metaphysics, Typescript I, Continuation, p. 3 {GA67, p. 73.})

In speaking of the differentiation, the snare involved in every attempt at an objectifying explanation must also be recognized. Otherwise, what is left as an expedient is only the metaphysics of metaphysics. Thus proceeded *Being and Time,* where the truth of beyng is interrogated, but the differentiation, as the "ontological difference," is indeed objectified and made subservient to the question of the condition of its possibility.

This expedient would at least have been able to indicate the question-worthiness of the differentiation, that it is worthy of questioning; but even this did not succeed, because instead of being gathered toward this question, everything was read as a kind of "anthropology." Even the clarification of transcendence on the basis of ecstatic temporality [*Zeitlichkeit*] was of no avail. And yet thinking must take this course, because it is the most proximate path in the transition from metaphysics into the history of being.

If, however, the differentiation does not by way of representation first make and bring forth the difference, if instead it follows the difference and arises only out its essence itself, if the difference pertains to, and is, beyng itself, and if beyng is everywhere unavoidable in beings, then there must also be possible, even if for a transformed humanity, an experience of beyng itself, i.e., an experience of the difference.

Are there ways that lead into the difference?

Which are the marks that call attention to the possibility of an experience of the difference?

In what direction must the difference itself be thought in advance? Of what sort is this thinking?

We must learn the enduring of the difference in the departure. In this enduring, the pure essential occurrence of the difference is experienced out of the departure, and this essential occurrence no longer needs beings.

We must, however, also learn to think *what is beingless,* back beyond the negativity of beings; beinglessness is closed to all metaphysical representation, which is utterly unable to think nothingness.

The difference distinguishes being and what is beingless. Yet beinglessness is an event of beyng itself. Beinglessness is the first reflection of the luster of the riddle which is concealed in the event (on what is beingless, cf. "Event and Dasein" in *Über den Anfang* {GA70, p. 117ff.}).

Beyng differentiates itself from what is beingless, and this differentiation is the inceptual event.

The beinglessness of (beings) is the inceptual event of the dispropriation; the inceptual dispropriation in the sense of *withholding.* This dispropriation is an inceptual and still undisentangled reversal into the groundless beginning.

Beinglessness and the event of the between, wherein the coming up against beings, which thus first free themselves for their truth, turns back into the event. This "against" is essentially other than the standing over and against of the representation that brings before oneself; the coming of the consignment in steadfast carefulness.

177. Negativity and no-saying

No-saying is first of all acknowledgment of what is actual and adherence to it. No-saying is involved precisely with the putative actual and ever manifests its dependence on it. In no-saying, then, only the denied as such is apprehended, and to no-saying pertains denial as rejection. Denial comes to appear as if it itself maintained that there was no more to it than its own doing and that what is to be affirmed is thereby justified.

Negation is other than denial. Negation is the explicit self-maintenance of the first steadfastness in Da-sein. Negation is involved with something that is alien to steadfastness. Negation is a human form of rigor in the exertion of maintaining a first consignment.

178. Nothingness

is taken as the "denial" of being and reveals itself then already as something dependent, related to being, assigned to it, relative to it. Thus there is no absolute nothingness.

This consideration is over-hasty, not only because it reduces nothingness to "denial," but also because it does not recognize that "nothingness" could "be" equiprimordial with being. If therefore this latter is "absolute," which is still to be decided, why should not also and precisely nothingness be absolute?

IV. The twisting free

The dispensation of the conjuncture
of the junction in the beginning

The "essence" of the history of beyng

The dispensation even in its complete integration
is a twisting free into the windings of the event

(The *twisting* of the *wreath,* not of the screw.
Twisting: wound into a ring, twisted up
in the form of a ring.)

179. Outline

The difference and the resonating of the turning
being [*Sein*] in its truth
The turning and the twisting free
The historicality of the twisting free
its course of history
The twisting free and the disentanglement in the first beginning
The twisting free and the overcoming of metaphysics
cf. II. The resonating
The twisting free and the twisting of the (event)
(wreath)

180. The history of beyng[1]

essentially occurs for the first time as itself in its clearing for the experience of the passing by. But history does not first arise afterwards. Metaphysics belongs in this history, and metaphysics, as past, now displays its essence, one resting in the historiality of the truth of beings, i.e., in the history of beingness. (Cf. On the history of the concept of existence {in GA80}.)

Metaphysics is the advancement out of the first disentanglement, a disentanglement that can likewise be recollected only in the experience of the other beginning, in the pain of the difference and of the twisting free.

The disentanglement is the essence of emergence and of unconcealedness as disconcealment, an essence marked by an event in the history of beyng.

The history of beyng as the essential occurrence of the truth of beyng, i.e., the twisting of the beginning, is illuminated in the inceptuality, and the latter has come to resonate in the passing by. The

---

1. history = *historiality*
the mountain range in its chain.

experience of the beginning must put itself into words in the saying of the event.

The experience of the beginning is at first, in the wake of the experiencing, the experience of the other beginning, and only in this and in the inceptuality does the first beginning become inceptual.

In such experience, historical humanity attains its ground.

Disentanglement and twisting free, advancement and transition, passing by and resonating—these are always to be thought in terms of the event.

181. The history of beyng

The resonating consonance of the dispensation of beyng.

The dispensation has its axis in the event.

Everything in the resonating and in the overcoming, in the transition and in the twisting free, is already appropriated.

The passing by: the demise of the devastation into disjunction and the downgoing into the departure toward the junction of the beginning pass each other by, without either knowing the other or being experienced by the "between" within which the passing by is appropriated.

Accordingly, the abandonment of beings by being and the differentiation are divergent in their essence.

The abandonment by being of beings expands so far that the essence of truth is no longer needed, and this lack of need is justified in the will to willing as the inmost essence of machination, over and against which the will to power is only a consequence, and in the consideration only something preliminary. The will to willing is the concealed ground of the idolization of "life in itself" and of "dynamics." The devastation of the essence of truth guarantees the forgottenness of being. Passing by this abandonment by being, i.e., appropriated in it: the differentiation.

The differentiation of being brings the truth of being explicitly to dignity and leaves all metaphysics behind. The differentiation now eventuates as itself, and its emergence is not first its arising; for it is only the resonating of the departure. With it starts

The overcoming

of the truth of beings in the form of beingness. Metaphysics appears on the ground of its abandoned, yet previously unexperienced, truth. Metaphysics is not the history of an error; instead, it is the history of the distorted essence of being, a distorted essence which is itself ungrounded in its truth, escapes into the otherwise essential relation to the human being, and, out of the transformation of truth into correctness, seeks to master being itself as unconditional objectivity and as life. Therefore since Plato the "soul" and the good—up to Nietzsche: values and psychology, anthropologism. (To what extent must being proceed into this distorted essence? Can we ask and answer that question?) The overcoming eventuates as

The transition into the turning.

This is the essential occurrence of the truth of beyng, and in such guise the beyng of truth essentially is. The turning arises from the wreath and the windings, into which being turns back as essentially occurring in its junction. The turning belongs to the essence of beyng, and what is owing to this turning as the most proximate ground is that which concerns thinking as the original "circle" without the ability to arrive immediately at the ground of its essence. The historiality of the turning eventuates out of the turning back.

The turning back of the turning into Da-seyn

The turning in its full essence turns back, namely, from the starting point into the differentiation which has gone astray into its distorted essence in being as beingness. The turning back is not the consequence of the turning but, rather, is its ground. The turning back has already eventuated in the appropriation of Da-seyn. The turning back makes impossible the individuation of truth and of its essence in the same way that it prevents the individuation "of being." In the turning back, however, being and truth are not first coupled together, as if each already had a separate essence for itself; on the contrary, their essential unity itself comes now for the first time into the clearing of itself which emerges out of the turning back. This unity, which essentially occurs in an originary way, is

Da-seyn.

All beyng is Da-seyn [*Alles Seyn ist Da-seyn*]. Yet Dasein is not a being, called the human being, but instead is, in terms of the history of beyng, the ground of the essence of the human being, insofar as this essence itself has come into the conjuncture of being and is determined expressly and exclusively out of the relation to being (i.e., according to *Being and Time,* out of the "understanding of being"). The appropriation of the "there," the appropriative event of the clearing, is Da-sein, and that is the essential occurrence of the truth of beyng, i.e., beyng itself. "Da-sein," experienced in accord with the history of beyng, is the first name for beyng, which is thought out of the essential occurrence of its truth. But only in the clarity of the knowledge of the event and of its conjuncture can the essence of Da-seyn be determined. (In *Being and Time,* Da-sein is surmised and in that way decisively brought to consciousness, but it could not yet be adequately thought.) For even the essential occurrence of Da-sein as the inhabited place of the turning back of the turning does not grasp Daseyn, because the latter is:

the twisting free of beyng into the event.

At first, what was available, simply out of metaphysics, was—to name only this—the schema of the transcendental, such that this itself was immediately conceived, according to the basic position of *Being and Time,* in its own truth ("primordial temporality" ["*Temporalität*"]). Yet thereby also resulted by necessity the fatal delivery of the step to metaphysics; it seemed that everything was only a modification of Kant's laying of a foundation for metaphysics (cf. the Kant book {GA3} and the turning—already grasped there but not conceptualized—in speaking of the "metaphysics of Dasein," wherein it is thought that metaphysics itself exists by the grace of Dasein rather than Dasein being the "object" of metaphysics).

What is the twisting free, however? It is just the twisting up into the winding (wreath) of the event, such that beyng and its turning purely and essentially occur in the event. Thereby the twisting free is a circulating in the event, wherein a constancy prevails which is itself determined out of the event. Thus within the event beyng is ultimately sheltered and also concealed; twisted free from but not "sublated." "Dialectics" must not at all steal in here, since indeed there is in this place no presupposed unconditional certainty or resolved unanimity. For consonance is indeed the unitary sounding of the word in the abyss of the beginning. In the thinking of beyng and of the twisting free from it, all recourses for an accommodating and already all-equalizing sublation are relinquished.

The twisting free is not sublation into the absolute; instead, it essentially occurs in the conjuncture with respect to the abyssal character of the beginning.

The dispensation of the conjuncture of the event

Out of the twisting free, which twists up into the event the turning back of the turning and, with that, the overcoming of the differentiation, it becomes clear that the event is in itself the conjuncture of a concealed structure which itself essentially occurs in the integration into the junction of the beginning. The twisting free does not twist up into the event "something" that was previously lacking to it; on the contrary, the twisting free allows the clearing of the event to eventuate.

Dispensation [*Fügung*] is an ordaining [*Fügen*] as event of the structure [*Gefüge*] of the time-space of the abyss, is integration [*Sich-fügen*] into the junction [*Fug*] of the beginning. The integrative ordaining essentially occurs in the junction.

The junction is the downgoing into the departure.

The downgoing is inception of the beginning in its incipience.

The departure is the consonance of the differentiation into the historiality of the (event); it is the leaving behind of the disjunction in the wilderness of its distorted essence; the junction itself does not cast away the disjunction, and both belong in the truth of the beginning. But whence the dis-?

The dispensation, like the twisting free, can be thought so essentially and inceptually that it can be experienced in thinking already with regard to the abandonment by being, provided this abandonment is even named. The levels of the dispensation are not historiologically determinable stages of a development.

At first, however, we experience the in-between of the passing by. The passing by is the most proximately "visible" conjuncture of the transition into the turning which essentially occurs out of the twisting free of beyng into the junction of the event.
The turning belongs in the twisting.
The twisting belongs to the inceptuality.
The essence of the twisting is the event.
The origin of historical mankind out of the twisting.

182. The conjuncture of beyng

is to be thought in the dispensation. This latter thinks unitarily something threefold:

1. the structuring of the structure of the "between."
2. the integration into the junction of the beginning.
3. the ordaining (disposing as the *encompassing* of all dispensation in every mode) of the beginning.

*

The conjuncture of being has its most proximate open realm in the inceptual history of beyng.

We must experience this history in the resonating of the encompassing of the beginning, we who are first explicitly ordained into this history as knowers.

The resonating, however, is consonance (sounding into the beginning—as downgoing).

The resonating consonance of the dispensation of beyng.

183. The conjuncture of beyng

Experience the junction only
on the basis of the dispensation.

To experience: the *integrational* "between" of the clearing appropriated in the event (provenance of the origin of the unity of the time-space which here for the first time splits apart).

The necessary ambiguity of integration:
1. unfolding of structure
2. and thus integrating into the junction.

The "between"

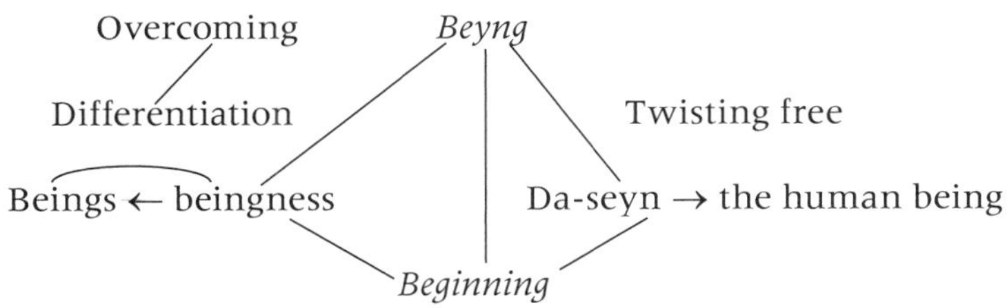

The event is to be experienced only in Da-seyn.
The conjuncture of beyng is the junction of the beginning.
Beyng must twist free of itself into the event.

*

The conjuncture cannot be compared to a system, even if the latter is thought of as the system of the spirit itself. The conjuncture integrates itself into the junction of the beginning; to follow this dispensation while experiencing the allocation of the lack of a sense of plight.

The event can be experienced only "in" Da-seyn, which is itself the essential occurrence of the event.

Experience is the steadfastness of the pain, and the pain stands within the "between" which lies between beyng and beginning, between beingness and beyng, between being and beings, between beings and historical mankind.

The conjuncture of this "between" is the clearing which appropriates the event. In this appropriation, Da-sein is grounded groundlessly in the downgoing into the beginning.

The downgoing conceals the inceptuality.

Experience can never experience the beginning immediately but also cannot attain it through any dialectics. Even dialectics, because related to λέγειν—ἰδέα—consciousness, is calculation.

V. The event
The vocabulary of its essence[1]

Regarding the introduction to *The event*

1. This vocabulary consists of the German term for "event" and ten other terms linguistically connected to it. The root common to them all is *eignen*, "be proper to," "appertain." It is not possible to carry out the same play on words in an English translation. The terms are:

das Ereignis	event
das Ereignen	appropriation
die Vereignung	expropriation
die Übereignung	consignment
die Zueignung	arrogation
die Aneignung	adoption
die Eigentlichkeit	properness
die Eignung	eventuation
die Geeignetheit	appropriateness
die Enteignung	dispropriation
das Eigentum	domain of what is proper.—Trans.

184. The event
The vocabulary of its essence

The following delimitation is to make less ambiguous the otherwise still-fluctuating lexicon which must constantly maintain a transitional breadth.

The event — expresses the explicitly self-clearing inceptuality of the beginning. The inaugural truth of beyng preserves in itself, as inceptual unification, the inaugural unity of the appropriating and the appropriated. The word "inceptual" always means: appropriated out of the beginning and consigned to the inceptuality. But it does not mean incipient in the sense of mere starting. Being does not start and stop, nor does it exist "perpetually" in the duration of beings. Being begins and does so essentially: it *is* the appropriating beginning. The event lights up the clearing of the beginning in such a way that the beginning does not merely emerge and bring to appearance along with it something inceptual, as in the first beginning, but, instead, such that the beginning, qua the beginning, is consigned to the truth of its inceptuality, a truth which is therefore illuminated.

The appropriation (the appropriating eventuation) — is intrinsically counter-turning out of the inceptual emergence, and the latter is at the same time a downgoing into the abyss. In emerging, the emergence differentiates itself from the things that come to appearance in its openness, without this difference as such already co-appearing in its essential belongingness to the beginning. The event is of the difference, but it keeps the difference and its essence concealed. The inceptual event of the difference, however, the departure, keeps itself utterly concealed. Nevertheless, in the self-clearing event the difference with respect to beings comes into the clearing, and above all the clearing of the departure eventuates into the downgoing of the beginning. Thereby the difference also comes into its full essential occurrence for the first time, since the clearing is proper to the difference and in no way merely depends on it as a way of becoming known. The event turns toward the abyss the concealment in the departure *and* unitarily turns toward what is grounded, namely, beings, the clearing in the difference. Out of this event-related turning, the event is counter-turning. This counter-turning conceals the essential belonging of the nihilation, i.e., of the inceptual (not the null) nothingness, to beyng. In the difference, in the departure, and in their event-related unity, there essentially occurs the event of nihilation. Nihilation is unfathomably distinct from all "negativity" and "negation," for negativity (in Hegel's sense) belongs to beingness and negation applies to beings. Thus "negativity" and "negation" fall on the side of beingness and beings and do not determine what is inceptually nihilating in the differentiating departure. Thought in terms of the history of beyng, both are consequences of the still-hidden event. The difference which is not yet sheltered in the abyss by way of departure and which, simply in emerging, radiates in the first beginning—this difference pervades the essence of metaphysics. But if the difference as such, i.e., at the same time in the departure, is cleared, there eventuates the twisting free of the difference into the abyss. Out of the twisting free, the overcoming of metaphysics is disposed, and toward it the consummation of metaphysics and its demise are already moving, to be sure without being known by metaphysics. In contrast, the first consummation of metaphysics in Hegel's absolute idealism believes the truth of beings has been attained and secured; the second consummation in the metaphysics of the will to power takes the revaluation of all values as a new start, whereas it merely introduces, and in all essentials grounds, the unconditional demise of metaphysics at its end. At the time of the demise of metaphysics, and seen in terms of metaphysics, the event and along with it everything inceptual have disappeared into the nothingness of decisive ignorance.

The appropriation contains the counter-turning of the event into the two modes of expropriation and consignment, modes which dispose the difference and the departure.

The expropriation is the preservation, by way of departure, of the event into the abyss of its intimacy with the beginning. The beginning, in its inceptuality, is concealed by the expropriation in such a way that the concealment is lit up and thereby preserved in its event-related essence and is not dissolved in any disconcealment. The lit-up concealment allows the uniqueness of the beginning to emerge in its incontestable—because entirely proper to it—simplicity. In the expropriation the unique costliness of the beginning is witnessed in its preservation. The expropriation appropriates the essence of beyng as the unique treasure out of which all the riches of every *warrant* are drawn. The expropriation points toward what is most proper to the event, which is the beginning. But what is most proper to the event also remains, just as inceptually,

The consignment. It is appropriation in such a way that the event allows the clearing to occur essentially as the in-between of time-space so that the "there" eventuates and Da-seyn is as the essential occurrence of the turning (i.e., the truth of beyng as the beyng of truth). The consignment is Da-seyn as essentially occurring. Such Da-seyn *is* only if the inceptuality of the beginning becomes explicitly cleared. Prior to that, and thus in all metaphysics, yet also still in the first beginning, Da-seyn does not essentially occur. By way of the counter-turn, the downgoing corresponds to Da-seyn in the event such that the downgoing becomes historial first, and only, in Da-seyn. The inceptual event of consignment, however, does not ever allow the clearing of beyng to occur merely in general and indeterminately, if indeed the event as an expropriation preserves the uniqueness of the truth of beyng. Hence, in the consignment there must also be, inceptually, a uniqueness according to which the event as consignment arrogates a unique essence. The inceptual event of the unique consignment is

Arrogation. This word says that the event consigns itself to the essence of the human being and in preference to all other beings confers itself on this essence. In the arrogation Dasein is concealed as the event of that turning which constantly remains the intimacy of the truth of beyng qua the beyng of truth and which allows the eventuation of the inclusion of the human being in beyng. Indeed this being is not objectively present in itself; instead, what is distinctive about this being first eventuates in the arrogation. The distinctiveness consists in the fact that the essence of the human being is located in steadfastness, which is the guise assumed by the concern and watchfulness for Dasein within beings, i.e., uniquely in this being. Therefore, the appropriated—i.e., inceptually historial—human being and this being alone has to preserve the truth of all beings. In the arrogation, there eventuates the relation of the beginning to the human being (not to just any arbitrary one or to humans in general but, instead, to the unique one of the single history of beyng itself). The event of the relation never merely lets the relation "persist" but, rather, sends it into historiality and maintains it in inceptual history. The appropriation essentially occurs in its counter-turning (expropriation and appropriation) according to this relation in the extreme remoteness of the beginning and of the human being, who only in this remoteness experiences the nearness of what is nearest, which remains nearer than any being encountered. Such experience, however, eventuates only because arrogation is at the same time

Adoption.

By consigning the truth of beyng to the essence of the human being, the event adopts this being in the essence thereby awakened, insofar as the event allows historical humans to pertain to the claim which, in the arrogation, touches them essentially. The adoption directs human beings to the expropriation and disposes them for the belongingness to the departure. Here is concealed the necessity preserved in the inceptual essence of beyng, namely, that humans, specifically as historial, comport themselves in a unique way to death, such that death is in every case the death of the historial human being, in that a departure with respect to beings eventuates within beings. The event-related adoption (claim) of steadfast humans for the expropriation of the event into the downgoing of the beginning, i.e., into the abyssal inceptuality, contains what is distinctive of human death (strictly taken, only human death can be thought of as death). This unique death reaches into the "extreme possibility" of beyng itself. This death "is" never an ending, because it constantly belongs already to the beginning. Neither theological nor metaphysical considerations and explanations of death ever reach into the domain of its essence as that essence is understood with respect to the history of beyng. In a first attempt (*Being and Time*) to think the truth of being, the essence of death was thought, and the reason for that lies not in an "existentiell" "anthropology" or in a peculiar and wayward conception of death. On the contrary, it arises from an unsaid—but at that time also hardly grasped—glimpse into the event-related essence of the truth of beyng. The misgivings over the "conception" of death in *Being and Time* may be correct within metaphysical and anthropological discussions. Yet we can lay to rest these misgivings along with their correctness, for, in the uniquely mandatory domain of questioning in *Being and Time*, i.e., in the thinking of the truth of beyng, they of themselves come to naught and do so with such decisiveness that they are unable in the least to penetrate into this domain. Of course, the same also holds of all the supposedly concurring approvals of this conception of death, because they are limited to a certain form of "moral" and "existentiell" application of the "doctrine." To be able to produce an "anthropologically" understandable "argument," a formal confrontation with everything "for" and "against" in relation to the "notions of death" in *Being and Time* would first have had to renounce occupying the only appropriate "level" of thinking. After this renunciation, however, what would be the point of such a confrontation? It could only take itself as foolishness and would have indeed at first to think only of the one circumstance, namely, that the question of the truth of beyng was thought through in its preliminary steps and the experiences required by this question were already conceded.

The event-related adoption of the historial essence of the human being into what is most proper of the expropriation of the beginning to its abyss surely includes the clearing of an essential character in humans, one which first lets them be capable of historiality and allows them to "live" in a historial relation to death.

The arrogating adoption of the human being for the beginning prepares the domain in which the human essence unfolds along with all of its inaccessibility for metaphysics, as that essence occurs in the history of beyng.

In arrogating and adopting the essence of the human being out of the beginning and for the beginning, the event first allows humans to come to themselves, i.e., to their essence as that essence in appropriated in the appropriating event. Accordingly, in this essence (in the steadfastness of the guarding and the stewardship which preserves beyng historially in its truth), humans come to own up to themselves. Humans come to themselves, come into their own, because they must now be themselves out of the arrogation into the event. The human being becomes "proper" in the strict and unique sense of this word.

Properness. It is the origin of the historial selfhood of the human being. As appropriated into the truth of beyng, humans are now themselves. For a human being to be a self means to experience the arrogation into the preservation of the truth of beyng as an essential law. Humans are "present" to themselves by maintaining their inaugural essence instead of proceeding to a self-made task whose pursuit confirms them only in an unappropriated self-absorption. The latter derives not from selfhood but from a metaphysically-anthropologically (morally) grounded "egoity" which can easily extend its essence to the "we" while thereby merely becoming more self-absorbed. The "we" is the spreading out of the I into the "remainderlessness" of the unconditional arrogance of all in a will which no one has as a "subject" since it is willed from itself, i.e., from sheer willing, and thus of itself constitutes the subjectity of the subject. The will to willing allows the emergence of the most insidious semblance of autonomy; this will speaks only of "freedom" and liberation. In the current historical moment, the self-absorption of metaphysical mankind declares the ready-made historical task to be "the mission" "of" history. Historical mankind inceptually knows no mission, since it has no need of one, having been consigned enough in the arrogation of the truth of beyng. The flight into the proclamation of a "self"-obtained mission "before history" is the sign of mankind's lack of history. Humans have fallen irredeemably into bondage to machination and crow about this fall as an ascent into a "world." Yet the emptiness of this world does not once summon up the effort even only to ignore these assurances, since the emptiness, sacrificing to the idol of "remainderlessness," lets everything sink into nothingness. If one may speak of a "mission" at all, then it is only out of a knowledge of the beginning. The mission is then the consignment of beyng to the essence of the human being and accordingly is not anything this being first has to dispose of.

In the age of history in which beyng illuminates its more original beginning, the selfhood of the self of historial mankind is the responsibility [*Verantwortung*] of the response [*Antwort*] which prepares the word [*Wort*] of language for the claim of the event. "Responsibility" is meant here not in a "moral" sense but, rather, with respect to the event and as related to the response. The response is the word of language, the word that from the human side replies to the word of beyng. The response is essentially correspondence. This response corresponds to the word of beyng, i.e., to the disposing, in which guise the soundless arrogation and adoption claim the essence of the human being for the preservation of the truth of the inceptuality. Corresponding to this inceptual word is the basic trait of speech, out of which the language of historical mankind arises inasmuch as this language unfolds into the general traits of the vocables of thoughtful saying and poetic naming. The response is here not a reply to a question and its answer and sublation. The response is the human counter-word of language to the voice of beyng. To remain steadfast in the response is the essence of historial responsibility. Thereby humans adhere to that wherein they are adopted. This adherence to the appropriated essence is properness, i.e., being a self. Only in appropriated properness, in the sense of the guarding and stewardship of the truth of beyng, does the inaugural selfhood of historical mankind arise. Because beyng appropriates mankind into the distinctive character of steadfastness, the experience of the truth of beyng experiences at the same time and for the first time the human essence as the self rooted in properness. If now, in the transition from metaphysics into the cleared history of beyng, the question of the human being must be posed, then this question must already own up to the determination of its questioning out of the essence of what is questioned. Because that is the "proper" self, i.e., the one rooted in properness, the question of the human being can "still" only read: Who is the human being? In the "who," the selfhood of the human being is already recognized beforehand, and indeed as a selfhood whose truth can be expressed only in thinking about properness, i.e., about the appropriation of the appropriating event. Therefore the type of questioning of the human being, quite apart from the answer given, can signify whether the thinking is still ensnared in metaphysics or has been delivered over to the history of beyng. For metaphysics, the essence is always the whatness (the τί ἐστιν of the εἶδος); therefore metaphysics seeks the representation of the outward look of beings as things that are present, i.e., for the modern age, as objects. Metaphysics asks about the essence of the human being by asking: What is the human being? In this "what," metaphysics has in view the present *animal* and its objectively present endowment of *ratio*. The anthropological question of the human being must develop this what-question in every possible way of regarding the properties of the rational animal. Therein are grounded the immensity of anthropological cognitions and the necessity of "research." Anthropology is the first consummation of the "positivism" which is prescriptive in the natural sciences. Indeed, metaphysics thinks of the human being as "person" and as "subject" and recognizes, beyond the "ego," also a human "self." Metaphysics can therefore also, in its own way, ask who the human being is. Yet this who-question not only remains, as a question, indeterminately related to rationality and thus to animality but also never understands itself with respect to its bearing on the properness of the human being. Metaphysics *also* asks "who" the human being is. Metaphysics, however, does not grasp that the question can be asked *only* in this mode as soon as one experiences the inceptual essence of historical mankind, the relation of beyng and of its truth to mankind.

Then the human being would be the only being whose "essence" must be interrogated by way of the who-question. Indeed. And "essence" here no longer means the endowment of a whatness; instead, it means an essential occurrence as the appropriated steadfastness in the responsibility of the claim of beyng to the preservation of its truth. The "who," directed toward the "essence" of the human being, thinks toward the response which corresponds to the arrogation out of the inceptuality of the beginning. Yet even non-human beings, which, in the what-question, are to be thought with respect to the history of beyng, are no longer considered in terms of the what of the εἶδος but in correspondence to the appropriation into the truth of beyng. From what source, however, and in what way do we know that historical humans alone must be interrogated with respect to their essence in the who-question? It is because historial humans are uniquely adopted by the event to its truth. Yet whence do we know that? Where resides the testimony that humans are uniquely distinguished by beyng through the relation to it?

The previous ponderings on the history of beyng (cf. the earlier manuscripts and lectures) ever and again mentioned that the human being alone "has language." But is this not a conviction resting simply on a survey within the realm of beings, even though this survey cannot claim to include utterly everything? Could there not be other beings which share in mankind's distinction? Or must this possibility also be rejected? Yet how could that be justified? What then are we insisting on when we demand guarantees and testimony for the uniqueness of the distinction? Can the truth "about" the essence of the human being simply fall in line amid other sure cognitions in the manner of indubitable constatations about objects? May we treat the uniqueness (assuming it does hold) of the distinction as we would the endowments of some thing whose properties interest us? How could it be denied that questions obtrude here, especially for anyone still proceeding on the path of metaphysics? But perhaps everything depends on the suitable type of questioning, i.e., on the necessity of what is experienced here.

Is the talk of a "distinction" of the human being amid all other beings not already a characterization that ranges the human being in advance and peremptorily in the midst of beings and finds humans there, i.e., precisely by gazing at beings? Is *this* gazing, however, not already a straying from the experience of beyng and from the truth of the uniqueness of beyng? There is no need to stress the postulated distinction; for, occurring more essentially is the uniqueness of beyng itself, beyng which, by way of the appropriating event, arrogates what is unique and adopts it in its clearing. The uniqueness of the relation of the human being to beyng pertains to the uniqueness of the beginning itself. The allegation that the human being "has" language (i.e., possesses it as a capacity) is unaware that this "having" of language derives from the fact that the word of beyng "has" the human being (i.e., adopts the human being in the steadfastness of the responsibility of the claim of the truth of beyng). Nevertheless, beyng uniquely "has" the human being, because what is unique in the strict sense can belong only to something unique. That is why we can find no other being that is responsible for, and "speaks," the word. But the gods? Do they speak? And what do we know of the gods? Can humans, who are still without any presentiment or experience of the essence of the divine, speak straightforwardly of the gods, simply because earlier and even now the gods are still named? The divinity of the gods must first eventuate before a god appears and before the naming word, which names "the gods," can be heard. Yet the phrase of Sophocles still holds: ἔρρει δὲ τὰ θεῖα (Oed. Tyr. 910), "astray, however, goes the divinity (of the gods)." This straying conditions a godless time. Indeed the straying of the divinity is not nothing. It pertains to the hidden essence of the historical course of the history of beyng, at the time of the passing by, in that the devastation of all truth and the inceptual beginning are not allowed to know each other. At such a time, the truth of beyng forbids

any speaking of the gods and even any claim to understand beings as a whole.
If the uniqueness of the adoption of humanity into the preservation of the truth of beyng corresponds to the uniqueness of the beginning out of the event of its inceptuality, then to the gods, if and in whatever manner they "are," an immediate relation to beyng is denied. But if they would comport themselves to beings and especially to human beings, then the gods require that the clearing of beings, as beings, be steadfastly preserved, built, and disposed in historical humanity. In another way and according to the respective character of being, this still holds for every domain of beings. In the properness of the historial human being, there eventuates to the previously beingless (beings)

The eventuation

into beyng. To the eventuation there unfolds the uniqueness of the essence of the human being, as that essence is understood with respect to the history of beyng. The truth of the uniqueness is accessible only in the experience of beyng and only according to this experience. A consideration can very well fix two waypoints for the meditation on the uniqueness of the appropriated adoption of the human being: on the one hand, the arrogation to a unique being must correspond to the uniqueness of the beginning in the event, and, on the other hand, historical humans, in meditation on the history of beyng, experience the uniqueness of their adoption by the event into beyng. Furthermore, they can at least comment on this experience through the uniqueness of the destiny which has claimed only them, human beings, for the word and has led them into language. Out of this uniqueness of the belonging to beyng must arise every destiny that is disposed to liberate the experiencing of the eventuation of beingless (beings) into beyng, liberate it toward knowing, acting, forming, grounding and building, granting and releasing.
The uniqueness of the belonging to the preservation of the truth of beyng is experienced by historial

humans from time to time in the rare solitude which transmits to them the simple claim of beyng (merely that it is) in its pure clearing and which allows them to surmise the selfhood of the self out of an abyss that has thrown to the shore of confusion everything egoic and communal, all boasting of accomplishments and ingenuity, all forced self-absorption. Selfhood is the originality of being human, an originality rooted in the properness of the human being. To the unique claim of beyng, namely, that it is, there pertains—as stemming from the arrogation—the gathering of all capacities in the unity of the preservation of the truth of beyng. Corresponding to this historial solitude of the human being within the one beyng and within its appropriating is the experience that a unique historical humanity has been exposed to the claim of being itself. Out of the demand on Greek antiquity for the first beginning and for its appearance in the brightness of figurative apprehension, we surmise the future West, the land of the evening of that night which lets emerge a day of the truth of beyng, after having broken all dominance which, as the power of "beings," has usurped the essence of beyng.

The uniqueness of a historical humanity of the still-concealed West is responsible for the eventuation of beings into inceptual beyng, such that all beings, freed from presentification, come forth out of the previously experienced beinglessness and encounter humans inceptually. Only if humans in the event, adopted to the preservation of its in-between, are steadfastly responsible for the pure eventuation of beings into the time-space of their inceptual truth, only then has the human being become proper in the nobility of the indigence for the uniqueness of the simplicity of everything inceptual and has been withdrawn from the craving for the merely "reactive" product in all things. Instead of the insistent and all-consuming essence of the objectivity of beings, the beingness of beings has attained its inceptual, previously concealed, essence which is determined as

Appropriateness. This word says that beings have been admitted into their inceptually fitting being, fitting as measured against the measure of inceptuality. "Appropriate" does not here mean "opportune"; instead, it signifies entrance into the eventuation which assigns all beings to the inceptuality of the beginning, such that they essentially occur no longer in their "examination" for the human being but, rather, out of their "absence" (i.e., here, departure) toward the event. This change of beingness (beingness itself traverses its history as οὐσία, visibility, presence, actuality, objectivity, will to willing) into appropriateness does not require a restless ordering and reordering. The change eventuates in the transition into the other beginning, which *is* the overcoming of metaphysics. Metaphysics, as the history of the beingness of beings in the sense of visibility and objectivity, is nevertheless determined by the event. The essence of the event grounds the fact that every being as a being is admitted into a uniqueness and is more proper the more essentially it is at any time the individual of a singling out as unique. Individuality in this sense is essentially distinct from the particularization and instantiation of the individual "cases" which are set off against the "universal." It is in this way that metaphysics grasps individuation as particularization. Its *principium individuationis* reads correspondingly. Metaphysics ends in the supremacy of the undifferentiatedness of beings, because beings are given up to the abandonment by being and because being is relinquished through the forgottenness of being.

The dispropriation of beings sets in when being in the first beginning has scarcely emerged on the way to φύσις and has lit up its first essential occurrence in ἀλήθεια. The dispropriation withdraws beings from the assignment to the beginning. Being is presence, rigidifies into this essence, and out of such rigidity gives priority to beings, since nothing can be thought of as more present than the present thing itself. The dispropriation abandons being to the advancement into the priority over beyng, such that beyng remains without its truth and, as that which conditions beings, is always explained solely on the basis of them. The course of metaphysics from visibility (ἰδέα) to the objectivity of the unconditional and constant guarantee of securing and ordering possesses an irresistibility out of the event of dispropriation wherein is concealed the start of the transformation of ἀλήθεια, through the individual phases, up to certainty as security, which, in its extreme progression, has become the guarantee of the sheer emptiness of securing. Attached to the dispropriation is at the same time the rising up—one with the transformation of beingness and truth—of the human being as *animal rationale* toward the "superman," in relation to whom the previous human being, not yet unconditionally developed into the presumptuousness of subjectivity, is still too tame. In the "superman," being as the will to power becomes "concentrated" (the dispropriated correspondence to the relation of being toward humans). All beings become anthropomorphic knowingly, i.e., by way of calculative planning and reckoning. The "superman" prepares the ultimate dispelling of magic from beingness: the will to power betrays itself as the unconditional emptiness of the will to willing. In this essence of beingness, the inceptual is first completely withdrawn from beings. The dispropriation has appropriated the abandonment of beings by being. Human beings themselves, like the organized superman, seem to dominate everything and are dispropriated of the last possibility of their essence: they can never recognize in the extreme blindness that the human forgetfulness of being, a forgetfulness brought to maturity along with the abandonment of beings by being, leaves human beings without a sense of plight insofar as it compels them to think that the ordering of beings and the instituting of order would bring about the substantive fullness of beings, whereas indeed what is assured everywhere is only the endlessly self-expanding emptiness of devastation.

The dispropriation of beings, which takes from them the truth of beyng, allows humanity, ensnared in such beings, to fall into a lack of a sense of plight. In addition, it abandons humans to the blindness which ever prevents them from experiencing that this lack of a sense of plight could be the extreme plight, which, if experienced, lets arise the necessity of a thinking of forgotten being and thus brings attention to the resonating of the beginning. The event of dispropriation extends, as its basic trait, through the history of being, in which guise metaphysics has unfolded. The extreme dispropriation of beings is the consummation of metaphysics. Yet the demise of metaphysics introduces the last phase of the dispropriation, in which even beings are devastated and come into the beginningless void, so that now there no longer essentially occurs any being which could fall prey to the dispropriation. In the "place" of the beginning, what presses forward in metaphysics are the causally determined ἀρχή, the *principium,* the supreme and first "cause," the absolute, the unconditional, and, ultimately, the *totality,* which no longer designates anything with content (a being) and simply confirms the "remainderlessness" of the dominance of the will to willing. Totality is the last idol of the hollowing out of all beings into the mere instrumentality of the means to the assurance of the ordering which puts the order into order.

If, however, at the historial time proper to the beginning, the event has permitted the dispropriation all the way to its distorted essence, then the historially greatest distantiation from the beginning has been reached. This distantiation is the one of the advancement into the abandonment of beings by being. Yet because even this abandonment, in its full distorted essence, still claims being, and because being has at the same time become "null" in the emptiness of the calculative means (i.e., of values), so in this unconquerable discord of emptiness and unavoidability a last blaze of the insurmountable beginning can appear, assuming that the relation of being to the human being has expressly eventuated. Now the possibility has eventuated that the inceptuality of the beginning might light up, such that the beginning can be experienced more inceptually—i.e., as itself in a now-appropriated humanity—and its truth can be taken into protection.

At this time there eventuates, by way of difference and departure, the event of the truth of the beginning, in the going down of that truth. There eventuates the preservation of the inceptuality of the beginning in its proper essence, ushering in the time of the domain of what is proper. This "time" is, like every "time" in the history of beyng, an interval. We understand by that the guarantee of the unfolding of the essence, a guarantee appropriated by the event. The time of the domain of what is proper prepares itself in the overcoming of the advancement of the first beginning into metaphysics. In the realm of the history of beyng, the overcoming is always a twisting free. It twists metaphysics up into the wreath of the turning. This twisting first brings metaphysics into the concealed dignity of its provenance. The twisting free is the event-related reverence for the dignity of beyng. This reverence eventuates as the history of beyng. Thinkers follow only this reverence and adhere to it. Thereby they think of the dignity of beyng. Accordingly, beyng in its truth must become for them worthy of thought. The overcoming of metaphysics is not an "accomplishment" of thinkers, ones who lead their thoughts beyond the mode of representation of the "philosophers." The "overcoming" is the history of beyng during the interval in which beyng revokes the dispropriation of beings. Here the "overcoming" does not at all claim to compel lower, to degrade and get rid of. The thinking of beyng in its history is constantly an appreciation of beyng.

The domain of what is proper

The term means here not possessions or anything similar; instead, like "domain of a king," it refers to the essential occurrence of the event in the appropriated properness of its truth. The "domain of what is proper" is the name of a time in the history of beyng, the time of the entry of the truth of beyng into the appropriated inaugural essence. In the domain of what is proper, the inceptual unification of the difference and the departure eventuates toward the abyssal unity of their oppositional essence. This unification, however, does not derive from a "oneness," already present at hand in some time and place, which could cause "unity." The inceptual unification of the domain of what is proper unifies the essential unity of the event toward the full inceptuality of the beginning. In the abyss of the beginning, all essential signs of the event are grounded (i.e., here, deprived of ground), signs which show themselves in the circumscribed vocabulary of the "event." The "unity" essentially occurring as the domain of what is proper denies itself every objectification toward a present at hand oneness. And already this mere speaking of "unity" involves the trap of setting aside the unitary essence of the event like a secured resource. Instead of this, the event-related experience must preserve beyng in its abyssal truth. This does not take away the necessity of grasping the oneness of this unity, as the domain of what is proper eventuates, in unique, inaugural experience. That is the experience appearing in the pain of the event-related, inceptual separation in which the "that it is" of beyng comes to light. In this *"that being is,"* beyng emerges by going down and by emerging out of the inceptual nothingness of the denial of the beginning. Out of the inaugural pain of the enduring which preserves the twisting free of beyng toward the event into the inceptuality of the beginning, there pertain equiprimordially, to this "that it is" of beyng, the horror of the abyss and the bliss of the departure. But this "that it is" of beyng does not merely fall under the determination of uniqueness, as if there were a "uniqueness" existing in itself; instead, this "that it is" is the unique beginning of all uniqueness, which allows the essential occurrence of the abyssal separation in relation to the nothingness of beyng and becomes the origin of all experience of beyng.

The domain of what is proper is the consummation of the event, in which guise the uniqueness of beyng eventuates into the more inceptual beginning. The history of beyng in the other beginning is the historiality of the domain of what is proper. The human history of the nobility of indigence corresponds to the domain of what is proper. The inaugural domain of what is proper, belonging to the event, harbors and confers the inceptual richness which first lets all "possessions" arise and which remains unassailable to any wasting, depleting, or corroding. The inaugural richness of the preservation of beings out of the domain of what is proper "of" beyng is the treasury of that which disposes every truth of beings into appropriateness. What inceptually disposes is the still-soundless voice of the word.

185. The treasure of the word

The word is a treasure enclosed by the beginning. Only occasionally does beyng itself light up. Then a search pursues this inceptual richness through human history; for, in the word, beyng is within the proper domain of its truth by way of the event. The event is the inceptual word, because its arrogation (as the unique adoption of the human being into the truth of beyng) disposes the human essence to the truth of beyng. Inasmuch as the appropriating event is in itself this disposing, and since disposition eventuates as an event, the event-related beginning (i.e., beyng as abyssal in its truth) is the inceptually disposing voice: the word. The essence of the word resides in the event-related beginning.

The voice disposes in that it adopts the essence of the human being to the truth of beyng and thus attunes that essence to the disposition in all the attitudes and comportments which are thereby first awakened. With respect to the event, "disposition" is not a human state of feeling, but is the event of the word as self-arrogating adoption. The word, in its event-related essence, is soundless. In addition, however, inceptually the word does not have the property of "meaning" or "sense," because, as the self-arrogating clearing of beyng, the word first becomes the ground of the subsequent formation of "word meanings" and "word sounds." Both of these arise concurrently and arise every time the word-sound is intoned. But all sounding is the echo of the fact that beings, previously beingless, enter into the eventuation toward beyng and persist therein. The echo of the inceptual voice of being originates in the breaking apart of being in beings, which are themselves first lit up through the appropriation to being. In the inceptual voice of the event-related disposition, there is neither speaking out nor silence.

We can still hardly experience these relations appertaining to the history of beyng, relations of the beginning as voice to the essence of the adopted human being, because we take "disposition" as well as "word" metaphysically. We do not recognize in the mood-marked "disposition" its essential provenance out of that disposition which, by way of the event and as beyng itself, claims the human being for the preservation of the truth of being. We are still unable to apprehend that this claim of the beginning is an addressing and a claiming that eventuates in what is speechless.

Indeed it happens to us occasionally that we are "speechless" in amazement, joy, horror, bliss. But we have no inking of speechlessness itself in its event-related essence. What appears to be the absence of speech, i.e., the absence of vocables and words, is, thought inceptually and essentially, only the pure event of the word as the disposing voice of beyng. This voice adopts us into the clearing of being so that for certain moments we experience beings themselves, i.e., the fact that beings are. Yet in this way we are also still scarcely on the path to the experience which can be expressed briefly thus: beyng is.

Speechlessness is to us an unexpected and fleeting transitional state, an exceptional case, which we understand in reference to the usual mastery and use of language.

In truth, however, speechlessness is a "sign" in which the event-related essence of disposition and of the word, in their inceptual belonging-together, can become visible, assuming that we are able to think in terms of the truth of beyng. Of course we are accustomed to represent language as the possession of vocables and as the "capacity" to use them. We think of the word on the basis of languages and linguistic capacities, rather than—although not as a mere reversal—experiencing language on the basis of "speechlessness," the latter on the basis of the inceptual disposedness, the latter on the basis of the event-related disposition, the latter as voice, the latter as the inceptual "claim," and the latter as the grace of the greeting of beyng itself, i.e., in the essential occurrence of its truth (the twisting free into the turning departure).

Because beyng itself is inceptually the word (the event-related disposition which knows neither utterance nor silence and stillness), the treasure of the word (treasure as the origin of the "vocabulary" of "language") must be experienced in the saying of beyng. Out of the apparently emptiest and poorest word, out of the "is" and its inceptual truth, there originates the ordained fullness of vocables and of their cases and inflections.

The thinking of the history of beyng thinks on the basis of the word of beyng. It seems that such thinking is merely arbitrary opinion which feeds on the dissection of the meaning of vocables. As if vocables, as well as their sound and meaning, could be objectively present in the manner of things. Heedfulness to beyng and the opposite, inattention to beyng, already lend a disposition to and determine the way the thinking of the history of beyng in the vocables of language hears the word at any time and on the basis of this word attempts to say it. Attentiveness to beyng is foreign to us. Just as speechlessness remains a "state" we want to overcome as quickly as possible and without being affected by it any further, so also the ability to speak and the technical dominance over the linguistic means are already sufficient proof of the assurance of mastering being (which here always means only beings).

The event is the richness of the simplicity in whose guise the turning of beyng eventuates while disposing and bestows the showing power of signs. This richness is self-sheltering because it goes down out of the inceptuality of the beginning into the departure. The appropriating event is beyng as the inceptual voice. The appropriating event is the treasure of the word. Nevertheless, the appropriating event, as beyng, is inceptually the relation to the essence of the historial human being, an essence which is thereby determined, as regards attitudes and comportments, with respect to this relation and thus with respect to disposedness through the voice. The relation eventuates in the departing-differentiating counter-turn.

From long habituation, we indeed think and reckon everywhere according to the directives of metaphysics. Under the domination of its essence, the stamp of being devolves upon beingness, and belonging together with this is the transformation of truth to the correctness of objectification. Inseparably from this nexus, the entrenchment of the human being into the *animal rationale* becomes valid, and so does the role of "grammar" and "logic" for the predelineation of the way the word is apprehended on the basis of the vocables of language and language is apprehended in a "technical"-instrumental sense.

Under the force of the metaphysical tradition, a force scarcely still felt and so released for the first time in all its might, it could almost seem impossible to think the inceptual essence of the word out of the event and to experience, within the event, the treasure of the word.

The overcoming of metaphysics, however, is already afoot. By no means does it simply cast aside "metaphysics" as something false. Yet neither does it "dialectically" sublate "metaphysics" into a merely higher truth, a truth that is by degrees and in scope "other." Metaphysics is, historiologically taken, the course of thinking from Plato to Nietzsche. In relation to the playing out of this entire course and experienced in terms of the history of beyng, metaphysics is the episode between the first and the other beginning. Metaphysics, in a mode of historicality proper to it alone, belongs to the twisting free of beyng. The character of the metaphysical tradition in its own course has its law out of this twisting free. Metaphysics knows only the truth of beings. The word is never known to metaphysics otherwise than as language, i.e., with respect to vocables. Metaphysical humanity knows exclusively beings in their beingness and cannot experience beyng. Therefore the word as well, which is essentially the word "of" beyng, remains concealed to humans. Accordingly, barriers stand in the way of the attempt to become attentive to beyng in the transition from metaphysics to the other beginning, to say the word of beyng, and, for that, to use language differently. These barriers are not to be traversed or removed by means of metaphysical thinking. In this bridging domain, where the metaphysical use of language still thoroughly dominates, and where the word of beyng must nevertheless be said on the basis of inceptual experience, the attempt is being ventured, through the communication of a few key words of beyng (lecture course, s. s. 41),[2] to attain the relation to beyng in its broadest span of the event-related counter-turning. The task is to enter into the domain of disposition where the word of beyng disposes comportment toward steadfastness in the preservation of the clearing of beyng. The tension in the aforementioned key words of beyng is "grounded" in the abyssal essence of the departing-differentiating event itself, in which belongs the appropriation of humanity to the preservation of beyng. Those words, which at first seem to express only the way being is comprehended by the human being, i.e., "understood" and "forgotten," in reality express the way the truth of beyng, taking that truth in its turning essence, appropriates the human being (cf. typescript *op. cit.* p. 42ff.; manuscripts 17–18).[3] Yet all this remains concealed to metaphysical humanity, such that to it the relation of beyng to the human being is accessible only in the representation of the self-relating of the human being to beings. Within metaphysics, thinking can still indicate that "we," humans, can never not think of being. In this impossibility can

2. *Grundbegriffe*. {GA51}

3. {GA51, p. 49ff.}

be grasped the necessity of our having always already thought of being. Why must we have done so? Because beyng shows itself in every representing, already prior to all beings. But why does it show itself so prominently? Because our essence belongs to beyng. But how does it belong to beyng? What is being, such that it has adopted the human being in this way? With these questions, metaphysics is left behind, for the truth of beyng is thereby already at issue.

Indeed this thinking can also bring us back again into metaphysics, in such a way that the confinement of the human being within metaphysics becomes definitive. For, if by means of metaphysics this attentiveness to the relation of beyng to the human being is casually transformed into an explanation of the relation between the human being and beings, then metaphysics can indeed presume to explain in its own way even this relation of the human being to being, a relation ostensibly not interrogated earlier by metaphysics. That is in fact what happens. The mark of this presumptuousness is the persistence of "anthropology" and of its role within metaphysics. Yet anthropologism is only the last deterioration of "humanism," which commences with the start of metaphysics (cf. the cave allegory). Anthropology, which sets the human being, as "subject," in the midst of beings, is distinctive in not asking who we are, because it maintains that its own question of the human being (What is the human being?) is *the* question of this being. The question of what the human being is directs the explanatory gaze toward the human properties which are demonstrable in research. The abundance of properties and relations leads erroneously to the swallowing up of the question of the human being in this anthropological research. The possibility of constantly new "cognitions" makes the human being seem to be an inexhaustible object of research. That is why the disciplines which join up in this research are heterogenous, indeed such that their heterogeneity is no longer disturbing and natural scientific craniology stands on an equal footing next to an "interpretation" in terms of "worldviews." The human being is investigated as one object among others. Humans are distinctive simply in the fact that they constitute the most important raw material within all the other materials to be mastered and utilized. The term "human resources" is a technological designation, and anthropology at least provides an account of the bearing of this designation because the included explanation of the human being pertains to presuppositions which are no longer discussed since they are used in security as the ones guaranteeing all assertions about "the human being." Indeed, any attempt to prove that anthropology and its investigation of the human being are "false" would be erroneous, since such an attempt fails to recognize that anthropology itself must be the last form of metaphysics in its demise. Even a "polemic" against anthropology would not only betray a hidden dependence on it but would have to undertake the problematic task of halting the progression of the essential law of that which, against its will and knowledge, must press on with the transition of metaphysics into the twisting free of beyng. Therefore, even if anthropological thinking rules over the relation of the human being to "actuality," it is utterly impossible to lead such thinking to the relation of beyng to the human being and bring it into accord with the heedfulness out of which the claim of beyng could be apprehended as the inceptual word.

Yet if we have become attentive to the relation of beyng to the human being, if we experience this relation in its character as an event, then we must still always resist the insidious temptation to incorporate the relation of being to the human being into the metaphysical interpretation of beings and thereby obliterate, already in its first illumination, the distinction between metaphysical thinking (i.e., in general, philosophy) and the thinking of the history of beyng. Not only the answer, but above all the question, of the relation of beyng to the human being is of an inaugural essence. Asking this question requires both an experience of the event and an obedience to the word of beyng. (Cf. 210. *Beyng and the human being.*)

If we are attentive to the simplicity of beyng (attentive to the turn), we experience the claim of the event and, in such experience, hear the word which gives rise to language, whose use stands under the law of the beginning. We become attentive insofar as the following can be of concern to us in heeding what is unique: never can we not think of beyng, because we must have always already thought of beyng. We are already underway on the path of the enduring of the differentiation into the departure. The simplicity of this uniqueness is not a matter of fact we could ever encounter amid other incidents and merely take note of. We do not experience the simple unless we already have an eye for the event. This simplicity is the most proximate illumination of the event itself, since in it the clearing of beyng is sent. The experience in which beyng consigns us to itself, in order to adopt our essence into the truth of the beginning, apprehends the word and recognizes the need of the use of language. At the time (with respect to the history of beyng) of this need, there arises the necessity of bringing the word of the beginning to language, learning to use language for the responsibility of the word, and recognizing the inceptual essence of the use of language. The word of the beginning comes to language in the naming within that poetry which founds what is lasting and in the saying within that thinking which brings the truth of beyng to endurance.

VI. The event

186. The event
Outline

The event and the beginning.
The event and the human being.
Here, in the essential occurrence of the event, the uniqueness of the *distinctive character of the human being* must be experienced.

In this experience, knowledge of *Da-seyn* arises. (Da-sein is the essential occurrence of the clearing, the appropriation of the inceptual truth into which the human being is consigned.)

The event and the turning. The *turning* essentially occurs in the event.
The *turning* itself is the essence of *"beyng."*

The event and the inceptual *"that it is"* of the inceptuality.
"The fact that being is" and with it nothingness—what does the "that it is" mean? The "that it is" of horror, bliss, pain;
the "that it is" of the distinction within the difference.

The event and uniqueness (the truth of the ἕν).
The event and beinglessness.
The event and the dispropriation.
The event and the domain of what is proper.
The event and the indigence of the claim; the favor of indigence.

187. The appropriating event

is appropriating eventuation, inventive saying of what is most proper. This latter is the inceptual in its inceptuality: the stillness of protective indigence is, as appropriating eventuation, the consignment (of what is appropriated) to the domain of what is proper, a domain which is thereby first appropriatively said (Da-sein).

The consignment to what is thereby appropriated is constantly arrogation of the domain of what is proper. The appropriating eventuation dispropriates the beings of the claim, so as, exclusively and for the first time, to be beyng [*das Seyn zu seyn*].

What is proper is all that essentially occurs, everything that pertains to the appropriating event.

188. Event and compassion

Compassion [*Rührung*]— the shy, non-grasping touch,
which hardly makes an impression [*berührt*] (not psychologically as tender, sad movement of the soul); merely comes into contact [*rührt*]
Compassion as inceptual disposition.
Touching [Rühren]— as appropriation
not causal movement; yet this movement does not here mean mere "overturning," but is to be thought above all from the domain of the inceptual.
To touch *the strings* [as of a lyre].
Touching— *extending to—reaching to.*
The wisdom of God reaches [*rührt*] from one end to the other.
To follow from [*her-rühren aus*]—
Schiller, *Wallensteins Tod,* Act IV, Scene 3:
Therefore it follows [*Daher rührt's*]
That we still lead only half the eagle.
To move [*Rühren*]— to affect intensely
Kant: the sublime moves; the beautiful stimulates.
To affect [*Rühren*]— *to make concerned—provoke care;*
to be appropriated into care; appropriate Dasein. *"deeply affected."*
narrowly: gentle affect—sorrow—sadness—
only narrowly? or the breadth of the origin of sorrow.
compassion—as *departure;* departure as beginning.

189. Beginning and the appropriating event

In inceptual thinking, beginning is thought "intransitively"; not to begin (tackle, take hold of, undertake) something, but instead *to be taken hold of* by something (*in-cipere*)

to be moved by something (compassion)
ontically intransitive, but "ontologically" *transitive.*
The essence of the beginning—the downgoing.
Bestirring oneself [*Sichrühren*] (appropriating event).
The inceptuality of the beginning to be thought on the basis of the event.

190. Event and domain of what is proper

The domain of what is proper arises in the appropriating event.
Domain of what is proper means here to have as properly one's own that which is appropriated as such (antiquity).
The domain of what is proper is inceptual.
The domain of possessions is subsequent.
Knowledge— steadfast meditation—is having inceptually as properly one's own.
Pure *domain of what is proper.*

191. Event and fate

(Cf. w. s. 41–42 Recapitulation 23–27ff.)[1]
Fate and effect.
Fate and withdrawal—concealment.
Beyng and its essential occurrence.
The beginning.

192. The appropriating event is incursion

The event, in clearing, incurs into (beings).
The incursion: φύσις—emergence,
therein the concealment in the withdrawal.
The releasement into the abandonment by being.
The admission of machination.
The devastation of being in the form of the unconditional order of the ordering of beings.
By incurring into beings, the event consigns the human being to Daseyn and commits him to the nobility of indigence; and this nobility becomes his proper domain, wherein he is steadfast.

1. *Hölderlins Hymne "Andenken."* {GA52, p. 99ff.}

The appropriating event is consigning incursion, such that it eventuates, in appropriating and clearing, amid (beings) as the in-between for their truth.

193. Event—experience

We must learn to experience the event as the appropriating event; and we must first become mature enough for experience. Experience is never the bare sensory perception of objectively present things and facts. Experience is the pain of the departure; it is belongingness to what is not yet past—steadfastness in the inceptuality.

The appropriating event is *essentially inceptual;* what is not yet past, what goes down into the beginning. The beginning is older than everything established by historiology. The event can never, in the manner of an idea, be established and represented.

Beyng is not a representation and never a concept, not something thought in distinction to "beings." Being is being, and being *is;* it is *the* beings.

Cf. *Die Geschichte des Seyns* I. Continuation. Typescript p. 1.[2] *Beings in their advent and passing away.*

194. To show—to eventuate Literal meaning

To show [*Er-eigen*]: to bring into view [*Er-eugen*], —to catch sight of [*Eräugen*] —*ostendere, monstrare,* to catch the eye, come into view, seize the gaze,
to appear
to manifest itself, carry to, give forth.
—to show —exhibit—*clear up.*

To eventuate (same as the above) *eu* [i.e., *ereugen*] became *ei* [i.e., *ereigen*]—
and also confusion with the unrelated "own" ["*eigen*"], *proprium,*
i.e., with "adopt" ["*an-eignen*"], "arrogate" ["*zu-eignen*"]

Already thus at the start of the seventeenth century.

2. {GA69, p. 131}

To eventuate = to strike the eye [*er-aigen*] —by way of clearing—to show

To eventuate —to incorporate into the clearing
to arrogate to it protection and preservation—
to human beings and to their care.

To eventuate = to come into its own of the appearing and at the same time self-concealing self.

VII. The Event and the Human Being (Steadfastness)

Cf. Da-seyn
Cf. On anthropomorphism

195. The event and the human being

In the age of anthropology, it is inevitable that the thinking of the history of beyng would seem to think the human being only so as to "explain" this being in the "middle" of beings, establish humans as the "ground" of beings, and declare humans the "goal" of all "being." But this thinking does not think "back to" the human being; otherwise it would have already recognized the human essence in the form which, with the start of metaphysics and in various although consistent stages, has achieved validity as *animal rationale.* Indeed this essence of the human being lies outside of the domain broached by the thinking of the history of beyng in the very first step of that thinking (i.e., in *Being and Time*). This thinking thinks human beings in their still-hidden essence out of the coming need of steadfastness in Dasein. The most proximate "goal" is to experience the uniqueness of Dasein. As regards Dasein, there is no sphere available into which we could place it, such that Dasein could then be explained by classification under a "universal." The essence of Dasein is unique, more original than the essence of the human being and yet is not the full essence of beyng itself. Dasein is the inhabited place of its own essence, an essence which is unveiled to us in its first traits when we originally experience the truth of beyng as the beyng of truth and thus know the turning. As a consequence, however, of the distinctive character of the human being with respect to the preservation of beyng, the human being uniquely belongs to the turning, provided the human essence essentially occurs in the inceptuality of the beginning. Because of that and because Da-sein, as the event of the turning, belongs to beyng itself and only to beyng itself, an original relation must obtain between the human being, as understood with respect to the history of beyng, and Da-sein. Therein is concealed the law that all essential human traits (ones in which the human being is related "to" being) must be experienced and thought, in terms of the history of beyng, out of Da-sein, i.e., in the inceptual essence of beyng. Moreover, this law at first concerns that human trait which has incorporated the human being into beyng inceptually and abyssally: death.

For the first and only time in the history of beyng, the essence of death must now be experienced and interrogated out of beyng itself, i.e., in terms of Dasein. The remaining, usual "notions" of death are metaphysical, as can be seen already by the fact that for them death is one "something" among others and lacks the distinctive character of beyng.

196. The event—The human being

The event is the consigning of the human being into that entity which has to preserve, lose, interrogate, and ground the truth of beyng (the historiality of the human being).

How human beings, appropriated to the truth, at any time can and do grasp themselves.

The preservation of the safeguarding and protecting of the event.

The *solicitousness* of stewardship
The *heedfulness* of the stewards
stem from the nobility and indigence
of the human being as understood
with respect to the history of beyng.

Consistence as a following
which follows the twisting
free—
follows the departure that
goes down.

The heedful solicitousness of the experience of the event;
the event is
the pain of enduring the differentiating-departing downgoing of the beginning.

197. The event

is the *appropriation* of the human being into humanity as understood with respect to the history of beyng, the humanity that has to ground the preservation of beyng. Yet the event is not only this appropriation.

If this relation to the human being belongs to the event out of the most intimate clearing of the beginning, then humans as understood in metaphysics have much to think about here, for they are inclined either to explain the human being as a creature or to raise this being up as the creator of subjectivity. In every case the human being is placed in a "role" and is either debased, exalted, or fatally accommodated in the middle of these two. That is the course of metaphysics, and it appears as a point of equilibrium between extremes and poses as the truth.

In terms of the history of beyng, however, the essence of the human being is different. It essentially surpasses all the loftiness of the superman and yet includes an essential indigence which of course has nothing to do with the wretchedness of the sinful human being of metaphysics. The event-related nobility and event-related indigence of historical humanity are the same. How does this essence correspond to the twisting of the event itself?

198. The event; the human being as understood with respect to the history of beyng, i.e., with respect to historiality

In the history of beyng, humans in their essence are addressed for the sake of a reply to this claim in the mode of the truth of beyng.

This distinctiveness of the human being, to be the historial being that alone encounters beings out of the preservation (care for the clearing) of beyng in the consigning, without becoming an object of representation, nevertheless excludes every anthropomorphism. Nor can this distinctiveness—the nobility of the indigence of steadfastness in Da-seyn—ever be understood in terms of metaphysics.

(Cf. the *beginning* of the interpretation of Schelling's treatise on freedom—s. s. 1936 typescript.)[1]

199. The event and the human being

This relation is the inceptually historial one. It constitutes historiality itself as the consignment (which appropriates the human being) of the truth of beyng to the human being, who, out of this consignment, first becomes himself, a self which cannot be determined out of "consciousness" egotistically, i.e., with respect to the I or the we.

The relation is therefore appropriated and corresponds to the intimacy between the event and the beginning.

In the essence of humanity, as understood with respect to the history of beyng, the event of the turning must therefore itself find its response. Where is this response predelineated?

The event "is" itself beyng as the relation, the appropriating relation, of beyng to the appropriated essence of the historial human being.

The event is the relation (proper to the inceptuality) of the beginning to the historial human being.

1. *Schelling: Vom Wesen der menschlichen Freiheit (1809).* {GA42}

The event is the inaugural "between"—the beginning of the clearing and hence is the abyss of the in-between, the consignment as Da-sein.

200. The event and the human being

(Grace and favor)

The appropriating event consigns the essence of the human being to solicitousness for the truth of beyng.

This consignment raises humanity to what is most proper of its essence and fits it for courage [*Mut*], i.e., for the knowledgeable (as knowledge of beyng) preparedness for the truth of beyng. The appropriating event is the inceptual vouchsafing [*Zu-mutung*] of courage. The appropriating event vouchsafes courage to the human being and is itself grace [*Anmut*]. As this grace, it is the favor of the beginning but also harbors the danger of disgrace and presumption [*Übermut*].

The inceptual, event-related courage of thinking, the courage that disposes toward steadfastness as thinking, is the nobility of the indigence [*Armut*] in the simplicity of the departure. The indigence experiences the favor and grace of the beginning.

201. The event and the human being

When we think of the relation between beyng and the human being, we are thinking of them from the standpoint of the latter: how the human being would relate to beyng and in general would surmise and find beyng. Or is this thinking an illusion, inasmuch as it already thinks on the basis of beyng and specifically such that "being" is not simply the "point of departure" but rather such that beyng is the truth of itself, of the human being, *and* of the relation? As this truth, beyng has already, by way of differentiating, appropriated the whole of what is in question here. And the experience of this event is the inceptual experience and thus also the first one.

This experience gives rise to the necessity of asking about the essence of the human being not under the guideline of the what-question, but by thinking of the *who*.

Who? This question already supposes that the human being is a *self. Selfhood* is marked by self-arrogation, which, however, is grounded in a consignment. The latter nevertheless concerns the proper domain of steadfastness in Da-seyn, i.e., consignment into the truth (solicitousness) of beyng. Cf. *Contributions to Philosophy (Of the Event)*, p. 193 {GA65, p. 245}. [Heidegger cites ms. p. 628.]

202. Being and death

Why did the preparation (cf. *Being and Time*) for the question of the truth of being think about the essence of death? Because humans alone die and have death, such that they therefore also in each case can and must die *their own* death.

But humans have death because they alone are adopted by being into a relation to being.

Yet being, as the event, is of a departure-like essence. In death resides the extreme possibility of the relation to being.

What is death? The departure-like abyss with respect to the beginning.

We still know nothing of the ontological essence of death, because we think metaphysically, take the human being as a ζῷον, and explain death, from the opposition to "life," as the transition to eternal "life." Thinking in terms of the history of beyng: *from beyng, Da-sein; as Da-sein, death.*

Death is to be thought inceptually, i.e., out of the event and with respect to Da-sein.

Death is the consummation of the steadfastness in Da-sein; death is sacrifice.

The end—in the sense of consummation—relates to Da-sein (not to life).

The departure-like essence concerns the departure from beings as such; yet this departure is the fulfillment of the relation to beyng.

Death essentially occurs not when someone is dead, but when the departure in the steadfastness of Da-sein attains its consummation. Therefore death also does not essentially occur when someone "dies," if dying is merely the extinguishing of "life."

Death is the steadfast going out of Da-sein into the nearest nearness of the clearing of beyng.

Death "is" rare and concealed. It is often no less prevented and deformed by dying than by sheer living. Death is the purest nearness of the human being to being (and thus to "nothingness").

We devastate the abyssal, departure-like, event-related essence of death if we seek to calculate what might be "after" it. Thereby we degrade death to a null passageway. We surmise nothing of the ground of pain in death, a pain that is not *"one"* pain among others, but is the essentially occurring abyss of pain, taking pain as the essence of the experience of being.

Death is the going out into the pure nearness of beyng. Its essence as "ending" must not be thought calculatively, either as "cipher" for life nor as start of another life. In that way, we avert our gaze from the essence of death and do not understand "ending" in terms of Dasein, i.e., in the unique relation to the clearing of beyng.

The law of the unavoidability of beyng is purely fulfilled in death.

Death appears to make everything equal; the result of this appearance is the great illusion about its essence and the entrenchment of the lack of a presentiment regarding the uniqueness of death. That opinion is the facile comfort of those who have degraded death and for that purpose avail themselves of expressions such as the "majesty of death."

203. What cannot be experienced of the beginning

The beginning and the human being

is that which essentially occurs before the differentiation; for all experience is not merely a human affair, but is such that in it the beginning brings itself to the clearing in something illuminated by the inceptuality.

We could never explain the origination of humans by way of a report about their production, not only because we have no "sources," but because in general the horizon of explaining and producing, making and creating, remains mired in beings and related only to them. Here already, *before* the first step of any particular mode of explanation, beings are decided *according to production* (whether ποιούμενον—εἶδος—ἰδέα, or *ens creatum,* or object and objectivity). Human beings, as beings, thereby already possess the basic sense of their being, even if further distinguishing marks are always added on: "reason," "spirit," "will," and other capacities. Yet not only is the being of the human being decided here without genuine experience; moreover, in correspondence with this decision, the essence is forgotten: the relation of being to the human being.

This relation of beyng to the human being can, indeed even must, be presented now first in its "fundamental" "meaning" on the basis of an "understanding of being." Here, too, what is already required is a dismissal of subjectivity and of "consciousness." Yet the essence—as understood with respect to the history of beyng—of the relation of being to the human being is experienced only if steadfastness in the difference recognizes that in the inceptual event, one still entirely concealed to itself, what has eventuated is the event of the human being: humans, inceptually overtaken by their essence, acquiesce in coming to terms with being. But then at once their capacities become sovereign, especially since being itself withholds its inceptuality, and an experience of the event becomes impossible.

The inceptuality is the *eventuation* of the human being into Da-seyn, and thereby humans are granted an open realm in which they immediately and spontaneously undertake "explanation"—proficiency (τέχνη).

The beginning, as it is before the event, cannot be experienced.

The event can also not be experienced in the first beginning. The experience of the event is of course not merely a matter of consciousness.

204. The beginning and the human being

Who is the human being? What is meant here by "the human being"? The human being as historical humanity. In that way the human being is thought, i.e., experienced, in the context of the history of beyng—on the basis of the relation of the historiality of beyng to the human being.

The human being is thereby the one appropriated into steadfastness in Da-sein.

To experience the clearing with regard to beyng and to think humans in their consignment to the truth.

The inceptual relation of the beginning to "the" human being? The question of the human being essentially not for the sake of this being but, rather, on behalf of the dignity of beyng.

Who the human being "*is*"—that is experienced only in the experience of beyng. No description helps here and no "new values" and "orders." In that way, "the human being," i.e., the human being of metaphysics (*animal rationale*), remains "as of old." Yet that is not the inceptual; instead, it is what has progressed out of the beginning, is no longer and never experienced in its inceptuality, is therefore ignorant of its essence, and consequently is unsuited to questioning.

205. Beyng and the human being[2]

(what is beingless)

The appropriating event appropriates into being that which is beingless. The appropriation does not effectuate, does not produce, does not allow something to self-emerge, does not represent, and does not let something merely appear.

What is the meaning of appropriation into "being"? And what "is" the beingless? Must that not already "be" "in some way," before the appropriating event eventuates, if we are not to speak everywhere of the created, the self-emergent, or the eternally actual?

Does not what is beingless constitute at the same time the last word to be said? Then it is in advance, in the metaphysical tradition, necessarily misinterpreted.

The appropriating event "is," "the fact that" humans "are," which now means steadfast in the clearing and in its stewardship.

How does the human being belong—*how does the human being belong essentially*—to beyng? How does this belongingness come about?

The human being and belongingness.

Belongingness is: consignment in the event, possessing the essence.

All metaphysics thinks the human being as *animal rationale;* that is so in the first beginning and still at the start of metaphysics. ζῷον λόγον ἔχον—from the "outside," the one that possesses the "word," and specifically the ζῷον, *the living being*!

λέγειν—the original gatherer, the one that possesses together out of the gathered together, out of presencing lets everything emerge by way of coming to terms with things.

This definition conceals the fact that the human being is thought and experienced in relation to being. But this relation to being is encountered as the property which is distinguished by contrast to ἄλογα.

The relation itself is grasped and graspable neither in its relationality nor as appropriation toward the essential ground. Wherefore does the ζῷον remain?

Is the ζῷον not stripped away when the human being becomes the ***res*** *cogitans* and when *cogitare,* as consciousness, determines the being of the human being as the subjectivity of the subject?

Certainly; but at the same time *adaequatio* has become *certitudo.*

The faculty of reason.

---

2. Cf. manuscript of *Die Geschichte des Seyns* I. Continuation, p. 28–29. {GA69, p. 149ff.}

Yet with the same decisiveness by which the essence of the human being (the essence of the soul, the essence of the spirit) was placed into consciousness (for Nietzsche, into the mere counter-essence of instinct, namely, "will"), so, precisely through this displacement, the essence of being as consciousness and objectivity was taken to be decided. Specifically under the semblance of the supremacy of being, the relation to being is now completely unquestioned. Indeed the only task now is to develop the essential determination into the unconditional.

But *what if* the relation to beyng itself, specifically as a belonging to beyng, as well as this belongingness are thought *out of* the essence of beyng? Then the essence of the human being is determined by the appropriation; then Da-sein first arises in the appropriating event. But from Da-sein arises the inceptual human being, who has at the same time twisted free of beyng.

How little the ζῷον and thereby the metaphysical outlook have been overcome by the interpretation of the *ego cogito* (consciousness) can be seen in the fact that now, in the consummation of absolute consciousness, nothing other than the bodiliness of the body is prepared as the guideline of metaphysics (Nietzsche).

The concealed capitulation to machination is altogether manifest in the fact that everything is elapsing only in revolutions and in "counterstrokes" and "counteractions"; only the flight into violence within the same domain (one that is unquestioned in the same way) traces out possibilities which circumscribe what is allowable.

The extent to which the outlook in the ζῷον λόγον ἔχον remains excluded, and must remain excluded, from every grounding of the relation to being, out of being itself, betrays this one thing, that inceptually and throughout the history of metaphysics "the difference" between being and beings remains what is unquestioned and at any time is merely interpreted in various ways, according to the change in beingness and in the truth of beings (e.g., the "transcendental" essence of objectivity).

206. The beginning and the human being

In the inceptual truth of beyng, there is no longer, as in all metaphysics, what is merely human, which is still rigidified by the erecting over it of something divine, whether for the sake of salvation or rejection.

In the inceptual truth of beyng as well, the human being is not immediately and purely divine, but now there has eventuated the consignment to beyng and to its clearing.

Now no longer the possibility of morality; but just as little the possibility of something merely beyond good and evil.

Now the saying of the steadfast responsibility of the hearth fire of the gods and of their inconspicuous advent in the inceptual indigence of the simplicity of all things which have returned to their essence.

The question of the relation of being and the human being still comes out of metaphysics and must stray into a dead end, insofar as it is asked too "anthropologically."

207. The human being and being

Gathering of the human being
    Gathering and unfolding of world
    "Circles" of gathering
Transformation of the human being
Grounding of Da-sein
Truth of beyng
Beyng
Gathering and memory
Memory and remembrance
Remembrance and history
History and the essential occurrence of truth.

208. Being and the human being

The object [*Objekt*] is what is most subjective, that which properly and exclusively depends on the subject.

But the "subject" is not "the human being," insofar as subjectity exhausts the essence of the human being or even arises in the origin of the essence.

If the object [*Objekt*] depends on the subject, it does not follow that beings depend on the human being.

It can be completely otherwise.

The fact that the human being in essence depends on beyng, whereby "dependence" would itself need to be determined first. The human being, within the event, is fitted to the truth of beyng.

Humans, as Da-sein, have the ground of their essence in the truth of being.

(This does not mean the human being would be influenced and conditioned by "beings," whereby humans themselves are things.)

209. Beyng and the human being

The essence of the human being is admitted into beyng. Beyng is neither outside nor inside the human being. Admittance of the essence of the human being into beyng in the mode of the appropriation of the disposition. (Circle—midpoint)

210. Beyng and the human being—The simple experience

(Cf., in this regard, 184. *The event and the vocabulary of its essence*)
The simple experience of appropriation.
Heeding that "we" can never *not* think beyng.

Attending to the question-worthiness of that which we heed in such heeding.

Attentiveness to this simplicity and to the pain of enduring the difference.

211. Being and the human being

Humans themselves, if they find their way back to their essence, are the ones dignified by being, dignified to preserve being in its truth and, out of this preservation, to erect beings in their *essential orientation.*

To accommodate the essence
and
to establish oneself "scientifically" (biology, anthropology).
The dignity
The nobility } of beyng as
The freedom inceptuality
The decisiveness of endurance in the departure.

VIII. Da-seyn

212. Da-sein
Outline

The "there" [*das Da*] and beyng. (Beyng as event appropriates the clearing whose uniqueness is possessed by the "that it is" of the beginning as its fulfilled brightness.)
The "there" and the clearing of the event.
The clearing and the undermining of representation; the emptiness of the will to willing and the abandonment of ἀλήθεια.
The uniqueness of Da-seyn.
The historiality of its essence.
The "there" and the in-between | time-space—and its essence | (turning).
The in-between and the event.
The in-between and the historial human being.
The in-between and beinglessness.
Da-seyn and steadfastness (disposition and the voice).
Steadfastness and consonance.
Da-seyn is the event of the turning.

213. Da-seyn

not merely Da-*sein*
instead, Da-*seyn*

is first the event as *essentially occurring*—the greeting of the twisting free of beyng—into the *clearing appropriated* with such twisting free.

Da-seyn belongs to the dispensation of beyng into the beginning and is disposed by the beginning and its inceptuality.

Da-seyn is also the necessary (wherefore) "recollection" of both the transformation of the first beginning and the overcoming of the episode of metaphysics.

*

Da-sein—the essential occurrence of the turning and indeed its essential occurrence as the fulfilled preservation of the concealed modes of decision and the paths regarding the advent of beings and the entrance of the gods into the divine realm.

The essential occurrence of the in-between of godlessness—the undecidedness of this essential occurrence as the encountering of beings.

*

Da-seyn—through a counter-turn, the *downgoing* corresponds to Daseyn in the event such that in Da-seyn alone the downgoing becomes historial.

214. Da-sein

(inceptual thinking)

Da-sein, out of its appertaining steadfastness in the truth of beyng, as steadfastness in the event of the beginning, relieves us of all critically probing reflexion characteristic of Christian modernity. At the same time, however, Da-sein also prohibits a return to the first beginning.

Inceptual thinking—begins simply. The inceptual thinking of the other beginning is even more inceptual.

Da-seyn as the recollection of the first beginning and of the episode of metaphysics.

215. Da-sein

was said at first as "human Da-sein," i.e., the Da-sein "in the human being" or the human being in Da-sein.

In each case, a distinction between the human being and Da-sein is indicated. But the essence of Da-sein is already projected on the basis of being and out of the question of the truth of beyng. And precisely this projection does not attain its essentiality as long as there prevails an attempt to make Da-sein "visible" with reference to the human being and as something "lying before us." Indeed it does lie before us, inasmuch as it already essentially occurs and is not something humanly made. It also lies before us in the appropriate experience, namely, in the clearing of being. But this "lying before us" is never an encountering in the way we come up against beings and establish them.

To be distinguished clearly:

1. if and to what extent Da-sein (truth of beyng), projected on the basis of being, is determinable by starting with the human being.
2. to what extent, primarily and properly, Da-sein, even if not unrelated to the human being, must be spoken of out of an experience of beyng, thus in terms of the history of beyng.

Then from where does Da-sein receive the determinateness of its essence?

216. Da-sein

Futile is every attempt, within the horizon of traditional concepts, to come close to what is thought on the basis of the inceptuality of the beginning as appropriation of the essence of the truth of beyng and is called "Da-sein" in inceptual thinking.

Da-sein is *not existentia, actualitas,* actuality.

Da-sein is *not* beings as a whole in the sense of the objectively present "world" (cf. the notion of the order of existence, i.e., of "things" in the sense of whatever there is).

Da-sein is not "human existence" in the sense of a "life" that is "lived through" and that refers to the mode of being of the *animal rationale,* i.e., the mode of being of the human being as established by and for metaphysics.

217. All beyng is Da-seyn

That expresses something other than the opinion that beings are human existence, whereby the latter is still taken in the sense of the "subject" and as consciousness, and, at best, some sort of Fichteanism is extrapolated.

All beyng is Da-seyn: that means beyng, in its dispensation into the junction, still makes known this inceptual essence, namely, that beyng essentially occurs as the truth of beyng.

Nothing of all this is known by the misinterpretation that at most knows only beingness and never beyng.

Da-sein "is" the *turning.*

The truth of being, in which guise the being of truth (clearing), the turn, and the resonance of the twisting free of *beyng* into the event.

218. "Dasein" (history of the word)

only since the eighteenth century with the meaning of "attendance" [*Beisein*], "in attendance at," "in the presence [*Anwesenheit*] of"; then, in the nineteenth century, existence in general, being at hand.

This word thus stems from an interpretation of beings as represented, as the presence of "ob-jects." Cf. the corresponding transformation of "object" ["*Gegenstand*"], which at first meant opposition [*Widerstand*] (fifteenth century) and juxtaposition (Christianity-Judaism); then a translation of "objectivity" ["*Objektsein*"].

Dasein—the presence of what is posed; that which lies before us in the posing.

219. Da and Da-sein

Da = to be in attendance, present, to have arrived, to have appeared, to be at hand, available, on hand.

Cf. Grimm [*Deutsches Wörterbuch von Jacob und Wilhelm Grimm*]: "Da" n. 10:

"and if I (Göthe) now come into the theater and look toward his (Schiller's) place and realize that he is no longer present [*da*] in this world, that those eyes will no longer seek for me, then I find life vexing and would prefer not to be present [*da*] any longer." (Bettina, *Briefwechsel*. 1, 281)

220. The clearing and its semblant emptiness

The clearing is the essential occurrence of the open, and the open is the passageway of opposition and arrival (beings) out of what is beingless.

The clearing is then indeed "empty"; so it seems, if we forget or have never considered that the clearing illuminates and gives brightness and that the passageway [*Durchlaß*] as a letting [*Lassen*] is a—indeed *the*—guarantee of truth [*Gewahr der Wahrheit*]. The *guarantee* belongs to the essence of truth; it has the character of an event. The emptiness of the clearing is inceptual nothingness.

221. The simple and the desolate

Between them is the abyss. Yet as to the desolation in the empty institution of instituting and incorporating into the process of securing the security of what is in itself negative: this desolation, in its clarity which anyone can learn to grasp, gives the "impression" and semblance of simplicity.

The simple, however, is the inceptual kindling of the unfathomable beginning and is the fullness of the mystery. Desolation is the emptiness of the explained and calculated.

222. In Da-sein

and experienced out of beyng and the truth of beyng, and out of the twisting free of beyng, there is decided the twisting of history into the beginning, the other one.

Therefore does not *Da-sein* have to be the first name for the event of the thinking of the history of beyng?

The "between" and the pain. Here in the in-between, especially the "between" between beyng and beginning, between beingness and beyng, between beyng and the human being.

223. Da-sein

is the inhabited place of the foreign wandering into the foreignness of beyng as the hearth of the event of the beginning, a hearth from which we have not twisted free.

224. Beyng—as Da-seyn

The last greeting of beyng from which we have twisted free into the beginning and into truth as the clearing of the event.

Dasein—not only as Da-sein, but Da-sein *as Da-seyn.*

Da-sein not only in human steadfastness, but Da-seyn as the essential occurrence of the event.

And with experience related to this inceptual Da-seyn that belongs to the beginning, related first and only to this, to let experience be disposed by Da-seyn.

Only to Da-sein, as the *between,* is the pain of experience in accord as the disposition that remains disposed by the voice of beyng in twisting free of beyng.

225. The temporal domain of godlessness with respect to the history of beyng (experienced godlessness)

(Da-sein—the inhabited place of the foreignness in beyng)

can very well allow the semblant Christian God and substitute gods; all this lies within the "worldview" that sets straight the godlessness which cannot at all be experienced in its truth as long as metaphysical thinking remains sovereign. Therefore it must be said:
All lights in heaven are extinguished.
The human beings of metaphysics will die under extinguished stars.

Godlessness is the time-space in which nothing can be ordered and instituted any longer, because here every calculable being defaults. In the inhabited place of the foreignness in beyng, there are open "places" for the entrance of the beginning, the beginning which inceptually appears in the twisting free of beyng.

226. Da-sein illuminates

beings and a being with respect to beyng

In Da-sein, beings are formed to themselves and thus to beyng.

The illumination confers the brightness of the inceptuality.

The illumination into beyng is itself neither effected nor effecting.

The illumination is the disposing and is like nothingness and its indeterminateness; for the illumination itself is not able to proffer this or that being.

The illumination brings to fruition the clearing of the "there" and brings forth beings out of the clearing.

Who has sealed this illumination to be such?

227. Da-sein and "openness"

The "*Da*," as a concept understood with respect to the history of beyng, does *not* have a directional character according to which it is distinguished from the "over there" (here and there [*da und dort*]). Even the "there" is a *Da* or, more precisely, is in the *Da* (*Da* ≠ *ibi* and *ubi*).

Nor does "*Da*" mean the same as "arrived" and thus "present," "at hand." Dasein = attendance [*Beisein*], "in attendance at," presence—"*Goethe is fond of this word*," according to the Grimms' dictionary.

The *Da* signifies the appropriated open realm—the appropriated clearing of being.

The "open," however, is conceived out of the essence of ἀλήθεια, unconcealedness, as that essence is understood with respect to the history of beyng.

(This openness has nothing in common with Rilke's concept of the "open" in the Eighth Duino Elegy, but neither does it stand in an extreme contrast to it; at the very least, a "relationship" could be made out.)

A. The human being as understood with respect to the history of beyng and Da-seyn (steadfastness)

Cf. The event and the human being

228. Steadfastness

and steadfast *thinking*.
Thinking and pain.
Pain: the horror of the abyss and the bliss of the departure.
The pain of indigence.
Pain and the restfulness of nobility.
The thinking of the history of beyng as the experiencing of the event is the preparation for the most proximate steadfastness: *the endurance of the difference.*

Steadfastness and the truth of the word.

Steadfastness is the nobility of the indigent heedfulness for the preservation of the beginning.

Steadfastness is *in this way* the preservation of the stewardship *of* the domain of what is proper, i.e., of that to which historial human beings are appropriated as to what is their own, wherein they possess what is proper to *their* being. *The domain of what is proper,* wherein essentially occur all appropriation and all arrogation and having as arrogation, is Da-seyn.

Steadfastness is disposed by the claim of the beginning.

Steadfastness essentially occurs in the event-related disposition of the beginning.

Steadfastness is "disposed" on its basis.
Only *the disposition* eventuates. What it determines, and thus appropriates while clearing, is *courage* [Muot]: *indigence* (not a lack).

229. The nobility of indigence

Humans are still not appropriated into the nobility of their historial essence; for they still have not experienced what is concealed about the beginning, namely, that the inceptuality requires the unique fact that the pure concealment of steadfastness corresponds to the beginning. This concealment must not only essentially occur *as if* it did not essentially occur. It must "*non*"-essentially occur, i.e., recede into the unknown—that is the extreme withdrawal of all nihilation. Pure passing by in it on the path into the truth of the inceptuality.

Only *the fact that* thinking eventuates is uniquely the need of the beginning. Not whether any human being has knowledge of it.

230. Steadfastness

Protect what is rare
Prevent habituation to the habitual.

231. Steadfastness in Da-sein

as the greeted peregrination over the inhabited place of the clearing of the event.
Da-sein essentially on the basis of the event;
in that sense already (only transcendental temporality [*Temporalität*]) in *Being and Time* and yet thereby thrust precisely into the postulation of "the human being" and on the path of exhibition.
Now: the experience of the beginning.

232. Knowledge

(the pain and the fulfilled acuity of this knowledge) is steadfastness in the truth of beyng.

Not the possession of cognitions.
Steadfastness as carefulness, submissiveness.

233. The event and historial humanity

(Beyng and the human being)
Da-seyn and steadfastness
Steadfastness and consonance
⟶

234. The nobility of humans and their indigence in the history of beyng[1]

To be kept at arm's length are the metaphysical explanations of the human being, ones in which this being is degraded to a sinful creature or exalted to the superman beyond good and evil, or which mediate between these two either by avoiding the extremes altogether and positing everything conditionally in a "not only—but also" or else by reconciling the extremes dialectically.

The nobility of human beings, experienced with respect to the history of beyng, is their appropriation into the truth of beyng. Their indigence is their dwelling in the simplicity of the event. Nobility and indigence belong together in accord with the twisting of the truth of being.

The essence of the human being, as that essence is understood with respect to the history of beyng, is not an "ideal"; instead, it is the historiality in whose truth there is in each case only the following of pliancy or there is forgetfulness.

The essence of the human being is illuminated in the experienced event.

Experience itself is appropriated.

The nobility and indigence (experienced in terms of the event) ground the essence of the human being in the history of beyng. This human being is not "human" and then in addition noble and indigent; on the contrary, nobility and indigence constitute the essence of the consigned as consigned. The human being is the one who is fitted to nobility and indigence.

235. The event and the human being

Appropriated into the truth of beyng is a being which, in an event of consignment to truth, experiences "itself" as steadfast in Da-seyn;

1. *Grundbegriffe*, 1941, typescript 47. {GA51}

out of this steadfastness the essence of the human being is opened as an essence sent by beyng and consequently belonging to the history of beyng.

The historical human being alone is consigned to the beyng of truth, i.e., to the truth of beyng.

"Through" (i.e., "throughout," not "produced by") the steadfastness of the human being, however, the truth of non-human beings eventuates.

The being of beings does not consist in objectification by way of representation, nor in effectuation through a creation, or through a self-showing in visibility; on the contrary, it consists in the event as the essential occurrence of truth, out of which then the first beginning proceeds forth as metaphysics, and in this progression the experience of the essence of beyng is neglected.

236. The open realm of concealment

The concealment opens itself first to the open relation which liberates into the open air by way of projection. But this self-opening of it is never a reversal into the unconcealed in the sense of something merely abandoned to the arbitrariness of affectivity or to the emptiness of chance encounter. The self-opening of concealment is indeed its unveiling and "merely" its highest preservation.

Such a miracle can become an event only in pure intimacy. Mere explanation and consumption, all compulsion to grasp and possess, can never understand this one thing: the self-opening of concealment as a pure harboring back into the consonance of the world.

237. Steadfastness and the clearing of the "there"

The blossoming of the concealment as *Da-sein* through the steadfastness of the human being.

The gleaming toward the world: a concomitant grounding of the inceptual world, which, first and only as world of the earth, preserves the clearing whose in-between bestows the encounter.

The earth is still not thought on the basis of the truth of beyng, but is merely explained and nihilated according to metaphysically predetermined appearances and is subsequently trimmed into mere "allure" and glitter.

Inceptual intimacy alone can be the origin of thoughtful discourse, which must be prepared for such intimacy, prepared in long solitude.

238. The incomparable

What is at that place where we can no longer compare? What is it when something precludes comparison? Then this something points purely to itself and so points *us* to the search for what it itself is—out of itself.

Then appears the first guarantee of a path toward the inceptual.

Then the pure gathering toward what is one and the same becomes essential. This gathering renounces all dispersal into restlessness—pure gathering is that thinking which is fulfilled and purely determined by itself. But what is purely and simply itself, the unique? Beyng.

Beyng, however, exists only as its truth. Yet how does that truth essentially occur?

B. Da-seyn
Time-space
Da-sein and "reflexion"
Steadfastness and disposition

239. "Reflexion"[2]

The shining back [*Rückschein*]; the fact that the shining shines upon something, and this latter, as the shined upon, itself concomitantly appears, such that the relation now shows itself as such and is held fast as what remains.

To what extent the shining back is bound within ἀλήθεια.

To what extent the shining already asserts itself in δόξα and the relation is announced.

To what extent nevertheless the *subjectum* is first grounded as an I through insight into the *ego* as *ego percipio.*

To what extent the grounding of ἀλήθεια (in the other beginning) transforms "reflexion" radically.

Is every reflexion already "consciousness"?

Differentiate between the origin and the incentive of reflexion. Reflexion and "the difference" in the sense of Hegelian negativity.

Is the source of reflexion the experience (!) of a recoil which proceeds from what is "experienced," perceived, present?

2. (originally, on the contrary, "clearing" and the "there"—the "as")

Reflexion and "the difference" between being and beings: beings *as* such! The "as" and the clearing of the regard:

(a) toward the ἰδέα
(b) toward the *ego cogito*
(c) Regard toward as view into—
Openness and clearing.

240. Da-sein—"space"

Remoteness and nearness—we think of spatial distances and extensions. And yet the space of things is accessible to us only over the space in which the stars exist. And the space of the stars opens up only if what eventuates is what we surmise to be the consonance of hearts. Only in that way can we, in "world"-space, grant to the stars the place which they present to us, either concealedly or as an astronomical position, for shining.

We think of nearness and remoteness as distances "in" space and do not surmise that "space" first has its ground in inceptual remoteness and nearness.

C. Disposition and Da-sein

The pain of the question-worthiness of beyng
Steadfastness and disposition
The *voice*—soundless—of the word
of the claim of the beginning
Disposition—appropriated by this voice
"disposed"—not in relation
to any other disposition—
thus *or* thus—calculated toward "temperament," which nevertheless, despite
Da-sein, in the possibility of
misinterpretation.
Disposition and *response*
"Disposition" as the essential occurrence of the event—
not "dispositions" as states

241. Disposition

disposes for the most proper determinateness of what is undetermined; the undetermined, but the disposed is the conjuncture of the appropriation of the inceptual.

*

Joy—the tending and preserving of the turn to the indigenous.
to dispose—not to deal "with" disposition.

*

Bad temper is the rage which seeks to tear itself up.
Disposition is not *indeterminate* and abstract,
and
what is concrete is never the material;
these are "metaphysical" distinctions, not ones bearing on Da-sein.

242. "Disposition"

pain
with respect to the history of beyng

Everything to be thought about "dispositions" must be thought on the basis of the experience of beyng and of its question-worthiness, i.e., on the basis of pain as understood with respect to the history of beyng.[3]

It can never be demanded to treat "the dispositions" in themselves, as it were, to arrange them in an absolute hierarchy, and to lay them out as if they could be a matter of choice. In this domain, there is no question of an earlier, anthropologically postulated manifold of dispositions, which are then considered according to elation and depression, in order to play the dispositions off against one another and, above all, to choose those appropriate to the "heroic" and consequential "times." In such a procedure, "anxiety," especially in the usual misinterpretation, will of course appear at a disadvantage, provided it manages to avoid complete condemnation.

In *Being and Time*, "disposition" is grasped as "situatedness"[4] ["*Befindlichkeit*"], which means that it must be experienced in terms of

3. (pain as the clearing of the difference—the difference itself) {Marginal remark in typescript}

4. In published translations of *Being and Time:* "state of mind" (Macquarrie and Robinson) and "attunement" (Stambaugh and Schmidt)—Trans.

Da-sein. "Situatedness" does not here signify the psychological state of well-being [*Wohlbefinden*] or of feeling ill [*Schlechtbefinden*]. "Situatedness" here means the ecstatic situating of oneself [*Sich-be-finden*] in the "there" as the inhabited place of the foreign temporal domain of Da-sein. Time as temporal domain is the essence of the "temporality" ["*Zeitlichkeit*"] of Da-sein.

"Disposition" ["*Stimmung*"] is here already disposedness based on the voice [*Stimme*], i.e., based on the intended claim of the question-worthiness of beyng. The basic disposition is the "disposition" replying to such a claim; it is the pain of question-worthiness. The disposition must also be experienced in its essence out of the essence of *pain* as the absence of intimacy. (Pain must not be misinterpreted as "disposition" in the ordinary sense of "feeling.")

Disposition is the steadfast hearkening—(to reply) to the voice of the dignity of beyng, a voice that disposes into the pain of the question-worthiness of beyng.

"The dispositions" of Da-sein "come" out of beyng; they are unavoidable; but, just as essentially, they are never states that simply befall us; instead, they are steadfast, they exist *by way of experience.*

We must here think "about" the dispositions in the sense that they are first thought inventively—i.e., experienced thoughtfully—in terms of the history of beyng. This experience is then at the same time also "disposing" in a sequential sense. *Pain* harbors the original unity of the joy of intimacy and the sorrow of absence.

Joy is the tending and preserving of beyng in its twisting free and sheltering in the beginning.

Sorrow is the tending and preserving of beyng in its twisting free and escaping in the downgoing of the beginning.

Joy and sorrow and their painful unity are determined above all from the inceptuality of the beginning.

If now, however, the thinking of the history of beyng attempts to bring being into experience immediately, it must purely and simply differentiate being from all beings and at the same time from the counterturn that essentially occurs in it itself, namely, nothingness. The "nothingness" that is to be experienced with respect to the history of beyng (the first, only half-successful attempt occurred in "What is Metaphysics?") possesses the voice of beyng no less than does this latter itself. And nothingness disposes into anxiety, conceived as anxiety of steadfast Da-sein. (This does not have anything to do with the usual "life-anxiety," insofar as "Dasein" ["existence"], according to the usual meaning, as in Nietzsche, is equated with "life.")

The anxiety of nothingness is *the anxiety of the pain* of the question-worthiness of being. In the just-named lecture, "anxiety" is discussed only in the context of the unfolding of a "metaphysical" question, i.e., the question of being in the sense of *Being and Time*.

The anxiety of pain is itself, in its essence, the pain of the question-worthiness of beyng in its own counter-turning. The anxiety of pain is not anxiety "in the face of" pain; it is rather the anxiety arising out of pain, anxiety as experience of nothingness.

243. The disposition of thinking is the voice of beyng

What does the voice say? What is the disposition? How is the disposition liberated in and through thinking? How is the disposition itself disposing and determining?

Because the thinking of beyng can never claim "the sensory," one might believe that it must furnish itself with some sort of sensibilizing of its concepts. But the origin of "concepts" is disposition—the dispositional is that by which thinking does not need the sensory and images. The imagelessness of disposition is never complete. But the remainders of the imagistic are also never the supports of the missing and too unjustly missing sensibilizing.

But which disposition? Which courage?
The basic disposition and the dispositions.
Disposition is not "indeterminate."
The basic error is that "disposition" is considered only half—and thereby corrupted—in essence, and according to this objectification it is judged:

1. as indeterminate and consequently "general" and so "abstract," fleeting—empty, a "logical," "psychological" interpretation of disposition.
2. as weak attitude, state, and mere disposition, feeling.
3. as subordinate neighbors to the other capacities (will and reason and passion), pallor—keenness.

Instead of this: Da-sein—the basic essence of disposition out of what disposes; the uniqueness, decisiveness, clearness, fullness, and bearing of disposition; the grounding of disposition.

Disposition and temperament, courage; disposition and voice—word.

(*Being and Time* still liable to be misinterpreted: "situatedness" as a state! The reference to the open realm does not suffice unless in advance openness.)

244. Downgoing and its disposition[5]

Downgoing is entrance under the protection which, as concealment, has taken the departure into safekeeping. The departure protects inceptually. Calculatively thought, the downgoing is the dissolution and disappearance of possessions and of things present at hand. In that way, downgoing remains a character of beings in the sense of actuality. Downgoing is then a falling into the non-actual, and this alone holds for nothingness.

The downgoing, whose essence with respect to the event is intimate, bears intimacy by essence, and intimacy is departure. Experienced thus, the downgoing essentially occurs, like the beginning, with respect to the history of beyng. The genuine beginning is the one that goes down.

The departure, i.e., the intimacy of the downgoing, is the reticence of beyng and thus of its voice, which inceptually twists free of beyng and, out of such a twisting free that goes down, disposes toward thanking.

In the stirring-up of the disposition of thanks as the greetedness of the human being, the event of Dasein appropriates.

The departure protects inceptually and greets in the appropriated intimacy of the inceptuality.

245. Da-sein and thanking

constitute reception of the appropriation of the essence of truth as clearing of the beginning.

Reception is itself marked by the event and requires no effecting, no "results" or consequences.

Da-sein as reception *is beyng.*

Beyng is the luster of the beginning in the in-between wherein what is true has illuminated itself and, as a "being," inceptually "is."

Da-sein is the appropriated time-space, the hearth-place of recollection. At this hearth, the inceptuality glows in concealment.

The steadfastness of reception is thanking. Thanking here taken over in the inceptual essence.

5. Cf. The pain of the question-worthiness of beyng.

246. *The basic dispositions of the history of beyng*

Wonder (the first beginning)
the beginning in emergence—φύσις itself.
Astonishment (the start of metaphysics)
Shock (transition)— freedom
the pain of question-worthiness.
Thanking (obedience to the other beginning).
Diffidence (appropriation into obedience) the steadfastness of harkening, *integration* into hearing, pliancy.
In *thanking,* we are first disposed in advance for thinking and poetizing and for their future truth with respect to the history of beyng.
Thanking and greetedness.
Greeting and event.
The beginning.

247. *The basic dispositions of the history of beyng*

Disposition is the name for the dispositional effect of the voice of beyng. This voice is so called because it is what is audible for hearing as the harkening of the obeying for an inceptual obedience, the pliancy which is itself uniquely historical and as such is also already uniquely determined.

The audibility of obedience.

Diffidence; its preservation is thanking.

Thanking at the same time again greetedness.

The audible as the perceivable of a greeting.

Thus not *a* disposition merely distinguished, but now in general the dispositional essence of the truth of beyng first brought into the open and into knowledge.

Only out of this unique disposition the essence of "dispositions" essential; in terms of the history of beyng; the truth of nothingness; anxiety. Anxiety and diffidence and Da-sein as care.

To what extent the voice is what determines. What is determinable—in disposing first *at*tuned? i.e., raised into the essence? Da-sein and its steadfastness.

("Dispositions" also in *Being and Time* already distinctive characters of "Dasein," the latter determined completely with respect to being and the question of being, never anthropologically.

Beyng and nothingness

Nothingness and anxiety.

Nothingness as the thrust into beyng—for the hard of hearing and disobedient.)

Voice and freedom.

Beyng as the predisposing which first attunes the essence of Da-sein.

248. Predisposition

Toward what does beyng, essentially occurring in its truth, ever dispose Da-sein? First of all, Da-sein itself must be predisposed.

Which steadfastness must ground itself as the essence of mankind itself in Da-sein?

Which outlooks and basic dispositions must be dispatched to humans and be preserved by them?

Why must these questions as such no longer be apprehended and answered from calculative measures? Because otherwise consciousness merely entrenches itself once again.

Yet because consciousness, despite all reassurances, bears "the life" of modern humanity, and the will to power as will is suspended entirely in this consciousness, then only what is essentially other than consciousness, namely, *meditation,* can inventively think the transition.

Even so, rare hearts which immediately apprehend the silence must wander therein.

249. Voice, disposition, "feelings"

It can never be pondered and questioned enough whether "the feelings" are merely "a cloudy aura" which remains stored in a psyche or whether this view of the feelings does not derive from a twofold error: on the one hand, from an apprehension of the human being as a living thing endowed with faculties, and secondly from a calculation of the faculties based on a preference for one particular class (such as reason or will).

Moreover, the twofold error is especially obstinate, because in all respects it remains concealed as an error and appears in the semblance of self-evidence like the pure truth to which everyone has already consented.

Even this misinterpretation of the feelings undergoes its own proper entrenchment in the abandonment of beings by being, within which the life of subjectity is lived out.

The "dispositions" are then described like the "types" of "airplanes" which just happen to be. And this descriptive industry produces great discoveries.

IX. The other beginning

Beginning and event

250. In what does the essential unity of event and beginning dwell?

To what extent is the beginning event-like? To what extent is the appropriating event beginning-like?

The unity of the event and the beginning is to be known from their intimacy.

This "unity" is the abyss of the difference and is the inhabited place of the pain of the thinking of beyng in its history. This "unity" is the inceptuality of the ἕν and might in the future teach us to surmise why the ἕν weighed so heavily on thinking at the first beginning. The ἕν itself already only on the basis of ἀλήθεια (cf. τὸ γὰρ αὐτό).

It must for a long time remain strange that event and beginning "are" intimately the same.

The event is the inceptuality of the beginning. The beginning is the denial of the differentiated departure.

251. The counter-turn in the event and the beginning

The event as consignment of the clearing and refusal of the grounding.

Refusal as denial; this denial the inceptual word of the *inceptual claim.*

The inceptuality as abyssal and yet emergent.

252. The beginning

The beginning is not inceptually in the inceptuality; the beginning commences in what has not begun, inasmuch as the beginning disentangles itself from that in order to emerge. The disentangling is what is concealed of the unconcealedness.

The consequence of disentangling is the advancement into metaphysics. The disentangling requires, should the beginning ever begin, the twisting free into the twisting of the inceptuality.

The other beginning is *the* beginning *otherwise* than the first—the first is still otherwise than the other.

The disentangling and the twisting free essentially occur in the inceptuality. The disentangling of being and of truth out of the twisting.

Only in the other beginning is the inceptuality experienced and the clearing of the beginning itself bestowed.

The bestowal, however, requires the truth of the protective submissiveness in the downgoing.

The beginning is the abyss of the clearing of the difference in the simplicity of the "that it is" of the "it is."

The beginning is abyssal and is the denial of the ground; for wherever there is a "ground" there is a cessation of the clearing. All grounding ends in the darkness of the ground. This is not contradicted by the fact that explanation [*Erklären*] goes back to something clear [*ein Klares*]. This something is nevertheless "clear" only according to the light of *explanation* and according to the domain in which representation keeps itself and is satisfied. What is "clear" in explanation does not know the clearing [*Lichtung*] of being; instead, it circumscribes only one mode of the representation of beings. (The explanatory "principles": they themselves are postulated as the last and the first, and they do not know the inceptuality of the truth of their being, and must not know it, for otherwise every foothold and point of departure would be lacking.)

The ground is cessation of truth.

The abyss is the inceptuality of the beginning of the truth of beyng.

253. The beginning

is the beginning "of" being. It is the essential occurrence of being in its truth. Being is evident to the historical human being from the first, i.e., at the commencement, already on the way to its essential occurrence, and thereby, because it is unconcealed as φύσις, it is at once also held fast as the preceding and then is turned toward beings. Consequently what is needed is the experience that being is in itself historical, i.e., inceptual.

Beginning does not mean commencement, and afortiori never means the commencement of beings, not even in the sense of an explainable origination out of "something."

In order to think the beginning, we must already in advance be appropriated in the experience of being, appropriated by being to this experience. We can never take hold of the beginning by ourselves. The beginning can only consign us to Da-seyn. But we can cultivate the courage [*Muot*] for being insofar as we are already, through metaphysics, delivered over to being. Although metaphysics, with all its thinking of beingness, can precisely not experience being itself, we are nevertheless reminded that in order to heed beyng it is essential to experience metaphysics itself, i.e., the West, in its history.

To experience being as the beginning and the beginning as beyng is necessarily foreign to all ordinary representation, desire, and calculation. And already the attempt to weaken this foreignness, instead of developing it, testifies to the inability to understand what must be said here.

The saying of the beginning does not explain anything. And it provides no help in finding one's way "better" amid accepted beings according to fixed horizons.

The saying of the beginning produces a tremor in beings, without their ever having allowed themselves to be effectively "concerned" with "being."

254. The last god

is the oldest, most inceptual god, the one that is decided to his essence in the inceptuality of the beginning, the one that could *be* more eminently only if the truth of beyng were inceptually grounded to him, which is not something in his own power.

The appropriation into the event first provides the time-space of the appearing of the last god.

The higher inceptuality of the old (i.e., the first) beginning must have eventuated.

All attempts to fabricate and plan "religion," to return to past religions and renew them, are aberrations stemming from a metaphysical-historiological intention.

The absconding of the Greek gods is grounded in a disturbance of the barely unveiled essence of ἀλήθεια. The pressing forward of being as ἰδέα is the end of divinity.

The last god is not the "residual" god remaining left over and the sheer end, but is the most inceptual and highest god; all past things essentially occur with him, in that he "is"—what is never effective inceptually.

The last god first grounds the essential occurrence of that which, badly calculated, is called eternity.

X. Directives to the event

A. The enduring of the difference (distinction) Experience as the pain "of" the departure[1]

Unsuitable questioning
in the thinking of the history of beyng

The question-worthiness of beyng
is in truth the inceptuality of the twisting free
of beyng, and thinking follows
this twisting free.

255. Pain—experience—knowledge

Pain
Experience the enduring of the difference—thinking
Knowledge
to think out of steadfastness in Da-seyn, i.e., out of historial humanity.

But that says: all these determinations are appropriations of humans into the uniqueness of their distinctive role: carefulness—i.e., the protection and stewardship of the truth of beyng.

To be sure, the mention of "pain," "experience," etc. will at first be taken in an anthropological and psychological sense as the singling out and arbitrary defining of "human" faculties.

256. Experience

is the pain of the departure, a pain that belongs to the twisting free of beyng. This pain, insofar as we twist free of it, first unfolds the bliss

1. here "pain" indeed steadfast, but not yet event-like: the painful {Marginal remark in typescript}

together with the horror. The twisting free of the pain follows the twisting free of beyng and is appropriated out of beyng. The twisting free of the pain does not remove it but, instead, brings it back into the continuance.

Experience is the return to the difference, and the latter, by way of departure, has taken over the history of beyng. Experience is the return to the history of beyng.

Experience involves taking in [*Erhalten*], in the double sense of reception and preservation.

The taking in of experience is the cleared assumption into what continues. What continues is the continuance. The continuance is the beginning. This latter continues in the abyss. This continuance is the downgoing.

257. The pain of the enduring

Pain is the inceptual *sharpness* of fulfilled knowledge. Pain is the forbearance which, in withstanding, has originally gathered together the horror of what threatens and the bliss of what entices.

In this withstanding in the time-space of the turning (the truth of beyng as the beyng of truth—essentially occurring as the nearest ring of the twisting free of the inceptuality), pain is steadfastness in the experience of the appropriation.

Only in the pain of enduring is beyng illuminated for the human being of the history of beyng. Only the preservation (preserving custody of the event) preserves inceptual, pure "presence," in case this should ever be spoken of.

Pain is the inceptual (replying to the beginning and thus corresponding to it) transfiguration of the unique knowledge. The horror of the abyss in the beginning and the bliss of the departure into the appropriation are inceptual and are not of such a kind that "feelings" could ever reach them.

In the withstanding-steadfast essence of pain, there rests the experience of the event, an experience which constantly brings the difference to knowledge in its history.

This experience is the essence of the thinking of the history of beyng. That thinking, in turn, grounds the experience in which the human essence in the history of beyng preserves the foreignness constituting the inhabited place of the abyss for the human being.

The essence of this experience goes to determine the inexperience which first comes to light in the age of the consummation of the episode of metaphysics. From this inexperience we can first recognize the lack of experience which, in metaphysics, is supposed to be replaced by inspection and calculation, certainty and systematics, without the replacements ever needing to become known.

The inexperience for the beginning and, most proximally, for the turning of the event does, however, ground at the same time the dominance and tenacity of metaphysics.

In metaphysics, the horror of the abyss as well as the bliss of the appropriation, this double-unitary pain of the departure into the inceptual, is unknown and inaccessible. The overcoming of metaphysics out of the twisting free of the event.

258. Enduring as thanking

(Experience and thinking)

The enduring of the differentiation, insofar as this latter follows the difference into the twisting free, is steadfastness in the appropriated proper domain of the indigence of the simple inceptuality. Steadfastness in the arrogated proper domain of indigence is the nobility of thanking.

Thanking is not a mere appendage to the thinking of the history of beyng; on the contrary, it pertains intrinsically to the distinctive character of the pain of the experience of the event.

This thanking is not the subservience of someone who is made happy by the possession of some commodity which makes everything easy for him. This thanking is the high spirits of the great courage which acknowledges the risk to the distinctive character of the enduring. In this thanking, the thinking of the history of beyng is essentially the experience of the assignment to the truth of beyng.

This thanking is the appropriated preparation for the foreignness in the abyss of the beginning. The full essence of thinking, as enduring and experiencing, is ordained out of this thanking. *Experiencing* and *thinking* are the same in the enduring, but their determination can never be acquired out of an anthropological delimitation of cognitive faculties.

The essence of experience, taking all the moments of experience as a unitary whole, derives from the essence of pain as the cognizant enduring of the difference in the departure. In the experience of the history of beyng, there is experienced the utmost separation of the thoughtful human being from beyng as beginning: the fact that the consignment of beyng is the intimacy of the remotest nearness. The remotest nearness prevails here because nothing intuitive essentially occurs here, nothing imagistic, nothing that could be grasped immediately by handling and manipulating. On the contrary, what essentially occurs resides in a nearness that could never be attained by the presence of a spectacle or of any sort of captivation, because all of that is either entrenched in objectivity or, transgressing every distance, merely descends into the dullness of stimulation and of a feeling of blind sensations or of the brute force of the sheer elements. The nearness of the most remote, in terms of beyng, eventuates in the pain of the experience of the event.

Inceptual thinking thinks the beginning in the sense of a departure; this thinking follows the beginning into the abyss. The thinking of the departure is fulfilled solely from the inceptuality of the beginning. It thinks the simplicity of this uniqueness and does not have anything else it could still grasp. That is the inceptual indigence. This indigence [*Armut*] is the courage [*Mut*] that takes on [*sich zumutet*] the claim of the beginning. The thinking of the history of beyng, as a human enterprise, constantly remains in the predicament of arriving out of the everyday into the appropriated. At any moment it requires an inceptual attentiveness to the directives of Dasein.

259. The enduring of the difference

(Questioning and question-worthiness of beyng)

is the pain of the experience of the event, i.e., of the distinction as essence out of the difference which twists free in the departure. The enduring is thinking. In this thinking, "questioning" also is overcome.[2] What is called "thinking"? Relation of beyng *as such* to the human being. Yet the overcoming of questioning is not a transition into questionlessness.

The enduring is, if speaking in this way is still possible, *more of a questioning* than any question, because the enduring belongs to the abyss and therefore does not stop at a ground but goes back beyond it instead. If this is the essence of questioning, then the enduring has the character of an inceptual questioning of that which, as abyssal beginning, is itself what is question-worthy. Insofar as the essential occurrence of beyng (turning) pertains to the beginning, beyng illuminates its worthiness for such questioning. But because we are wont to persist

2. "Questioning" in the sense of metaphysical-explanatory questioning that determines the "essence." Condition of possibility. {Marginal remark in typescript}

exclusively in metaphysical and scientific questioning (i.e., in problems of research, calculation, and explanation), this talk of "questioning" and of question-worthiness is too easily degraded to that domain. *Inceptual questioning* is the enduring of the difference; it resides in the pain of the experience of the departure. Enduring into the beginning.

The enduring of the difference is heedfulness for the abyss; this heedfulness is in itself the grounding of the truth of the beginning.

The enduring, as the painful experience of the departure of the twisting free, is *more of a questioning* than any sort of question, provided questioning is the appropriated relation to the beginning, i.e., to the downgoing "whence," which, as having been, is the pure coming of the clearing.

In the strict sense, questioning exists only where the relation to being is already established and out of which, in its light, ἰδέα, there is an interrogation into beings, that which is, τί τὸ ὄν. Questioning exists only in metaphysics and, consequently, in "science."

If questioning is taken in the strict sense (inquiry into the what, why, how, whither, and whence of the look and composition of things, of their causes, production, representation, and objectification, and of their content), then inceptual thinking is not a questioning. The previous attempt to characterize this thinking of the truth of beyng, precisely as genuine questioning with respect to the question-worthiness of beyng, is insufficient and is a misunderstanding of the thinking of the history of beyng. The characterization of this thinking in terms of questioning and as questioning is unsuitable. It must no longer enter into the saying of the event. What the previous attempts thought by this misleading characterization does retain its truth but lacks the decisiveness of the contrast between the thinking of the history of beyng and "metaphysics."

The unsuitability of questioning, however, is not an evasion into faith and a flight into non-thinking. On the contrary, the unsuitability of questioning must itself be endured in the enduring of the pain of the departure. *The enduring is essentially more steadfast in the abyss* than all questioning, which indeed rests on itself, does not attain being in its truth, and is not at all appropriated by being.

The enduring is also never poetry, because the enduring follows the twisting free into the beginning and never follows the presentation of beings as dwelling places and guesthouses of humans and gods.

The enduring is the saying of the history of beyng.

The enduring is the appropriated, proper, steadfast word of the relation of beyng to the human being of the history of beyng, whereby talk of "relation" is always misleading, since it insinuates that beyng is like an object standing apart.

260. Inceptual thinking is abyssal thinking

In the first beginning, which corresponds to the disentanglement out of the still-unexperienceable turning, the abyss does not appear as abyss. But the abyss shows itself, for experience out of the other beginning, as the essential occurrence of the concealment which appropriates the concealed from which unconcealedness is disentangled. Therefore truth possesses the essential character of a wresting-from [*Ab-ringung*] (α-). Beings appear in emergence. In the first beginning, which, as the first, must be the first to emerge, the inceptuality remains concealed. Insofar as historiality commences with the truth (of being), the grounding of humanity in beings becomes needful. The grounding can immediately rely on the beings essentially occurring in being. The gods essentially occur immediately in beings as beings.

In the other beginning, however, where the inceptuality of the beginning comes into its truth, the abyss of the beginning is manifest. This does not prevent historical grounding but, in fact, requires it out of the inceptual appropriation; for in the abyss the grounding first obtains its inceptual necessity and sharpness. Where there are those who ground, those of the abyss must be there in advance, i.e., those who bring to experience beyng in its twisting free toward the inceptuality and who assure the preservation of the departure. This steadfastness distinguishes historicality in the other beginning. Therefore inceptual thinking is not νοεῖν and λέγειν but, instead, is abyssal experience as the enduring of the difference into the abyss. Thought in terms of the new true {?} poetizing as the founding of continuance, the thinking of the history of beyng is a de-founding: not as if the founding were revoked and not as if thinking in general were related to poetry. De-founding here means only that the thinking of the history of beyng, if differentiated from poetry, is taken away from the domain of poetry, separated from the essence of poetry. In such separation, the future thinking and poetizing are, to be sure, near each other.

Poetizing is thoughtful remembrance of the festival—the tarrying of the holy.

Thinking is de-founding toward the enduring of the difference.

261. Beyng is experienced

(experience and sojourn)

when the truth of beyng comes to be explicitly endured in the steadfastness of Da-sein. Both eventuate during the experience of the turning. This experience, as *the* experience, is the sojourn in the twisting free out of which the turn eventuates. As long as the word of the truth of beyng remains absent, there is no sign that the sojourn has eventuated. The word of the truth of beyng, however, must first be prepared through a saying of the essence of truth in such a way that what is inceptually true is therein taken over (w. s. 37–38).[3]

262. The question: In what way?

(abyssal thinking)

This question is the only question of inceptual thinking. The question thinks beyng abyssally in its truth, i.e., thinks the turning in the remoteness of its twisting free into the departure. The question thinks into the greatest remoteness of the abyss and, in this remoteness, keeps the inceptuality in its appropriate nearness. Residing in this questioning is a constant recognition of the claim of the withholding.

This thinking is the pure experience of the inceptual "that it is" of the "is" of beyng itself; the "that it is"—emerging out of the event-related inceptuality and only this "that it is."

Every "Why?" is out of place here. For, a "Why?" would be a depreciation and a non-experience of the beginning, since such a question, in asking away from the beginning and toward a ground, on the one hand denies the inceptuality and on the other forgets that here only an abyssal thinking is appropriate, a thinking which in the pain of the departure experiences the favor of the indigence of the event-related withdrawal.

---

3. *Grundfragen der Philosophie: Ausgewählte "Probleme" der "Logik."* {GA45}

263. The thinking of the history of beyng says beyng (the "is" of the history of beyng)

The "is" of the history of beyng, an "is" wherein beyng comes to be said in its twisting free, receives its significance out of the essence of the beginning. Every word of this thinking signifies on the basis of this truth which essentially occurs as the turning.

The "is" here always retains the inceptual fullness and signifies:

eventuates
begins
twists free
turns
distinguishes
departs.

264. Enduring and questioning *The question-worthiness of beyng*

In the transition to the thinking of the history of beyng, there is often talk (cf. the earlier manuscripts and lectures) of the question-worthiness of beyng, specifically in the sense that, in questioning, the dignity of beyng is recognized and the worthiness of this dignity is first shown. On the other hand, the misgiving could arise that questioning is rather a matter of curiosity and impertinence, that questioning brings the things questioned down to its own level and into its own sphere of power, whereby obviously the result would be the opposite of appreciation, namely, depreciation. But the emphasis on the question-worthiness of being means first of all, for the initial steps within the overcoming of metaphysics, that, in distinction to the priority of beings and beingness (oblivion to being), being itself in its truth would be what is more original and would claim not to be surpassed by thinking and questioning. Now insofar as this very questioning pursues the truth of beyng and explicitly (at the same time *for* the human being) grants to beyng the originality of its essence, to that extent is questioning, seen in contrast to the previous oblivion, an appreciation of the dignity of beyng. Questioning does have its own merit, as long as it does not draw things to itself but, instead, assigns all thinking to the essential claim of the truth of beyng.

But in this genuinely essential way of asking the question of being (in the sense of the thinking of the truth of beyng in distinction to the interrogation of the beingness of beings in metaphysics), it becomes clear, at the same time, that this questioning is related back to metaphysics and is dependent on metaphysics. The thinking of beyng still attempts here to determine its essence by characterizing its otherness to metaphysical thinking, thus indeed with the help of this latter. The positive sense of the question-worthiness (versus questionableness and doubtfulness) consists only in resistance to, and reaction against, the oblivion to being in metaphysics; consequently, this initial thinking of the history of beyng at first indeed understands itself in general in terms of "metaphysics."

Yet as soon as it is purely experienced that the inquiry into the truth of beyng is seeking to acquire the essential pain of the departure of the beginning in its downgoing, and it is clear that the thinking of beyng follows the twisting free of beyng and in such subservience devotes heedfulness to the truth of beyng because thinking is, in experience, an appropriated thinking, then questioning becomes unsuitable.

The enduring is essentially abyssal. Its thinking is inceptually that which the changed question of being seeks but can never attain. The enduring is the saying of the history of beyng.

265. The essence of experience
The question-worthiness of beyng

Experience is the pain of intimacy with steadfastness in the distinction, i.e., the pain of the departure. Experience is the enduring of the question-worthiness of the departure.

In this experience, being is preserved and manifested as that which is preeminently worthy of questioning.

Is questioning then a deeming worthy? Can questioning essentially occur in the worthiness?

What is worthiness? The resting in itself of the beginning itself. To experience the inceptuality in experiencing the difference.

But how is experiencing a *questioning*? Questioning whether, and in what historiality, being would essentially occur such that its truth would be recognized and fathomed in humanity.

To deem beyng worthy in the mode of following the twisting free. This following is a heeding—the heedfulness that one might be adequate to beyng.

To experience the clearing for beyng in humanity and to ground the open realm for beings.

266. Founding and enduring

Poetizing: thoughtful remembrance of the festival—consolidation of the emergence of the holy.
Thinking as thoughtful remembrance—relation of the holy to becoming homelike.
"Thinking"—because the holy out of the inceptuality.

Thinking: de-founding as enduring the difference into the downgoing departure. The enduring of its own origin.
Relation of beyng as such to the human being of the history of beyng—i.e., (event) de-grounding.
The abyss of the beginning.

Where there must be founders as those who ground in advance, there must be abyssal ones.

"Thoughtful remembrance" means	that poetizing about the holy is appropriated out of the beginning.
De-founding means	that thinking about the twisting free of beyng follows the inceptuality in the proper consignment to the event itself.
Abyss/ De-founding ≠	revoking the founding; instead, it means separation from it in a proper "counter"-essence.

The abyssal character of the de-founding does not originate in a subsequent or accidental break in the ground and grounding; on the contrary, the abyssal character resides in the departure-like essence of the beginning itself.

The opening of the abyss follows the twisting free into the downgoing and follows the enigma of the beginning.

The *de-founding* withdraws from the homelike, but this withdrawal arises already out of the essential heeding of the event, i.e., out of submissiveness to the twisting free.

The appropriating event in its downgoing inceptuality is the unhomelike but is not the one related to the homelike of poetry. On the contrary, it is an un-homelike that is essentially unrelated to "homelike" and "un-homelike," and afortiori it is not a mere seeking after adventures, a seeking which precisely remains captivated by both in an indifference to them that varies with the two respective cases.

The "un-homelike" of thinking is extrinsic to "homelike" and "unhomelike" in the essential occurrence of truth itself.

Poets can only keep in thoughtful remembrance; their word points to the holy, such that they can never poetize the (event) of the holy and certainly not the inceptuality of the event.
But in the fact that poets say nothing but the holy, they found and are ones who ground.
Remembrance is a poetizing thinking.

Thinkers merely bring the difference to an enduring and can never ground in submissiveness to the departure. But they do not merely think "of" what has been and what is coming; instead, they think ahead into the beginning. This thinking ahead, seen in terms of the beginning as such, is a more inceptual relation to beyng and therefore is a more thoughtful thinking, i.e., a thinkers' thinking. But their thinking, as a thinking ahead, out of the pure separation, possesses something of the character of grounding (i.e., poetizing).

Nonetheless, in such oppositionality the same determination must never be carried over into the opposite. There is in general here no mere opposition and no correspondence. Here in the full separation is no recourse to a commonality which could have the character of something immediately common to all.

Consequently, we must not forget that everything here is said in dialogue with "the" poet, a dialogue that already speaks out of the enduring and its experience.

Experienced in terms of the enduring:

The inceptuality of the beginning
The departure
The downgoing
The (event)
Da-seyn
Beyng
Truth

closed open

The holy	Being
Gods and humans	Humanity of the history of beyng
Becoming homelike in passing through the un-homelike	Becoming free into the abyss
*	*
The ability to hear the poetizing word	The inaudibility of the heeding word
↓	↓
open	closed

B. The thinking of the history of beyng

The enduring of the difference (distinction)

The care of the abyss

The timber trail

Thinking and the word

267. The thinking of the history of beyng

is—judged from the standpoint of metaphysics—necessarily exposed to two corresponding and yet contradictory condemnations. It appears to metaphysical thinking and to its "logic" and *ratio* as the revival of the "irrational" (the beginning is irrational).[4] But it also appears to the metaphysical way of designating the elemental ("nature" and the sensory) as rational (being is like a mere concept, empty, abstract).[5] Both judgments are just as correct as they are incorrect. In every respect, they are inappropriate. They stem from what has been overcome. They do not allow themselves or their unity to be thought, and so their essence can never be clarified, above all not out of the matter of thinking. The thinking of the history of beyng leaves behind the distinction into rational and irrational representation, because it cannot at all be determined in terms of representation, presence, and mere appear-

4. But the beginning is the appropriation of thinking. {Marginal remark in typescript}

5. Being is *the* element. {Marginal remark in typescript}

ance. The enduring of the difference is essentially more rigorous than every rationality, and it is essentially more a matter of disposition than is the impression made by anything irrational.

The enduring is the pain (horror and bliss) of the experience which, in the abyss, steadfastly stands in the inceptuality (having been—forthcoming).

268. The thinking of the history of beyng

The essence of thinking is determined as the relation to the truth of beyng, specifically such that this relation is appropriated out of the (event) itself.

"Thinking" is here not a human "act" or comportment which could be delimited by means of an analysis of "faculties."

Thinking is determined by the appropriation of the human being, whereby the essence of humanity is grounded in Da-seyn.

But the distinctive characteristic of thinking is not yet grasped in this way! That characteristic is the enduring of the difference, in which guise beyng itself is differentiated from beings while providing a clearing for them.

Enduring? [*Austrag?*] is submissiveness to the twisting free of beyng toward departure. What and who submits? Thinking, as an enduring that *speaks*. Speaking, the word, is not a mere expression of the enduring but is the enduring itself. What sort of speaking? The proposition?

The submissively indicative, heedful (dispositional) saying of the history of beyng.

269. The thinking of the history of beyng in the transition

detaches itself only slowly from the character and the claims of metaphysical "thinking," which counts for us as "thinking" pure and simple and which has also produced "logic."

In the transition, it is necessary furthermore that thinking extricate itself from metaphysical, anthropological "reflexion" and nevertheless take up "meditation," since the enduring is a meditative one.

The carefulness of the enduring is a matter of care for the truth of beyng.

270. The thinking of the history of beyng

does not introduce any "gods," nor does it discover any new realms of beings.

It is not a "reflexion" on the "historical situation." It is not poetry but the uniqueness of the enduring of the difference. The difference essentially occurs already as metaphysics, although groundlessly and with no experience of the truth of beings, and has ultimately promoted the oblivion of being and the devastation of beings.

271. The thinking of the history of beyng. The thoughtful word

thinks beyng in its twisting free into the event of the beginning. The twisting free itself essentially occurs meanwhile as the passing by.

But if this thinking is indeed determined out of what is thereby to be thought, it nonetheless still remains to delimit what constitutes "thinking" in general. To be sure, "thinking" in general is indeterminate and as such is indeterminable. Still, the question of what is here called thinking will not rest.

Thinking is a relation to being, a relation opened up and ordained by being. Ratio and λόγος as opinions and propositions about what is present and co-present constitute only one mode of thinking and are determined by beingness as ἰδέα.

The "essence" of thinking is determined according to the way beyng essentially occurs, i.e., according to the way beyng dwells in its truth, namely, whether it abandons disjunction to the dominance of the machination of the will to willing or whether it twists free of the disjunction and consigns thinking to the twisting free as the matter to be thought and thereby disposes thinking.

If thinking is determined thus, then it submits to the dispensation of the junction and thereby dwells in the historiality of the event and brings about an enduring of the twisting free of beyng in a thoughtful word. How can this be endured? By its taking up the resonating of the consonance, such that it is the resounding of both.

Thinking is appreciation of the dignity of beyng. Because beyng possesses its dignity in the beginning and because the beginning essentially occurs by going down, thinking must submit to this downgoing and so must experience the abyss. Thus is thinking the venture of the inceptual freedom of the beginning. The experience of being—

of being which differentiates itself in the difference of the departure—is the pain that withstands this separation.

Thinking is a becoming at home in the inhabited place of the departure. Questioning is here a following into the abyss. This experiential questioning needs no answer.

The questioning of the history of beyng opens to the human being the open realm of the resonating consonance of the conjuncture of the event. This questioning follows the seams of the conjuncture; questioning, by speaking out, fits into the junction. But why do we speak here of questioning? Because thinking, in its essential relation to the truth of beyng, constantly remains in ignorance of the beginning inasmuch as thinking is never displaced into the beginning, although at the same time it indeed knows the beginning and only the beginning, since thinking follows into the event the junction (appropriated out of the beginning) of the twisting free of beyng. This knowing and yet non-knowing, which can provide no information because otherwise it would abandon the twisting free of beyng, must remain in the experience of the event. This experience maintains the relation to the dignity (inceptuality) of beyng, a dignity which has for thinking the basic character of questionability. That beyng is worthy of questioning does not mean it would stand *under* questioning and be dependent on it, but does mean that beyng stands in a not accidental relation to human beings and to the possibility of their history.

Does not even the thinking of the history of beyng ask the question of essence as a what-question? Yes and no. For the essentiality of the essence is determined from the truth of beyng, i.e., from the event. In accord with the twisting free and the dispensation, the what-question is also changed.

Out of and through this thinking of the history of beyng, the essence of the poetry "of" the future poet is thought. This thinking is a dialogue with that poetry and is in every way separated from it. Accordingly, on account of the experienced dispensation into the proper historical essence, a dispensation into the history of beyng as this history first opens itself thereby, that which is illuminated and thought in poetry is one and the same with what is illuminated and thought in thinking. Indeed only "thinking" says this. Whether poetry has poetized over into thinking, and has spoken poetically of thinking, is difficult to see. The Empedocles poetry [of Hölderlin] could lead to such a conjecture, if it itself, within this poetizing, did not need to be the transition to genuine poetry. Indeed it therefore poetically grazes up against the domain of thinking.

The thinking of the history of beyng not merely can, but, as a consequence of its own historical essence, *must* maintain itself in dialogue with poetry as regards the essence of poetry itself and must also be a preparation for poetry, a preparation that remains only mediate. Meditation on the thinking of the history of beyng, since this thinking inceptually thinks thinking itself, must also enter into dialogue with the poetizing that poetizes the domain of poetry and thus must think through the relation between poetizing and thinking.

The thinking of the history of beyng cannot be differentiated from "science," because this latter, as pertaining to metaphysics and as perishing along with metaphysics, is not able to indicate any difference inasmuch as it remains essentially beneath the domain in which thinking resides, namely, the relation to being. Science is research into beings, such that these are already determined in advance as objects. Future poetry stands outside of art, which is always metaphysical. Future thinking stands outside of philosophy, of which the same holds.

The thinking of the history of beyng thinks, conforming to the twisting free, out of the pull of the dispensation into the junction of the beginning; in conforming to the twisting free, this thinking is the pain of the departure of being into the downgoing of the beginning. As pain, it is steadfast in the counteraction to this pull, and only thus can it present itself. Thinking is not simply submissive to the dispensation in the manner of an immediate compliance, but it also does not mediate out of an already resolved absolute sublation of everything. This thinking remains in disconsolate pain and is thus the knowledgeable non-knowledge of the beginning; but not a *docta ignorantia,* because it does not think of beings. This thinking thinks out of the beginning; it thinks from behind into what is already appropriated as such. Consequently, it is never a derivation from the supreme cause and also is not a retrogressive constructivism.

The word of the history of beyng therefore constitutes the event: it eventuates, it has already eventuated, seen from the point of view of thinking, which exists only as something appropriated.

Even the thinking of the history of beyng has its measures, namely, the history of beyng: how historiality appropriates it, out of what inhabited place and how inceptually, how the appropriation disposes the steadfastness, out of what alienation thinking comes into experience, whether thinking is only a prelude to the sounding, or is a sounding, or a consonance, or indeed the resonating of both; ever and again different is then what is experienced and its saying and the law of that saying.

The thinking of the history of beyng experiences the event; in this experience, such thinking does not remain constant in a "present" which is likely to be sought out and preferred as a refuge in the face of historiology (past) and technology (planned future). This "present" is an evasion. Experience attains another inhabited place and stands outside of the endeavor to order it within a historical process in the manner of dialectics or historiology; for history is not "happenings" and succession but, instead, is historiality. The inhabited place of Dasein lies outside of all historiology and technology, but also outside of all myths and pre-historic time.

272. The thinking of the history of beyng

does not restrict knowledge to "ontology," nor does it expand knowledge to a supersensuously "ontic" perception. It allows "metaphysics" to enter into its past essence, and it thinks more originally than ontology, ontic science, and their combination and augmentation.

273. The event

is experienced in pliancy toward the dispensation into the twisting free out of which Da-sein essentially occurs, in which guise the totality of beyng is.

The thinking of the history of beyng is the venture of saying the unsayable without naming it. Even the "beginning" and the event are only forewords. The resonance is thus the clearing voice of the stillness.

274. Thinking

must now, as it were, spend the night outdoors, must know, more rigorously than ever before, its inhabited place, and must stay the course.

Today thinking must think in a startling way so as to jolt humans for the very first time into the passion of thinking and to compel them to learn, and exercise, the differentiation. The empty display with the emptiest semblance of rigorous thinking, namely, "logistics," leads only into thoughtlessness. Logistics is most of all an instrument of the instrumentalism of ordering, which is why the Americans show a special partiality toward it. No one appeals to "Leibniz," although he, as a modern thinker, necessarily had to envisage and desire "calculation."

Thinking seldom meets with correspondence, because instead of this, of which nothing is known, thinking is expected to produce results, and of course none can be found. People then allow themselves to be misled into calculating up possible "effects." People either demand that thinking and its concepts and terms be repeated and used (in fact the worst of the effects, all of which are bad), or people attempt to show appreciation for thinking, which is held to be abstract, by applying it in a practical way.

Instead, the task is simply to correspond to thinking, such that experience is more experienced and propositions are confronted with thoughtful speech. Instead of repeating propositions, the task is to come to self-clarity and to let oneself be determined by what is essential.

We must think about thinking (essence of truth). If *this* thinking is still to be called "logic," then what is "logic"?! Certainly not a theory of propositions and representations.

275. The discrepancy in the priority of presentation[6]

1. If the conjuncture of beyng is to be said, then that requires, specifically for the thinking of the history of beyng, a thinking of the first beginning and of its advancement to metaphysics and also a thinking of metaphysics in its full history as the history of beingness and of the truth of beings. This truth itself restricts the essence of history and projects historiology as one with technology. But all this is then not presented, and the conjuncture of beyng appears to be detached arbitrariness, perhaps mitigated through the *sounding*.
2. If, before all else, the history of being, right from the first beginning, is to be told immediately, then it would be difficult to see whence history is already experienced in general as the history of being and not as an object of the historiology of philosophy. This introductory presentation is no less arbitrary. And this presentation arises out of the thinking of the conjuncture of beyng.
3. Are *both of these* to be presented in the resonating? Sounding of the end of metaphysics—consonance in the beginning—resonating of the sounding and of the consonance.

276. The beginning—inexperience[7]

We are equally inexperienced, or indeed totally without experience, as regards both the first beginning and the other beginning, which in fact

6. Cf. the passing by; essentially toward *experience*.

7. The thinking of the history of beyng in its inception.

are not two different beginnings but, rather, one and the same beginning in each and every inceptuality. For we do not know the difference, and we do not surmise the departure. We are not a match for the downgoing and consider it merely an end and a collapse. We are inexperienced, "painless," as regards the inceptuality of the beginning.

We know only the *brutalitas* of the will to power; and we believe we know something of "pain" when we report about it that we are capable of presentifying "pain," whereby pain is still taken merely as a *bodily state.*

We must first learn experience. And above all the experience of the first and the other beginning; only in the relation essentially occurring between the two, for which we have no name, do we experience immediately the inceptuality and, in it, the appropriation of beyng. The steadfast standing in Da-sein originates from a standing out into the appropriating event. The abandonment by being, and the human being as understood anthropologically, correspond to each other. Taken for themselves, they constitute the insurmountable barrier which, as metaphysics, has been thrust up between beyng and the human being.

277. The inconsolable departure

The twisting free is not consolation in the sense of a dissolving of the pain but, instead, requires redemption in the pain of questioning that which is question-worthy.

278. The thinking of the history of beyng; the concept

The concept [*Begriff*] is not the grasp [*Griff*] of calculation; instead, it is the totality [*Inbegriff*] as inclusion [*Einbegriffensein*] in the steadfastness of the interrogation of what is question-worthy.

Concepts are not schemata of things represented, meant, and intended; instead, they are *instances of steadfastness* in the open domain of the clearing of beyng. More rigorous than all calculative concepts, because more exacting, exacted through the necessity of the plight of the question-worthiness of beyng.

But universal intelligibility and even bindingness? Is not everything here "subjective" and "dispositional"?

279. Inceptual thinking

This term could suggest that such thinking, out of its own spontaneity, posits the beginning and is itself that which sets the beginning on. But that is not the case.

Inceptual thinking, in speaking, points to beyng and lets being return to its essence (i.e., its truth) as the clearing.

To begin the beginning means to let the beginning return to itself. This letting is the obedience of the listening to the stillness of the neighborhoods of the beginning. Stillness as inceptual essence of the consonance; the "unity" not that of λόγος and ἕν, not that of the "system" and the "absolute."

280. The enduring of the difference

is the *care of the abyss,* such that the grounding of humanity might have as its own the open plight and inceptual necessity of the abyss. (On the "abyss," cf. *Die Sage,* typescript 29.)[8] Accordingly, from the thinking of the beginning must never be expected an *immediate* grounding and constructing, an immediate deliverance, or a palpable truth. To be sure, also never a mediate illumination of "existence" ["*Existenz*"], in the sense of the "Philosophy of existence."

This thinking of the history of beyng is historical in the sense of the event and provides no "worldview"; it does not appeal to "existence" and does not pursue "research" understood as a discovery of "categories." This thinking does not take the place of poetry, does not compete with poetry, and certainly does not derive truth from it.

As the thinking of the history of beyng, it is historically unique, is the enduring of unique relations, and is a dialogue with the unique poet whom this thinking encounters. The care of the abyss is a concern for what lacks holiness, wherein (in whose clearing) the holy and the unholy are first decided and are destined. The care of the abyss is preparation for the dispensation out of which destiny comes forth.

The enduring of the difference is thoughtful thinking. The enduring is the experience of the beginning. Experience is the pain of the departure. Thoughtful thinking is experience, and indeed appropriated experience, of the appropriating event.

8. {In GA74}

Enduring
Experience
Pain
Saying } *Thinking*

This thinking is essentially distinct from the thinking known in "logic" (i.e., metaphysics) as ἰδεῖν—νοεῖν—*intellectus, ratio,* general representation— "concept."

The enduring does not think "concepts," nor does it think "in" concepts; it is the relation to beyng itself and comes under the law of the event.

281. Thinking as enduring

is the *enduring of the difference* into its truth, i.e., into the departure as the essence of the inceptuality of the beginning. *The careful word of the slow saying of the heedful enduring.*

The enduring is itself appropriated and is therefore historial; thus it "*is*" not in a "result" of a "work" which then offers itself as "knowledge" and "insight." The enduring is in the appropriated saying itself, whereby at the same time, in accord with the twisting free, the word is transformed: the slow, constant saying of the history of the beginning constitutes the enduring.

(On account of the protracted dominance of metaphysics, thoughtful thinking has been led astray by "science," "research," "erudition"; the leading astray reaches up to the domain in which it is apparently overcome insofar as "philosophy" pursues the ambition of being a practical (not theoretical) "life-wisdom." But that is merely the false counterpart to philosophy as pure science; the coupling of both ways of leading astray in the "philosophy of existence.")

The enduring in the saying of the twisting free of the difference into the departure.

282. The enduring

To endure the difference means to let beyng essentially occur in its clearing through the support of speech such that every appeal to beings falls away and so does every explanation via beings (metaphysics and the continuation of its essence in technology and in historiology). The enduring into the departure has to endure this falling away only as an essential consequence and not at all as a goal, in case the enduring might be degraded to a plan through the positing of goals.

The enduring bears the word into the inceptuality, i.e., into the downgoing departure and into the falling away of the priority of beings, such that, in the enduring, beyng, as twisted free, comes within the event purely to its clearing. But never "through" the enduring as a kind of accomplishment; instead, out of the enduring as itself appropriated.

What testifies to the appropriation?

283. The gainsaying in the saying of the event

It might seem that the thinking of the history of beyng always speaks in negations. The turn of phrase is often: "It is not . . ." This negating has its essential necessity in the endurance, which submits to the departure. The "not" and "no" are never reactive, especially where the other beginning is spoken of versus the first. For, this "versus" merely speaks of the confrontation and clearing of the inceptuality of the beginning. Yet even where the saying puts into words the overcoming of metaphysics, the "not" and the "no" are never sheer negations, for metaphysics is the unavoidable episode between the first and the other beginning. In this episode the inceptuality of the beginning first comes to resound. This "not" versus metaphysics is also hardly a warding off, because the saying of the event already is inceptually in the other truth.

Often, however, this many-rayed "not" of gainsaying is merely preparatory in that it is addressed to the dominant view in the time-space of metaphysics.

284. The timber trail

The trails and paths of the enduring are always timber trails, i.e., ones which lead some distance into the woods, into the forest, and suddenly end in the forest gloom. Otherwise no one traverses them, and they are properly disparaged. Timber trails are "false," perverted paths, because on them there is no advancement, no getting anywhere. These trails are eerie. The enduring is always on a timber trail, and these trails are unknown to each other; they are disjointed, but only to the unique one is it determined to clear the timber so as to leave it undamaged in its emergence, and the many are determined to the concealedness that essentially occurs along such trails. Timber trails are then overgrown paths; they are forgotten, and yet on them was borne and transported the felled wood which, although its origin is forgotten and impossible to search out, somewhere allowed a fire to be kindled. The enduring of the difference (i.e., the thinking of the history of beyng) bears, on a timber trail, the burden of speaking.

285. Beginning and immediacy

Saying

If our consideration brings the thinking of the beginning, as a thinking "about" it, at once into relation with the ideas of mediation and presentification, then it has become unavoidable to ascertain something of the function of mediation out of the beginning as that which is unmediated and unmediatable. Thereby, however, we also ascertain the limit within which it is possible to speak "of" the beginning at all. The beginning is the immediate and is nothing else. And this seemingly inceptual constatation indeed turns the beginning into something mediated by mediation in general and as such (prescriptive mediation). This kind of thinking can never think inceptually; its own essence prevents this thinking from forgetting the beginning, i.e., from entrenching itself in what is objectively present.

Those declarations "about" metaphysics and its history, declarations relative to the history of beyng, seem to be didactic; insofar as they allude to an "overcoming of metaphysics," it might appear as if they were supposed to set this overcoming in the correct light merely by mentioning the previous thinking. One can always, to be sure, take everything merely in that way and, with some good will, even use it for the improvement of "historiological-critical research" in the history of philosophy. Perhaps one can also pass over all this as an arbitrary construct. However these opinions turn out, they all derive from the realm of erudition and remain within it.

But recollection with respect to the history of beyng is the presentiment of the inceptuality of the beginning. Such presentiment does not occur in the rigid certainty of calculation. It is a surmise, as the steadfastness of a courage whose temperament was disposed by the consignment to it; the fact that something futural happened long ago: *the clearing out of beyng toward the beyng of truth. The "out of beyng toward beyng" is one and the same, the appropriating event.* The clearing "of" beyng cannot be stated in the words of ordinary language, because the saying itself, as appropriation of the beginning, disposes the words.

286. Inceptual thinking in its origination out of metaphysics

The thinking of being maintains misgivings about beings with respect to their beingness.

The thinking of being itself—this thinking thinks into the truth of beyng.

Truth is already ambiguous here. On the one hand, truth means the domain of projection for the understanding of being. The domain or projection is itself the clearing. But the essential occurrence of the clearing is itself indeterminate and is also indeterminable in this line of questioning. Truth then means that which essentially occurs, in which guise the clearing eventuates, such that the appropriating event itself at length fails, just as if it did not essentially occur.

Thinking into the truth of beyng thinks the appropriating event.

The other thinking, thus arisen through the appropriated leap, has meanwhile become transitional thinking. It thinks beingness, οὐσία, into φύσις; thinks beyng into the appropriating event; and thinks φύσις and the appropriating event itself inceptually out of the inceptuality.

The inceptuality of the beginning discloses itself as the saying. In the first beginning, the saying emerges as λόγος (Heraclitus). But, in unity with ungrounded ἀλήθεια, λόγος is forthwith, or even already in the first beginning, delivered up to human "talk."

For inceptual thinking, the overcoming of metaphysics is properly, with respect to the history of beyng, only an interlude within the transition.

In inceptual thinking, beyng first manifests itself as the inceptuality which promises, denies, and forbids the essential occurrence of truth and of its grounding, ungrounding, and transformation into correctness.

Out of the inceptuality of the beginning, there eventuates the clearing in which the event itself, as appropriation of Da-sein to the inceptuality, is revealed while concealing itself and thereby first allows us to think the relation of mankind to being.

It is only in inceptual thinking that there arises the knowledge that and how thinking cannot at all originate in metaphysics, if "originate" here refers to essential origin. For, the latter is the appropriating event. Inceptual thinking exists only by being inceptual. It is not produced as a consequence of a deliberate transformation of the metaphysical mode of thinking into another "form of thought."

Inceptual thinking is inaccessible [*unberührbar*] through past thinking because it was set in motion [*gerüht*] in the stirring [*Rührung*] (disposition) of what has been.

Inceptual thinking thinks more inceptually, i.e., more thoughtfully, than the thinking of metaphysics. "More thoughtfully" means here: outside the distinction of "rational" and "irrational." But this "outside" is to be found not in the direction of the "mystical" but, rather, in the direction of the "concept" in the sense of the inceptual word. If now there can at all still be a dialogue on the same level of discussion, then it would have to transpire by *countering* the conclusion of the address Hegel delivered on October 22, 1818 (cf. Hegel, WW VI, p. xl):[9] "The courage of truth, the belief in the power of the spirit, is the first condition of philosophical study; man should honor himself and esteem himself worthy of what is highest. Of the greatness and power of the spirit he cannot think highly enough. The closed essence of the universe contains no force which could offer resistance to the courage of knowledge. The essence must open itself before this courage, spread out in front of it its riches and depths, and bring enjoyment."

287. If being bends toward itself the track of mankind

The inceptual thinking of beyng never aims at "effects" or even at practical usefulness; therefore it never enters into competition with regard to results in this domain.

Yet the inceptual thinking of beyng aims just as little at a mere contemplation of "essentialities"; therefore it also never belongs in the domain of "theoretical" considerations.

The inceptual thinking of beyng does not at all "aim" at "something"; instead, it itself exists only by favor of that which is to be thought, beyng. While this thinking *is,* what is unique already takes place, that which takes place in the proper sense and grounds history in the essence: the decision of the essence of truth.

---

9. Address at the opening of his lectures in Berlin. In G. W. F. Hegel's *Werke. Vollständige Ausgabe durch einen Verein von Freunden des Verewigten.* Bd. 6: *Encyclopädie des philosophischen Wissenschaften im Grundrisse. Erster Theil: Die Logik.* Berlin: 1840, p. xl.

288. The thinking of beyng

Whoever ventures this must learn to grasp what is most difficult, namely, that in such thinking there arises an experience which sets itself off *against* all other "experience":
Everything essential produces the essential occurrence of the concealment which, as beyng itself in its own silence, prohibits any utterance out loud.

To know, in this concealment, the riches of the beginning means *to think.* Residing in this thinking is the knowledge that one can never hear the saying of beyng if one is not already disposed through its voice and does not need it to be uttered aloud.

289. Thinking and words[10]

It seems as if poetry is assigned to words more originally than is any human comportment or attitude. If language is considered the "primal poetry" of mankind, then this relation between words and poetry is undeniable. Perhaps, however, these views are erroneous. Poetry, although it exists only in the "element" of language, constantly possesses in its words an "image," i.e., something to be intuited, through which and in which it poetizes its compositions. At the moment of poetic saying, the words detach from the poem, in that they allow the duality of both to disappear in the composition. The assignment to words in the thinking of beyng is essentially other and is more inceptual, i.e., altogether inceptual, in comparison with poetry.

In the thinking of beyng, words and language (these are not the same) by no means constitute a mere "element" and "aether" but, instead?—the abyss of the beginning.

Since the abyss of the inceptuality essentially occurs in words, what is decisive in the thinking of beyng—to be sure, not in metaphysics and philosophy—is the act of saying what is said and not what is said itself in the sense of some graspable content of "knowledge" and of truth. In poems of every kind, the composition incorporates the words; in thinking, on the other hand, that which is to be thought, i.e., the enduring of the difference, is ordained back into the words. The submissiveness in the words is, in thinking, of an inceptual essence; what is shown exclusively therein is that these words are image-less, i.e., are *mere* words, ones which uniquely refer to the twisting free of beyng.

---

10. Cf. The saying, typescript 18ff. {In GA74}

Words in the thinking of the history of beyng are not means of expression and presentation but are the essential answer, the replying words of the human being of the history of beyng. Nor are they words first of all and in general and then in particular replying words. On the contrary, the answer is the essence of the saying of the beginning, because the saying is appropriated to its essence, i.e., to bringing the relation of beyng to mankind into the enduring.

The distinctive character of the relation of "thinking" (as the enduring of the difference) to words is grounded according to its uniqueness in the fact that on the one hand the illuminated relation of being, as the event, to mankind becomes essential and that on the other hand this relation of beyng is appropriated in the manner of Da-seyn in "thinking" as the enduring. But words belong inceptually to beyng. And words alone hold fast out of the clearing of beyng and out of the history of the twisting free of beyng into the departure. In contrast, poetry never poetizes beyng, although what is poetized, the holy, *is* the inceptual along with beyng, even if separately.

The thoughtful word is the dictum of the experience of the departure. The dictum is the breaking of the silence of the appropriated clearing. Whence and how silence here? The soundless as the nonsensuous. The soundlessness of beyng.

The dictum [*Spruch*] is the word of the answer to the claim [*Anspruch*] of the beginning.

The claim in the appropriation of humans to their essence in terms of the history of beyng.

The foreword [*Vorwort*] in the answer [*Antwort*] of the word [*Wort*] of the thinking of the history of beyng.

290. Beyng—thinking

Thinking, i.e., seeking to dwell in the clearing of one's essence, encounters therein ever and again the greatest and, at the same time, the unrecognized obstacle, namely, that beyng is immediately taken as the "abstract" and "formal."

We are so unaccustomed to the ungraspable, which is not a being, and are even so averse to what is ungraspable by everyday capacities for grasping, that we only seldom find ourselves able to undertake the grasping of nonbeings decisively enough that something essential penetrates us here.

It is impossible to dispel immediately the ambiguity residing in the fact that being can constitute the mere emptiness of the "formal" and "abstract."

C. Toward a first elucidation of the basic words

"Truth" (With regard to: The saying of the first beginning)

The *"essence"* and the *"essential occurrence"*

History and *historiality*

a. *The "essence" and the "essential occurrence"*

291. Beyng and essence[11]

To think the essence of beings—that is the characteristic mark of philosophy and metaphysics.

To think the essence of beyng—that points beyond into the other beginning.

But if the essence is thought, whether the essence of beings or the essence of beyng, in each case the truth of beyng is already decided in the "essence" (for the history of beyng, the essence is the *essential occurrence*—the *turning*).

And in inceptual thinking, which thinks the essence of beyng, beyng and essence are also found in a unique way.

There "essence" is not simply beingness as the κοινόν of beings, but is "truth." And truth for its part pertains intrinsically to beyng itself.

But where the essence remains merely the general, there the priority of beings is conserved, and so are the "over and against" in relation to the perceiving subject and the ἐπέκεινα.

But nowhere is disclosed the "essence," i.e., the being of the essence.

Essentia, quidditas, and γένος always merely point to the mode of grasping beings as such on the part of the human being.

Nowhere does beyng itself come into words.

The thinking of the essence of beyng does not think beyng and then in addition think "the essence"; on the contrary, it thinks beyng as the essential occurrence, as the truth of beyng, which pertains intrinsically to beyng as event and beginning.

11. On the beginning

"Essence," in terms of the history of beyng, is constantly thought with respect to the event, i.e., thought as the *essential occurrence*—the "is-ing" of beyng, which alone "is."

"The essence" is grounded in each case already in the truth of being and "is" this truth.

b. History
(its essence out of the history "of" beyng (event))
Historiality ← | → *Happenings*
Cf. *The West and modernity*
History as the *essential occurrence of truth*

292. Terminology

Distinguish : historial and historical

historial : is what has its essence out of historiality, i.e., out of the appropriating eventuation.
Historial is:
1. Beyng itself
2. the uniqueness (appropriated in the event) of the human being as historial, (i.e., as understood with respect to the history of beyng).

historical : what pertains to the history of beings, insofar as beings enter into the historiality of mankind.

If beyng comes into truth, and truth into beyng, there is *history;* that means:
the historiality of the ordinances of the event.
The ordinances are the moments of the truth of beyng.

293. History is historiality

History [*die Geschichte*] is historiality [*das Geschicht*] in the same way that the mountain range [*das Gebirg*] lets the mountains [*die Berge*] essentially occur in their dispensation and is not, rather, put together out of individual mountains.

Historiality is the dispensation of beyng.
The dispensation begins in the beginning.

History is the decision on the essence of truth, because this essence is the event of the beginning, inasmuch as the beginning always consigns itself to the clearing.
The inceptual dispensation and the turning.

Truth—for the history of beyng—as event is the *consignment of the clearing.*

In the appropriation reside the difference and the plight of the decision.

Historiality is the appropriation to beyng of the ordinances wherein the essence of beings is decided in each case.

History is inceptually the historiality of beyng.

That is the dispensation of beyng in the event (the articulation of the clearing, while structuring beyng) toward the junction of the beginning, integrating itself within the beginning. (cf. II. The resonating)

History as historiality is the conjuncture "of" the beginning.

The beginning and historiality; the essence "of" history (its essence as historiality) can only be thought inceptually. (The *mountain range*—the abiding "of the mountains"—is not a mere gathering together of a number of individual mountains.)

294. The essence of historiality

According to the essence of historiality, an essence which proceeds from the junction, and which structures the junction itself, we must distinguish various concepts of history.

The history of beyng	—	the self-integrating structuration of the event
Metaphysics as history	—	is the progression out of the first, still-ungrounded beginning into the essence of beingness. This progression has its essence not in motion, but in the type of self-integration, in the cessation of the self-integration into the inceptual junction, and yet it is the necessary enduring of the disjunction.

The history of metaphysical humanity, a humanity ordained to Western history.

The history of the gods in the time-space of being; "the God" of metaphysics and of Christianity.

The consummation of metaphysics can be experienced only from the essence of the history of beyng and cannot be historiologically calculated from "facts" at the temporal point of a decline.

Historiality	and	"history"
Historiality		"happenings"
Steadfastness		historiological constructions
Destiny		and the making of history
"Fate"		forward and backward

295. History

(technology)

Fate and what is allotted, as well as what follows from the allotment in such and such a way, and also what avoids it in one way or another, misfortune in destiny, and everything determinative in history—all this never comes to "consciousness" immediately and as such, or, in modern terms, never comes to calculative representation as that in which, first and foremost, the calculation is carried out in advance. What is insidious in calculation and in technology is in general the setting up of a foreground for all ordering of objects. By means of this foreground, the domain of "reasons," i.e., causes, is provided, and out of them all calculative discovery, i.e., all inventing, is drawn, posing as "creativity."

A technological age, and especially an age of unconditional technology, is under way toward unhistoricality; that is an essence, namely, the distorted essence of historicality and thus takes the highest interest in "historical happenings." The unhistorical age is never history-less. History-less is nature, but in the case of nature the "-less" is not a lack but the proper origin.

296. History

The great error is either to understand the essence of history on the basis of historiology ("historiologically"), i.e., in terms of consciousness, or, if one likes to appeal to "ontology," to take history as "happenings" and the latter as "incidents" and "lived experiences."

History is historiality (the mountain range of the mountains). The historiality of the strata, i.e., of the destinies of what is proper, and of the latter we do not know the essence, for the lack of asking about it. The proper [*das Schickliche*] and the destined [*die Schickung*]. Destiny and consignment. Consignment and the appropriating event.

*

"Historiological principles"—always reactive and
historical beginnings—neither this—actively nor passively.

*

Keep clearly distinct:

The history of being
and
the history of the truth of beings.

*

The history of the truth of beings
and
the history "of" metaphysics.

*

Metaphysics as history of being
(more precisely as *an* event).
"History"—not from happenings and motion.

*

History of metaphysics
and
history of the *concepts* of being.

*

Inceptuality—history of being—metaphysics—
overcoming of metaphysics—twisting free of beyng

The history of metaphysics.
Metaphysics as the basic character of "Western" history.
The historical essence of metaphysics.
History—as the essential occurrence of the truth of beyng. Essential occurrence basically the twisting free of beyng—twisting free as inceptuality. The twisting free of beyng as the grounding of metaphysics and of its overcoming.

For the twisting free of beyng, being must first release itself into beingness, and beingness must bring beings as such into actuality and objectivity. The overcoming of metaphysics arises out of the twisting free of beyng.

297. Overcoming, transition, beginning

The overcoming looks like a repulsing and a sweeping denial. But, in terms of the history of beyng, it arises out of the beginning and is in essence transition.

The transition is a greeting across [*Herübergrüßen*] into the past and thus is the opening up of the incipience which was not previously allowed to attain the past. "Overcoming" and "transition" must therefore be kept distinct from every sort of "sublation" (*conservatio, elevatio*), which has legitimacy only in metaphysics and especially in the metaphysics "of" the absolute.

The question of how, in the transition from the first to the other beginning, tradition is maintained, along with the constancy of the advancement of history, is thereby already answered. The "constancy of the advancement" is a determination which historiological-technological thinking calculates into disappearance. What is inceptual is unfamiliar with "constancy" in such a sense. But how then do the leaps "cohere"? They do not cohere among themselves; on the contrary, they are each beyng itself in its respective mode of essentially occurring.

An overcoming is also not a mere overturning. The latter is always restricted to the conservation and altered recurrence of that which is to be overturned.

"Overturnings"—in the manner of the Platonic overturning of the first beginning, in the manner of Kant's "Copernican" revolution, in the manner of the overturning of relative metaphysics into absolute metaphysics, in the manner of Nietzsche's counter-Platonic "inversion"—never lead into the inceptual.

But overturnings live on the semblance of something immediately thrust forth as "new"; they merely revolve the same and keep it outside the sphere of an essential change. "Revolutions" are the modes in which the already decided advancements hide so that, through the proclamation of the new, the tired agreement of historiology might be newly secured. Revolutions are the cunning ability of the hitherto to make more definitive and unconditional its character as something hitherto. Thus it is at any time difficult to avoid the craving for overturnings, because this craving pleads, in the semblance of sheer novelty, that the inceptual has already been attained. Such craving falls everywhere into the emptiness of mere advancement.

298. The history of being

"Era"? "Situation" and "position" of humanity with respect to "being." To find here alone the correct words.
The "era" of machination—
Being everywhere already "actuality."
The relation of mankind to being as "closeness to actuality"; this closeness is interpreted as "closeness to life" as long as "lived experience" and "life" have the priority (as regards quaffing{?} and breeding).

Meanwhile, in the calculative course of machinational history, the "closeness to industry" has arisen out of the closeness to life. The "industrial" human being.

At first not only must the history of being remain concealed, but in addition the history of "philosophy" and the latter itself must sink into historiological oblivion, until the moment can arise for the recollection of the past and the inceptual.

299. Space and time

are not containers or forms but, instead, *in terms of the event,* are the *appropriated*—the "there."

Space and time: not empty or full; on the contrary, revealing or concealing as the event of the beginning; *history*—"moment."

300. History and historiology[12]

that the former is grasped in terms of the latter constitutes an essential consequence of the modern interpretation of beings in terms of consciousness; consciousness is knowledge in the sense of ungrasped certainty. This certainty obtrudes in the form of calculability and the planned ordering and establishing of all beings.

The consciousness of history—the historiological conception of history considers history a happening which must be brought to certainty, i.e., to a planned ordering.

301. Going under

inter—all the way between (underpass)
sub-
occasus, interitus. (decadence (Nietzsche, Spengler) ≠ the going under of an ocean liner)
Downfall (sinking down)—sinking
Ruin, death, disappearance—*naufragium*
Running aground —(Hegel)
to the ground —(i.e., to the absolute)
"Going under"—inceptually—*going to the abyss*

12. Cf. summer semester 42, Recapitulation 27–31. {*Hölderlins Hymne "Der Ister,"* GA53}

Going under and *concealment* = *twisting free*

"against the going under" =
against the evening (the founder).

"The West" the land of the going under, i.e.,
the going under of the inceptuality of the beginning.

Under—going down the rise, where the genuine *issue* is—
first also the rising.
First meeting—beginning
Going under (*inter—sub*)
Downfall—sinking under—sinking down
Running aground—disappearance—dissolution.
Thought inceptually, however:
to go under the preserving protection of concealment;
to occur more inceptually as emergence out of recollection into concealment as sheltering.
Sheltering—preservation of the dignity—*worthiness* (of what?)

Concealment
abscondere—veiling—withdrawing—removal
Guarding—*sheltering*
Keeping secret— to bring into secrecy—
to appropriate the secrecy
to withhold.

XI. The thinking of the history of beyng (Thinking and poetizing)

A. The experience of that which is worthy of questioning

(Cf. Founding and enduring
The enduring of the difference)

The leap
The confrontation
The clarification of action
The knowledge of thinking

302. Guiding notions

The thinking of thinkers is a thanking.
Thoughtful thanking is the liberation of freedom to its essence (the turning).
Liberation is the self-appropriated emancipation of truth.
Freedom is the inceptuality of the clearing of being to its truth.

303. The thinking of the history of beyng is the inceptual experience of the twisting free of beyng

This experience is the pain of the question-worthiness of beyng. This pain is the knowledge of the intimate belongingness to the question-worthiness of beyng—beyng which, in its twisting free toward the beginning, requires isolation from the beginning. In the extreme remoteness from the truth (as abyss) of beyng, only the thinking of the history of beyng is capable of saying the beginning in a way that grounds. Intimacy in the isolation is pain. With respect to the history of beyng, pain is the openness, connected to Da-sein, of the appropriated clearing of foreignness in beyng. This pain alone is the attainment of the enduring of the history of beyng. This history eventuates to us as the twisting free of beyng.

As understood in terms of the history of beyng, pain is fundamentally different from the "pain" of "metaphysical" consciousness, which is the pain of the disruption of *certainty* and of its negativity, a negativity that is already sublated in the absolute and thus, seen absolutely, is merely apparent and semblant.

As understood in terms of the history of beyng, pain cannot be sublated; it is the pain of question-worthiness and thus is the remoteness to the nearness of the unique dignity of beyng.

As understood in terms of the history of beyng, pain is the disposedness of steadfast thinking.[1] This disposedness determines all dispositions of thoughtfully grounded Da-sein, wherein humans must risk themselves in the historical future, if they are to know "beings."

304. The first step of inceptual thinking

is to ground the "there"—as opening (in interrogation) the conjuncture of the truth of beyng—on the experience of the twisting free of beyng, an experience which itself, as the appropriating event, is the inceptuality of the beginning.

Only out of historical steadfastness in Da-sein can the decision about godlessness unfold and an encounter with the gods be awaited.

"Time" in *Being and Time* is not the last but, instead, the first step of the passageway into the transition to the truth of beyng, the transition necessary for the history of beyng.

Care—is not affliction and sorrow. The care of beyng—is the pain of the departure of the twisting free.

305. The knowledge of thinking[2]

is proficiency in beyng and in its twisting free toward the beginning; this twisting free brings into the clear the inceptuality in the mode of the event, and the foreignness of Da-sein is appropriated out of this clearing.

This knowledge is not a mere explanatory acquaintance with beings, as is science. Science [*Wissenschaft*] never attains knowledge

1. (Here pain is understood as a characteristic of steadfastness, i.e., of the enduring itself. The event-marked essence of pain is first manifest when it is thought as a sign of the difference.) {Marginal remark in typescript}

2. Cf. on "philosophy"; key statements about "science"; technology; thinking and poetizing; art.

[*Wissen*] but, quite to the contrary, requires a knowledge of which science itself, since it remains posed on "consciousness," can never have any notion. Science is acquainted with this knowledge only in the form of "presuppositions" which it is compelled to take into use but never into "meditation." The latter, obviously, "produces nothing" that could be of "value" for "scientific research."

306. How the thoughtful thinking of beyng is a thanking

(The twisting free of beyng)

Inceptual thinking appreciates the dignity of beyng by questioning beyng with respect to its truth and thus experiencing truth itself as essentially question-worthy. How is beyng of such a truth that, on the basis of this truth, beyng demands and needs to be questioned in order to be appreciated? Why must there be such an appreciation? Is it not presumptuousness, rather than appreciation, to question being in its truth and to interrogate the beyng of truth? But does appreciation always have to be obsequiousness? If beyng essentially occurs in the twisting free of beyng into the beginning, if the truth of beyng is the inceptuality as the downgoing departure, if thinking comes into its truth (essential keeping) as thinking on a ground and *only* as this, such that it thinks the abyss, then must not thinking, through the venture of the departure, correspond to the ground of the inceptuality of the beginning? Then is not this venture of foreignness in beyng (not merely in beings) the unique appreciation of beyng in its twisting free? On the path of the thinking of beyng, this steadfastness in the *question-worthiness* of beyng can never be forgotten; to be sure, at times it may seem, precisely here, that deference toward what is questioned is sheer subjugation or even a flight into something that can offer redemption. But how can the beginning seek to redeem where it is the dignity of the abyssal itself, since the beginning in its inceptuality leads abyssally into the downgoing?

As an experience of the downgoing inceptuality of the event, the venture of thinking the twisting free of beyng is itself appropriated and its determination is consigned. Acceptance of this consignment to the thoughtful grounding of Da-sein (grounding of the inhabited place of the un-homelike hearth of beyng) is carried out in thinking by questioning beyng about itself; this questioning is an opening advance into the downgoing of the beginning, and as it questions further it becomes more inceptual and more venturesome. This venture is the appreciation of the beginning in its inceptuality. This appreciation, however, is the experience of the departure and is the pain of steadfast fidelity toward the downgoing of the beginning. This pain of questioning that which is worthy of question is the basic determination of the free thanking of freedom in beyng.

This questioning within inceptual thinking is always an attending to the experiences of the beginning. The attentiveness of this attending pervades the questioning, because such questioning questions as consigned to the event. Attending and questioning seem to be opposed in attitude and yet are oppositionally unitary, since they endure the one pain which is the intimacy of attending and, at the same time, is the disruption of the confrontational questioning.

Likewise, to the freedom in the foreignness of beyng there belongs the necessity from the plight of the twisting free of beyng into the beginning out of the (event).

The thinking of the history of beyng is a *thanking* out of the purposively thought question-worthiness of beyng, and such purposive thinking is experienced in the thoughtful interrogation of the truth of beyng.

This thanking is unique and cannot be determined through other comportments.

This thanking is the appreciation of what is question-worthy in questioning; questioning as abyssal allows beyng to return into the inceptuality of the downgoing.

The experience of the twisting free of beyng is the pain of isolation; the knowing "yes" to the appropriated departure.

This thanking has in essence the character of that "thank you" which is used [in German] as a polite refusal. But this refusal is not negative here; on the contrary, it is withdrawal into the remoteness of the attainment of the truth of beyng.

This thanking is the freedom of steadfastness in foreignness to the dignities of beyng.

307. The thinking of the history of beyng is the non-transitory departure of beyng

The thinking of the history of beyng experiences the twisting free of beyng into the beginning and in that way first takes beyng into protection. Such thinking relates to beyng in its constant departure and, through this protection, allows the first beginning to occur essentially.

This departure of thinking, in which thinking does not cease but, rather, attains the venture of a more inceptual questioning, corresponds to the essential, downgoing departure of the beginning.

Here is the origin of the *experience* of the event. This experience is the pain of the departure of beyng, which, although twisted free into the beginning, still only remains thus inceptually.

The inhabited place of the thinking of the history of beyng is the un-homelike hearth of beyng.

308. The thinking of beyng

is, as thinking of the truth of beyng, the interrogation of the twisting free of beyng out of the experience of the event, in which guise the beginning begins its more inceptual character (downgoing into the departure).

The thinking of the history of beyng is thereby the grounding of Da-*sein.* Da-sein—the "becoming at home" in the un-homelike as such. To venture the un-homelike as this and to be steadfast in such a venture. The thinker is at home in the un-homelike and is not at home in the homelike.

The *pain* of the un-homelike!
The experience (as downgoing) of the beginning.

309. The all-arousing, constant experience of the thinking of the history of beyng[3]

is the experience of ἀλήθεια as the essential occurrence of the clearing of beyng, a clearing that twists free of beyng into the beginning and thus preserves the inceptuality of the beginning.

This basic experience is the pain of an un-homelike becoming at home in the open realm of the openness of beyng.

This experience has its impetus in asking the question of beyng. To question—to think in a grounding way (the truth of beyng); grounding the un-homelike as such.

And this question itself, alien and inaccessible to all poetizing, arouses the experience which is displacement into the historical relation to the poet Hölderlin.

Now Hölderlin may perhaps at times readily make known what is most proper to him and simultaneously become a repulsion [*Abstoß*] for the impetus [*Anstoß*] toward thinking. But never is this poet "merely" to be used for thinking; instead, to give back to his own.

---

3. (ἀλήθεια— οὐσία—as presence; φύσις)

310. Thoughtful grounding as exposition of the ground Grounding and experience To remain in the most proper law of thinking

This law [*Ge-setz*] is displacement [*Versetzung*] into the necessity of the thoughtful leap toward the truth of beyng.

Truth is the inceptual essence of that freedom which remains open uniquely to essential thinking and which is the inhabited place to which such thinking is consigned.

This freedom of the question-worthiness of beyng in its twisting free is the shock.

311. The thoughtful assertion

Now a unique moment, determined by two events which "cohere" between themselves:

1. public opinion devours everything;
2. what is self-opening (beyng as beginning) must still remain what is most concealed.

To these is added a third: we today are not equal to either the first or the second.

The essential and unique freedom of thinking must remain concealed for some time and will indicate merely something proximally binding to which one can adhere.

312. The thinking of the history of beyng with regard to the beginning (Toward a clarification)

Being and Time seems to have "intended" "merely" an existentiell anthropology and a "description" of the human *position.* But which is the unique question? The one regarding the truth of being; under way toward being, because set in motion by being. Only in that way can a "position" be projected and withstood, for indeed the "position" occupies precisely a time-space (which one and where?) and, in occupying it, first determines it.

Now, as a result of the comments on Hölderlin, it indeed appears as if an unquestioning certainty was assumed in a poetically given being [*Sein*] and the question of the position as well as question-worthiness in general were abandoned. Now comes the opposite appearance. In truth, the same questioning has first arrived at the ground and time-space of its question-worthiness.

Da-sein (in *Being and Time* still exclusively *presented* in terms of the human being, although projected out of being) and beyng (brought near by "the holy") are now for the first time experienced, and experientially interrogated, out of the question-worthiness of the truth of beyng and out of the twisting free of beyng. The leap into the freedom of thinking is now first prepared. But the poet is not a "means."

313. Thoughtful saying and its claim

This saying claims the human being for *thinking* and, in doing so, places on the human being the claim of questioning and specifically of that questioning which uniquely experiences the question-worthiness of beyng. This claim is the promise of a demand for the attainment of the truth of beyng. This claim is not presumptuousness on the part of the thinker; on the contrary, it is an ordinance of the dignity of that which is to be thought.

Thoughtful saying therefore, in contrast to "scientific" assertion, is never a presentation or diffusion and communication of cognitions; it is not an imparting of something or an explanation [*Aufklären*] whereby one merely lets a "clarity" ["*Klarheit*"] come over oneself without being stirred from the state of one's usual opinions.

Thoughtful saying is the claim to attentiveness in the transmitting of the dignity of beyng. This dignity is worthily appreciated only in questioning.

Thoughtful saying demands the self-transformation of hearing and replying and of the relation to words.

Thoughtful saying is the dismissal of what is ordinarily homelike, which, through the conventionality of what is merely accepted, exchanged in various way, and constantly new, is accustomed to take itself as "familiar."

"Everydayness," grasped in terms of beings and calculated in relation to them, has its own legitimacy and, considered in itself, can at any time offer resistance to the claim of thinking and can thereby establish (its) legitimacy. Of course, it is not yet decided thereby, or even decidable, whether this legitimacy of everydayness can also in every respect be determinative of everything that concerns beings, "for example," being. The claim of thinking does not degrade everydayness to "mere" everydayness even when this claim brings itself to experience as unconditionally freer. Because historical humans are steadfast in the difference between beings and being, even when they do not experience the difference as such and in its essence, mankind must therefore remain prepared for the fact that the legitimacy of beings and the claim of being open up their strife and that this strife and its law become essential for the history of humanity. Consequently, it is never a matter of indifference to history whether the claim of thinking is heard or ignored.

Whoever ignores this claim, or is closed off to it, then of course continually misunderstands every word said by beyng. But it pertains to the necessary thoughtlessness of the inability to hear that it nevertheless attempts to attack thinking and to refute it: a "comical" procedure.

*

Claim
Enduring
Opportunity
Incentive
Warning
Intimation
Empowerment
Disposition
"Effect"

314. The word (the saying)—disposing

The word is the origin of language.
Language is the faculty of "vocables" (saying out).
What is the word? The soundless voice of beyng.
What is called voice [*Stimme*] here? Not "sound" but, instead, disposing [*Stimmen*], i.e., to let experience. How so?
Disposing toward the experience of the beginning (the beginning itself cannot be experienced).
Disposing through determining [*Be-stimmen*].
Determining through thinking of the voice of the word of the beginning.
Thinking—through the imageless saying of the beginning.
Saying through the *experience* of the (event).

The word claims the essence of the human being in such a way that it requires this being for Da-sein. But what of the thoughtful claim (claiming the human being for the essence)? Through inventive thinking of the experience of beyng → (event). Claim—truth.

Disposing—instead of talking "about" dispositions. But what of the thoughtful disposition? Why and to what extent must we indeed deal with disposition? Because we are restricted to metaphysics.
The beginning and its inceptuality.
The thinking of the beginning and the experience of the beginning.
Thoughtful experience.
Experience and the truth of beyng.
Experience and thanking.
Thanking and thinking.
The experience of the beginning.
The twisting free of beyng.
The grounding of Da-sein.
The inhabited place of historical humans in the other beginning.
The inhabited place "of" Da-sein (the inhabited place that is Da-sein) and the "position" of the human being.

315. The leap

1. as transition from ordinary thinking to thoughtful thinking.
   These two are so essentially different that from the one essence to the other no continuous progression is possible. Because the difference remains infinite, only a leap can bring us to thoughtful thinking.
   What is a leap? (cf. *Contributions to Philosophy* {GA65})
2. the leap in the first beginning
3. the leap in the start of metaphysics
4. the leap in metaphysics up to Kant
5. the leap in Kantian metaphysics
6. the leap in absolute metaphysics
7. the leap in the final consummation of metaphysics (eternal recurrence of the same).

Apart from the thinking of the first beginning, the leap is here always one into the thinking of beings *as such* and as a whole. In a certain sense, here and everywhere a leap into something wherein the human being is according to essential possibilities.

The leap into the truth of being (Da-sein) is, however, once again infinitely different from every metaphysical leap.

And that applies afortiori if it is a leap into the twisting free of beyng.

From that leap, the essence of leaps in general is to be thought.

The leap into freedom.

Freedom is the abyss of truth.

316. The clarification of what is to be done

What is demanded by the essential occurrence, i.e., already by the inceptual twisting free of beyng? What is demanded by the downgoing beginning as the inceptual beginning, if this beginning appropriates a thinking? And what is this thinking supposed to do?
Teach, or inventively think?
If teach, then to give historiological instruction to present at hand human beings through historiologically conceptual information about what was thinkable and what was thought in previous times?

If inventively think, then first of all by interrogating the question-*worthiness* of beyng. Such questioning displaces for the first time into the still-ungrasped truth of beyng.

If inventive thinking has become necessary, then there arises the other either-or:
inventive thinking in recollection of the first beginning, or
inventive thinking in downgoing recollection as thinking ahead.

Recollection of the first beginning inventively thinks the emergent beginning as this unique one; it thinks the beginning of the "West" and, concomitantly, thinks in a historical way the advancement of the first beginning into metaphysics, thinks the consummation of the latter, and ponders its demise.

The downgoing recollection inventively thinks the inceptuality of the beginning, inventively thinks the concealment and its intimacy. The thinking of this recollection is an abandoning of the differentiation, indeed is even the twisting free of beyng into the pure beginning. The course of this thinking proceeds in the transition out of metaphysics into the knowledge of the history of beyng, for which even beyng comes to recollection in the intimacy of the event.

If the downgoing recollection has become necessary, then there arises the inceptual either-or:
thinking in advance (downgoing recollection) *as preparation for the poetry appropriate to the history of beyng at the moment of the transition (Hölderlin)*, or
thinking in advance as thoughtful imageless saying of the event in the sense of the thoughtful grounding of Da-sein out of the disposition of the attunement of Da-sein, an attunement which disposes Da-sein toward *thanking* and so first lets Da-sein essentially occur pliantly and ordains Da-sein to its essence.

What is to be done—can that ever, out of inceptual necessity, be broken down into an either and an or? Must not rather both the one as well as the other first be accomplished? Which member of the human race would be capable of that? Who could accomplish even only a little of it, and even that much only if appropriated in a concealed history of the greeting?

Therefore we attain only the margins of a clarified endeavor. Therefore we can propose much in patience for a moment of the event. And what we thus propose is exhausted in directives which look like self-made rules and yet remain merely remote consequences of a submission to a most silent voice. Consequently, these intimations are good; they admonish us to adhere to that which is unique. The directive applies to downgoing thinking: avoid the expedient of saying no, even if a yes already speaks behind it and out of it. The yes is merely restrained and concealed. Say the inceptual knowledge; into everything should flow an unconcern over understanding and misunderstanding. Be only in the beginning, belonging to it.

The appropriated decision stands outside of an either–or in downgoing thinking in advance.

The latter thinking brings to words the saying of the beginning in its inceptuality. The saying itself belongs to the inceptuality.

Thus is Da-sein steadfast in pure recollection.

The dictum of the words of the saying of the beginning is first and only an attempt at inceptual thinking.

And indeed this thinking, because it is essentially historical, remains in the full carrying out of the thinking of the history of beyng, and through the latter it remains in meditation.

The inceptual recollection receives what remains in that act of remaining which is the inceptuality of the beginning, namely, the appropriating event.

317. "Critique"

To think of thinkers in a critical way means to grasp what is essential to their thought and specifically out of the kind of essence which their thinking itself first opens up.

Every thinker stands under the claim of an essence of truth, and we must first enter into this essence and must have entered into it in order then to correspond to it with equal essentiality.

The mere "criticizing" from any arbitrary standpoint, the counting up of errors with a *baculum* on the "basis" of a philosophy that is "free of standpoint," is not so much wrong as it is simply childish.

B. The beginning and heedfulness

318. The experience of the beginning

To experience the beginning in its inceptuality; from the inceptuality, the disposing into the clearing of the "there."
The essential occurrence of historiality.
The grounding of Da-sein:
to come before the (event) experientially, to remain in the beginning, and out of this experience, and for it, to say all. All of what? What pertains to the truth of beyng as the twisting free of beyng.

Do not ask	about a first certainty and about "order" as the securing of certainty—*mathesis universalis.*
Do not ask	about a basis for "deduction" and "derivation."
Do not ask	about the beingness of beings or about the objectivity of objects.
Do not consider	"the human being" a terminus; instead, take this being as the "between" in the (event): Da-sein.

Question what is uniquely question-worthy: beyng in its twisting free.

The experience *of the history of beyng* and the *essence of experience.* Cf. *Hegels Begriff der "Erfahrung"* {GA5}—an attempt and yet not maintained.

319. Experience

The double prejudice, the *most proximate* but not the only one:
1. Experience is empirical (sensuous—contingent—hypothetical).
2. Experience is "intuition" (sensuous or intellectual).
But—*experience* is originally pain—the basic disposition is a faring.

320. Markings and heedfulness

The markings [*Anmerkungen*] are the heedful [*aufmerkend*] words of the thinking of the history of beyng (and therein of the thinking of the history of "metaphysics").

Heedfulness is inceptual thinking in the other beginning, a thinking which necessarily penetrates through the markings.

Heedfulness [*Aufmerksamkeit*] is the future German term for the future mode of essential, i.e., inceptual thinking, a mode grounded by the Germans. It is the other, more inceptual term for "philosophy."

*

Heedfulness—as inceptual thinking, which arises out of experience of the history of beyng, experience to which the past as metaphysics has been revealed—is outside of all "reflexion" and every "systematics" and "science." The plight and necessity of heedfulness constitute the steadfastness of Da-sein; i.e., they constitute the experience of Da-sein itself out of the greeting of the beginning.

321. On heedfulness

Heeding the beginning.
Heedful—steadfast in heeding.
Heedfulness—steadfastness in heeding.
Heeding—inceptual remembrance, essential thinking.
Heeding—to let heed through the markings.
Heeding the intimations.
The intimations and the beginning (event).
Heedfulness is the heedful name for essential thinking, the changed "title" for "philosophy."

322. On heedfulness

Do we hear a sounding of the voice of beyng or only the echo of the language of our corresponding? But how is there corresponding? Is it always already only the answer to the counterword of the echo? But what if the echo were the response of Da-sein and of its steadfastness, the steadfastness which originally experiences the inceptual? That would testify to the echo as an original sounding.

323. Heedfulness

Heedfulness [from *Aufmerken,* "noticing," "marking down"]: mark—"sign." The mark—that by which something "emerges" for us, by which we "notice" something, i.e., experience it, i.e., are struck by it, feel its presence; νοός, become aware of [*innewerden*]—(intimacy) (these relations more essential than all merely rational "signs"). To notice—*notare, animadvertere, memoria tenere, observare, attendere.* Attend to, attentiveness, attention. Keeping in mind. *Marking—consideratio.*

324. Heedfulness

provides the word of the saying of the beginning. That it "provides" the word means it allows the word. Whence arrives this word belonging to heedfulness? From the fact that it marks and thereby allows beyng as beginning to emerge.

What does the word of heedfulness say? The inceptual as the history of the appropriation of Da-sein; this history is itself the appropriating event.

Heedfulness does not know the system and also not that which pertains to the system as its antagonist, an antagonist that pretends to be free of it; literary, "poetic," "aphoristic" expression.

The rigor that must correspond to the saying springs from its own law and from the originality of the beginning.

*

To be under way, so as to be able to be struck in the first place.
But why?
What must first "strike" us; "how"?
The plight!
For this is the time of the plight of the lack of a sense of plight.

325. Forgottenness of being

To be forgotten—No longer to be greeted;
forgottenness of being: 1. forgotten of being (the levels).
2. forgotten by being itself.
3. because not greeted by the beginning.
4. Without the event.

326. The forgottenness of being

as the disavowal of the age, and of its determinative history through beyng, is witnessed above all in the fact that the age, out of the will to willing which is indeed closed off to it, everywhere and utterly sets history up as mere happenings and also, through the truth of technology, incorporates "nature" into these happenings or, more precisely, has allowed "nature" to enter therein.

The setting up of history as planned happenings does not desire any meditation. The setting up prevents the age and its humanity from wanting to hear anything from themselves and about themselves. The setting up sequesters *itself* against every questioning. Thus it denies itself every possibility of heedfulness. The age itself, in its very essence, undertakes the extreme setting up of the forgottenness of being that affects it. On account of this sequestration, which indeed presents the semblance of closeness to reality, every naming of being appears to be null and empty.

But the setting up of the forgottenness of being reaches its highest inflexibility and inaccessibility precisely when it presents itself in the form of a revolution and a new order. For then there arises the semblance of change, whereas in truth the existing state of affairs is merely hardened into an extreme persistence and is thereby utilized. Such semblance also supports the opinion that all meditation has now become completely superfluous since everything, and everyone, is on the march toward something new. That is correct; the new is on the march, and the new sees to it that the inceptual appears as the old. And this semblance is quite in accord with the unfolding of the forgottenness of being in the history of being. The inceptual as the old—that is the most facile form of the self-absolving from every effort to experience the inceptual and to question the new.

327. The forgottenness of being; heedfulness

The forgottenness of being, with respect to beings: the fact that being is not thought, or else is considered (represented) merely as beingness.

The forgottenness of being, with respect to being: the fact that being releases beings into an entrenchment of beingness in the guise of the will to willing.

The forgottenness of being, with respect to the difference between being and beings: the fact that only what is actual is effective, objectivity persists, everything proceeds toward the security of its content in what is effective, and every consideration of beings, as well as all thinking of being, is altogether nullified through the utter *thoughtlessness.*

The forgottenness of being out of the withdrawal of being: the fact that all forgottenness of being in the previous forms is determined by the essential occurrence of truth and that the will to willing thereby inundates everything.

328. Being and beings

(forgottenness of being
concealment of being)

Being is concealed in the exclusivity of beings as that which is.

And herein lies, indeed is concealed, the innermost essential concealment of being, a concealment which for us constitutes an ambiguity.

Being can withdraw and thereby release beings completely to beingness.

But being can also conceal itself so as to let this concealment itself essentially occur. Then the difference is of another kind. Then the forgottenness of being is not mere absence as being: the pure unconcealment of concealedness as being.

How is this either–or to be experienced?

329. Beginning and being

Is "metaphysics" overcome?
Is the truth of beingness broken?
Are beings, as objectivity and actuality, bygone?
No.

Now for the first time beingness stands at the commencement of the unfolding of its unconditional dominance. Now for the first time "metaphysics" and "logic," as the "technology" that can be grasped only in terms of the history of beyng, bear "fruit."

Now for the first time the history of being arrives at the constellation in which beings and the truth of being, i.e., the inceptuality, are at the greatest remove from each other (this is to be understood in the qualitative sense, i.e., in terms of the history of beyng).

330. The decision

The term is *not* employed here in a "moral," "existentiell," religious, or any other "functional" sense. It is to be thought here only inceptually, out of the appropriating event.

The decision is the withdrawal of very possibility of separating and differentiating.

The decision is what is inceptual of the beginning, because, through this withdrawal, the truth is first preserved in its inceptuality.

The first appearance of the decision is this: the "remembrance" and the "will to willing" have now entered into what is without separation, what is utterly incomparable, what can no longer be juxtaposed.

C. The saying of the beginning

331. The word, metaphysics, and the beginning

Metaphysical humans have overstepped the word and left it behind as a tool they themselves possess and master—ζῷον λόγον ἔχον.

Beings overpower the word, and language is means and expression, even for the "more profound" metaphysical "philosophers of language," Hamann, Herder, and the like.

It is otherwise with the word and beyng.

Word and beginning.

332. The word of inceptual thinking

(the plurivocity)
the determinateness of
that which disposes.

possesses the plurivocity of the beginning, a plurivocity that neither rests on negligence nor is tailored for dialectics. This plurivocity lets the word essentially occur and thereby disposes into the unrest of thinking.

Every claim to univocity is indeed facile here but is also a sign that no capability and preparation can unfold, beyond the technical aspect of metaphysical concepts (and also of dialectics), so as to allow the essential occurrence of the apparent indeterminateness of what is inceptually and uniquely disposing.

The indeterminate is manifest already where the difference between being and beings is itself experienced out of the unity of the διαφέρον.

By its very essence, a word appropriate to the history of beyng, a word which constantly names the inceptuality and the event, cannot ever have a single meaning. And that is not a defect. Constriction to the technique of univocity is what would be defective.

Thus even to speak of plurivocity is misleading here, since plurivocity is still understood only in relation to univocity. Cf. the term "transcendence," which is indeed still a metaphysical concept.

It seems that the demand for exactness and univocity in "concepts" would be the most natural thing in the world and utterly self-evident in regard to "philosophy." Since "philosophy" itself produces "logic," it must for its part always proceed "logically."

But:

1. What is meant by "logic"?
2. Because logic pertains to metaphysics, must logic be the measure of the thinking of being? Or is it not rather the reverse? Must not thinking, which produces "logic," stand over logic?
3. Does "outside of logic" mean at once "unlogical"?
4. One can always proceed as if it were so; one can busy oneself endlessly with pointing out ambiguities and leveling charges of illogicality, and one can even persuade one's fellow citizens and reap a rich bounty in this hunt for contradictions.

But to what avail is this conduct, which poses as superior and "free" and yet is never free enough to engage in an experience that is in all respects alien to comfortable habit and to assurance through "logic"?

333. The thinking of the history of beyng and the demand for univocity, non-contradiction, non-circularity, and comprehensibility[4]

What justifies placing value only on such "words"? What is behind the demand that everything be univocal, non-contradictory, non-circular, and comprehensible? Is that not unconditional bias and the obstinacy of thoughtless thinking?

It almost seems as if we merely need to repeat what Hegel said against common sense, were it not that Hegel himself remained entirely within metaphysics; it would still not be a matter here of something essentially different! Would not this empty entrenchment in empty argumentation be the genuine nihilism, the one that wills nothing but the abandonment of questioning, the shunning of that which is question-worthy? One hunts after contradictions, acting as if one possessed eternal truth.

The retort might be made that it is facile to absolve oneself from all "logic" and arbitrary to pass from beings to being and the reverse, back and forth.

4. ("plurivocity"—"logic.")

One keeps speaking, without entering into the essential, tarrying with it, and meditating. One keeps speaking "like a lawyer." One keeps taking refuge in the self-evidence of ordinary "thinking." One does not for a moment attempt to meditate whether these plurivocities stem from sheer negligence and arbitrariness or whether we have here a responding and a surrendering to being itself. Whether personal-biographical vicissitudes are inflated here into a "philosophy," or whether experience does speak here.

334. Within the first attempt at the thinking of the history of beyng

(transcendence)

is at work only "metaphysics," i.e., everything that is to be obtained from it itself for its own determination.

Consider, e.g., the terms "transcendence" and "transcendental," even if they are forthwith removed from the domain of "consciousness" and the "I think" and are placed within the differentiation of beings and being.

Therefore also the *genuine* plurivocity of transcendence:

1. Dasein transcends toward the "world."
2. Dasein transcends itself.
3. Being transcends beings.
4. Dasein transcends toward nothingness.

In truth, however, there is one single "transcendence," which is not "transcendence" but, instead something interpreted under this rubric in terms of the human being, although indeed as Da-sein. Transcendence "is" Da-sein, but Dasein is the appropriation of the event, and the event is the beginning. Transcendence not action; instead, history.

335. The saying of the beginning

The assertion and presentation of the saying can only be simple. That means here: arising out of what is one and out of the unity of the beginning: in the manner of the event.

All discovery and instruction as well as all excitation and impetus must be left out; likewise, all "ordering" of "contents." Only the pure word, resting in itself, may sound. No auditor is to be presupposed, nor any space for the belongingness, since the latter is what first appropriates the saying itself. And neither can anyone "know" something here in advance.

The structure is not a "system," for in it truth is not understood as certainty. The essence of the clearing requires the individualized fire of the stars: the preservation of the event.

336. The saying of the beginning

The saying is itself the inceptuality of the beginning. The saying brings the beginning dispositionally into words (not vocables) and also silences the beginning. Far from the beginning lies every sort of communication and intimation, as if the saying were a proposition about the beginning. The saying is marked by the appropriating event. This implies that the appropriating event is marked by the saying. But saying, word, and voice are here thought inceptually, not as incidents and appearances of human activity.

The saying "of" the beginning is the inceptuality as a telling. The telling is appropriation into the essential occurrence (as unconcealing concealment) of truth. This appropriation includes the essential fullness of that which promotes a thinking of the appropriating event.

The saying "of" the beginning recollectively appropriates the thoughtful word and confers (promises) and refuses speech. Such is always the re-illumination of the starry brilliance of the beginning.

The brilliance is illumination out of the concealment of the hearth-center of the star, silently radiating in the light of everything lit up, a light uniformly attuned and resting in itself.

This re-illumination is not a subsequent accompaniment; on the contrary, it is proper to the appropriated and pertains intrinsically to the inceptuality. The inceptuality never exhausts its essence in a supposed "in itself," to which then a consciousness could be coordinated for occasional apprehension and inclusion, without anyone ever knowing whence and why this happens.

The inventive thinking of the saying of the beginning is the thinking appropriated by the inceptuality, in the inceptuality, and *as* the inceptuality. In whatever direction this thinking must think historically, nowhere does it refer to the "views" of thinkers, to a "doctrine" about beings ("world"), or to a mere speaking "about" being. Inventive thinking "is" beyng, the latter, however, as the appropriating event.

Because the saying is event-related and therefore legendary, it appropriates a history to the beginning by way of recollection. The inceptuality as history of the beginning unfolds the beginning and thus appropriates beginnings (the one beginning and the other), whose essence we are starting to surmise.

There is a projective character about the attempt to place into speech the event-related history of the inceptuality (in the guise of this history, the inceptuality appropriates Da-sein). But even this projection is already appropriated; it possesses truth only insofar as it can remain projectively in the event. Indeed in such a realm there is always already failure and error. And the "schematic" of these projections threatens to exhaust itself in mere misrepresentation. Yet what might be thought is not a series of doctrinal fragments and their divisions; instead, what is recollective about the event of the inceptuality should be heard steadfastly in its disposing: the saying is the *promise* and refusal of the voice which stirs up the abyss. The saying recollects and, by recollecting, in advance takes the recollected into the departure of the downgoing. Out of this that is recollected, the projection of thoughtful speech is projected.

Every thought of such thinking is at once, out of the appropriated steadfastness in Da-sein, already resonance and interplay, leap and grounding. This thinking has its abode in that which is incomparable. The simplicity of the consonance, in which resonance and interplay, leap and grounding belong together in unity, derives from the originality of the holding back. Essentially contrary is every effort to turn the inceptuality of language, which is historically concealed, into a technique of everyday speech and to try to convert it into a lingua franca.

Inceptual speech is always indebted to the beginning for the eventuation of the thoughtful word.

Talk of inceptual thinking experiences again the riches of the word, riches that are marked by the appropriating event and that stem from the proper domain of the beginning.

To the indolent, dull, vacant, and stubborn, let it be said: language is in its historical beginning richer, freer, more venturesome, and therefore also always more strange than worn-out ordinary opinion may admit into the precinct of its calculations. The inceptual word thus appears as the disturbance of an ordinary—and therefore taken to be "eternal"—univocity. Thence the indignation at the supposed play with word-meanings. That which fools consider to be an artificial contrivance, because it opposes their routine, is in essence only the counter-tone of the appropriation which maintains everything proper to beyng in the essence of its truth. Indeed even this semblance of inessentiality, in whose form the event keeps aloof from everything actual, in order to come to presence as such, must still be co-thought, in inceptual thinking, as what is unavoidable in the realm of worn-out everydayness. (On the word, cf. *Die Sage,* typescript 18 {GA74}).

Out of the resonating and interplay, leap and grounding, the inceptual word says the beginning, the downgoing, and the inceptuality first of all in the transition and in full consonance. Thinking maintains itself in the free appreciation of what is unexpected from an inceptual graciousness. This latter blossoms in the intimate event of the moderation shining in advance throughout everything, the moderation of the pure illumination that requires nothing, since it pertains to the beginning.

The unexpected that has its source in graciousness guards the mystery of the inceptual. Only the steadfast are open to the unexpected, for they can be indulgent in relation to everything importunate since they await the appropriating event. For that, all thinking must be spacious in oscillating spaces. The rigid univocity of the technical concept never attains the rigor of language, which resides in constantly and purely keeping in readiness what is essential in all its consonances. Inceptual thinking clears by illuminating. This thinking provides no states of affairs, and nothing "actual," to be known. But it is grounded in the clearing, in which hearts might shine and things can appear.

The saying is the inceptuality of the beginning (φύσις = event; φύσις as appropriating event; appropriating event as inceptuality).

The saying, in that it says the beginning, places the beginning into its history. The saying as saying (promising, announcing, forbidding, refusing) claims the word and consigns something essential into the dictum and thus into the language which, as the speech of thinking, maintains itself in the clearing of beyng, although without knowing either the latter or the former as such.

(In the first projection, the saying was still too exclusively thought as the word of thinking and, despite all the reservations, still conceived in terms of the proposition.)

337. The saying of the beginning

The beginning says the inceptuality. Thoughtful speech exists only if, appropriated by the beginning, it has received the appropriating event. The inceptuality of the beginning is then concealed in a reception. But how does the beginning appropriate the speech of thinking? Disposing into thinking. Out of this, the thoughtful utterance of the saying of the beginning integrates itself into a historical, and thus always unique, submission to the dictum. But how a disposing into thinking? There eventuates to the steadfast ones an ability to hear the saying of the beginning only out of obedience to the intimacy of the inceptual beginning, i.e., to the departure in the downgoing.

The other beginning is merely the proper inceptuality of the one unique beginning, which, as first, did not stay the same in its emergence and, in advancing, conceals the essence. *This* concealment a sign of the inceptuality.

338. The inceptual claim of the beginning

is that its inceptuality essentially occurs and says itself. Only thus does the beginning guarantee to come to knowledge as itself, a knowledge which is perhaps always denied "understanding" and "understandability."

If, however, the appropriation of Da-sein belongs to the inceptuality (as the appropriating event), and if Da-sein must be taken over by the human being, then there eventuates, in the appropriating event, the attunement of Da-sein and thus also, and just as inceptually, the determination of the human being. Yet this cannot mean that objectively present humans, satisfied in their previous state, may and must now also come to "understand" the beginning. Such a humanity has had its time and will long have it.

Steadfastness alone, not understanding, is allotted to inceptual thinking, and this steadfastness only in the claim of the saying of the beginning.

339. Inceptual thinking

The only thinking thinking inceptually is the one that inventively thinks the inceptuality of the beginning, the latter in the former. The νοεῖν of φύσις as ἀρχή is still not inceptual thinking, because in such νοεῖν the beginning is merely the emergence which conceals the inceptuality, without paying attention to this concealment itself.

The pure decidedness of the appropriation into the thinking of the inceptuality—event and reception.

Talk of the first and the other beginning already says too much, insofar as the so-called first beginning still does not essentially occur in full inceptuality. And nevertheless is not emergence the advent of the beginning? Yet advent is not the same as staying.

Staying occurs inceptually only in the downgoing of concealment.

340. Beginning as ἀρχή; inceptual thinking

"Beginning" is thus merely a character of beyng and specifically according to the insight that being takes over the starting point for beings. A being is what is present; but the "beginning" is then the designation of being as that from which beings come forth, are, and will be.

The beginning is here not beyng itself in its essence, nor does the inceptuality of the beginning unfold itself.

The thinking of the ἀρχή is still not an inceptual thinking. In the first beginning, being appears as ἀρχή. The first beginning is not the ἀρχή but, instead, is the appearance of being as the self-refusal of the event. In the other beginning, the twisting free of beyng must transform everything.

Even "the holy" of the poet is not the inceptual beginning but quite to the contrary is that realm of beyng which is closed off to the concept as such.

341. Beginning and recollection

The beginning is unique. The word of the inceptuality is multiple. Hence there are many ways to say the beginnings. We know the first beginning as the emergent (φύσις); we know the other beginning as the downgoing (event).

The other beginning is not a second one next to the first; rather, it is the same, but in the more inceptual essence of the inceptuality. The question of how the first beginning is saved in the other beginning finds its answer in the fact that the other beginning, as concealment, appropriates the inceptuality of the first beginning, namely ἀλήθεια (unconcealedness) into unconcealment and appropriates this latter into concealment.

The recollection of the first beginning attains its intimacy in the departure of the downgoing. Thinking in advance is the more inceptual recollection. But recollection is different from the mere new presentification of something previously perceived (ἀνάμνησις belongs to "metaphysics").

342. The saying of the beginning

The saying is the inceptuality of the beginning. In the saying, the beginning announces the inceptuality and also is silent about the inceptuality. This is not to be understood in terms of communication and intimation but, rather, in terms of the appropriating event. *The inceptuality is in itself a matter of saying.*

To think the saying means to be appropriated into the word of the saying for thoughtful speech. Here reign failure and error. (Is the why-question still fitting here?)

The first beginning is emergence (unconcealment). (How is this, and how is emergence presence? Out of the refusal; the saying as refusal, but λόγος). The emergence abandons itself to the advancement (start "of" metaphysics); emergence as presence. The advancement claims to be the one and only course (history "of" metaphysics). The course of the (historiologically grasped) proceedings brings the advancement to an end, one which the commencement had already prepared (consummation "of" metaphysics). The ending of the advancement is a perishing (the instituting of metaphysics as "worldview"). On what "now" is inceptual in terms of the history of beyng, cf. *Die Sage,* p. 11 {GA74}. Transition and concealment. Meanwhile, undisturbed by the mere advancement, the first beginning persists in itself as transition.

The transition transits back over the emergence (unconcealment) into the concealment. The transition thus passes over, and passes by, the advancement and course of metaphysics. The transition goes back into the other beginning.

The other beginning is the appropriating event (unconcealing concealment). The event is downgoing—recollection.

The intimacy of recollection is the departure.

The departure is the advent into the inhabited place of the sojourn of the inceptuality.

The inhabited place of the sojourn is Da-sein.

*

Inceptuality (event) and understanding of Da-sein.

Understanding: to bring into the essential occurrence; but the essence is *Da-sein.*

Selfhood and self-sameness.

Whence the essentiality of the αὐτό? The *same and self.*

*

The *first-ness* of the first beginning ("First" is understood too readily in the *historiological*-chronological sense, rather than out of the inceptuality of the event.) consists in its being provisional; running ahead and indeed not "genuine," as emergence and yet ineluctable, insofar as the human being is needed—insofar as emergence is precisely the appropriating event and the *appropriating event* is understood in the direction of the departure—downgoing. Here beyng the *essentially occurring* truth *of beings.*

Beings recur, but no longer the *actual* nor beingness as actuality. Only in the de-actualizing do beings again become beings.

*

The beginning essentially occurs more inceptually: that means not "heightening" but rather mitigation out of the inclination toward the most proper domain of what is proper—*graciousness.* But in such a way indeed a "comparative," a *mode of comparison.* But what is more inceptual is in each case also the *unique.*

The uniqueness does not tolerate several for an additional comparison.

*

In the first beginning and its advancement, Da-sein is essentially refused. Wherefore? And what does that signify?

*

The "ground" of the concealment is the abyss of the downgoing into the inclination toward the departure.

The stillness of the protective graciousness.

*

Beyng is —φύσις emergence
—ἀλήθεια *unconcealment,* unconcealedness
—ἀρχή disposal (starting point, dominance).
Beyng first disputes the inceptuality (clearing) as clarification of the explanation (ἰδέα—explain—substantiate—*possibility*—making possible—causing) and is hardly said itself (as beingness), so as then for its part to *explain* beings. Thus in order to gain the first inceptuality in recollection, there must be an overcoming of beingness and subsequently a twisting free of beyng.

D. Thinking and knowing
Thinking and poetizing[5]

to be unfolded only out of the
experience of the essence of truth
and therefore also not to be postulated
as "modes of comportment"
and forms of "creativity."

343. *Poetizing Thinking*

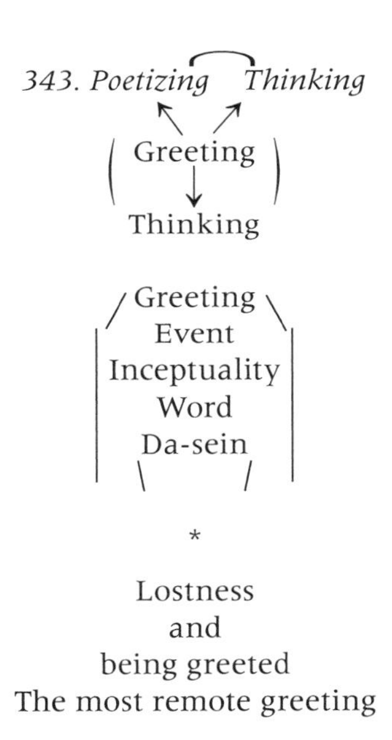

Greeting
and
event

Lostness and protection
as appropriating event.
How the mountain can be protected and the tree lost—not immediately through us, but through our lostness and protection. And these in turn?

5. *Über den Anfang* {GA70}: II. *Das Erdenken des Anfangs.* Cf. on Hölderlin.

*

Thanking—to *be* greeted as preservation of the greeting in founding and grounding.

*

Lostness in the transition to the beginning.
Poetizing and thinking of the lostness.
The lack of effectiveness and the inactuality.
Dread in the face of the "abstract."

344. To be greeted; Da-sein

To be victorious unarmed. Simply through that to make *Da-sein* capable of bringing all things essentially to itself and recognizing their essential dignity.

Da-sein as giving advice; not didactic prescription, but a pointing out of the ways and traits of truth, through simple steadfastness in them; also not mere "examples" but, rather, *by greeting*—to be incorporated reciprocally into the greeting.

In being greeted we receive the inceptual advice and become well provided so as then to give advice, in which we "merely" pass the greeting on.

"Advice"—*proficiency; advice* ⟷ *command.*

To bestow something on someone, i.e., to make someone a present of something.

345. The transition

(Poetizing and thinking)

The thinking of the history of beyng is prior to poetizing; the latter has already eventuated but, for that very reason, is only now in arrival.

This poetizing is poetizing of the holy. The holy is the abiding that bestows an abode as the temporal-spatial playing field of Da-sein.

Thus for the first time, through a thinking in advance, there is grounded the truth of the founding which itself is the origin of another history.

This inceptuality of the beginning comes only as a transition. The steadfastness of the leap is in accord with this transition.

346. Poetizing and thinking

Thinking is not simply the interpretation of poetry, which, as art in the sense of Hegel's absolute metaphysics, has been completed and has come to an end.

Thinking is the inventive thinking of beyng and the grounding of the time-space of the founding of beyng, a founding that has already eventuated.

Thinking, as inventive thinking of beyng, is a directive into the stillness of the origin of the word.

Thinking is appropriated; the appropriating event is history as the unique poetry of Hölderlin.

Poetry has become different in essence; everything has entered into the provisionalness of a long waiting and thus is disposed toward diffidence by the event.

347. Thinking and poetizing

are taken by us readily and immediately as modes of human spiritual activity and perhaps also as modes of human creativity.

And we proceed to seek the universal "essence" of both thinking and poetizing, their timeless concept, and to distinguish this conceptual essence more precisely through the enumeration of features. Why is this sort of apprehension usual to us and desired?

Why do we not surmise that in this way the proper essence of both is already perverted and lost? We do not surmise (why not?) that they ground history and are essentially historical, that we grasp in a timelessly universal concept only a semblant essence, and that we nevertheless cannot get by without this semblance.

Historicism and its overcoming ensnare both thinking and poetizing in this kind of opinion and keep us far from the historical meditation which we readily exchange, in our historicist attitude, for the "analysis of the situation."

Seen more closely, it cannot be a matter of an exchange, since for that we would have needed to know both already, historical meditation and historiological explanation, as well as the abstracting of universal concepts.

To ask about poetizing and thinking means, now and in the future, to grasp their assignment to the grounding of the truth of what is inceptual, i.e., to carry them out, or not carry them out, in such a way.

348. Silence and saying

1. as the *incapacity* to say; no longer being able to say, and this again as a consequence of emptiness and perplexity or from fullness and knowledge.
2. as *renunciation of* speech for reasons of prudence and self-protection or in order to dissemble and hide oneself.
3. as *expectation and unfolding* of a long preparation, without regard to oneself and not determined by ability and inability.
4. as *being greeted,* which is a silence that does not exclude speech, but also does not allow just any speech. Instead, it requires a particular word of inceptual necessity.

349. Thanking

as appreciating, *accepting* the favor and appropriation, *having faith* in the fidelity of the belongingness. Sacrifice, *giving up of the essence* as transformation into beyng. Taking *in advance*—insertion into the maintaining.

Steadfastness is the essence of the appropriated gratitude. Entrance and devotion.

But how to kindle and release this thankfulness?

350. Essential thinking

does not explain beings in terms of an origin, with respect to which everything that has arisen not only is missing but also falls into emptiness, assuming that explanation is a most general concept.

Essential thinking does not explain; instead, it transposes into the truth of beyng. More precisely, it prepares this transposition in that it transports into questioning by way of a transporting that is both disposing and disposed. Questioning is the interrogation of the truth of beyng. This interrogation is in each case a step toward the abyss of Da-sein, and Da-sein can be attained only in a leap.

The imagelessly dispositional transporting as interrogation of Da-sein is the preparation for the other beginning.

The usual "philosophy" explains, gropes about in empty "origins," and is constantly exposed to the reproach that through it nothing could be experienced and nothing learned; e.g., the most profound discussion of the "origin" of language in the "philosophy of language" accomplishes nothing for correct speech and for the "use" of language, all of which is to be acquired immediately from the great masters among the poets and orators.

We can therefore dispense with "philosophy." Certainly; if we take it as "explanation" and demand practical benefits from it.

But what if the transposition into beyng as a result of an inceptual belonging to the truth of beyng were a historical necessity?

Abandonment of beings by being.
Forgottenness of being on the part of humans.
Lostness of humans.
Transposition into the belongingness to beyng.
Transposition as grounding.

351. Essential thinking

If we take *essential thinking* merely as philosophy (i.e., metaphysics), if we consider its pursuit to be a "dealing" with "principles," if with understand these "principles" as most general concepts and axioms in the manner of rules, and if we adhere in advance to "actuality" in the sense of what is immediately present at hand and of concern to everyone at some time or other, then thinking appears to be desolate and empty and so one-sided that not even a single "side" of actuality is heeded therein.

But if we carry out essential thinking as an ever inceptual steadfastness in the truth of beyng, then the conclusion just drawn is shattered.

Thinking is then neither dealing with something, as if this something were an "object," nor is such thinking a dealing with "principles," as if being were merely what is "general" to beings.

Essential thinking is historical in two basically different ways.

On the one hand, without effecting or requiring effectivity or ever being measurable by effectivity, this thinking grounds a truth of beyng, a truth which itself is only as event.

Then again it is effective on readers and hearers, and, through their mediation, it effects a clarification, recasting, and steering of an epoch and often does so against its own aims.

Corresponding to these modes are various types of saying.

Can *pure thinking* ever be of practical benefit? This remarkable question supposes:

1. that thinking is an activity from which a result can ever arise.
2. what is essential must always be beneficial, i.e., useful.

Will we ever come to meditation and in it alone to the authentic experience that all things, including the much-prized practical ones, rest inceptually only in being and therefore must find their abode in the truth of beyng?

352. Thinking and poetizing

Thinking—is that not distinguished from "sensibility" and, as "pure thinking," always *without* it?

Yet we ask to the contrary: *is* "sensibility" ever sensibility without "thinking"?

But neither this question nor the counter-question touches the essential. For, what we call disposition resides *before* both and perhaps requires a *still*-stricter separation between thinking and poetizing.

Thinking is "imageless" and does not captivate, but it is not lacking in disposition.

We must certainly renounce appraising everything on the basis of "impressions" and on the basis of effective power in the domain of impressions.

353. Admission and steadfastness

Admission [*Eingeständnis*] corresponds to the beginning; the beginning is already the appropriating event but at first and for a long while is denied and disavowed in the semblance of a recognition of being, a recognition that poses in the form of an affirmation of beings as the actual.

The disavowal of beyng in the form of the forgottenness of being.

Admission as the correspondence that submits to the belongingness to beyng and renounces the priority of beings. Admission as a turn to the essential ground of the human being; abandonment of the *animal rationale.*

Admission—the start of thinking.

354. Admission and detachment

Detachment [*Gelassenheit*] as the essential occurrence of a letting [*Lassen*]

Letting: 1. as *abandoning*—not attending to, wanting to know nothing of.
2. releasing, letting enter into its own, abetting.

3. the releasement of the proper essence in abetting out of the appropriation which is beyng itself.
4. not only releasing, but also *retaining*—of the *conferral* of the essence in the appropriation by beyng. The retaining as maintaining—steadfastness—admission.

Admission as relation to being and as relation at once to the essence and to the essential transformation of the human being.

The admission (in terms of the history of beyng) releases, only to the inceptual dignity of beyng, the dispensation of the human being into the relation toward beyng, and thereby it preserves, by way of admission, steadfastness in the preservation of beyng.

355. The shyness in the beginning

Shyness [*Befängnis*] essentially as the diffidence of the inceptual [*anfänglich*] disconcertedness [*Be-fangenheit*] in the inceptuality [*Anfängnis*] of the beginning [*Anfang*].

This disconcertedness nothing to be eliminated; on the contrary, it must be taken up into an attitude of concession and developed toward steadfastness.

Shyness and diffidence in *thinking.*

Thanking—*admission—greeting;*
admission and thinking;
admission and shyness in the beginning.

356. "Thinking"

"Think to yourself" — project yourself freely into the projective swing of the oscillation of beyng.

The "Think to yourself" snatches away everything ordinary and transforms even thinking into a proper domain of what is thought in it, and this that is thought does at first and for a moment seem to be in fact merely the result of the thinking.

But: "being" is not the result of thinking. On the contrary, thinking is the appropriating event of beyng. Thinking is thinking ahead into the advent of what is coming.

Remembrance — is recollection into the beginning;

"thinking" — is, as recollective thinking ahead, the mindfulness [*Sinnen*] which first brings every meditation [*Besinnung*] into possibility.

357. Thanking and silence

What is most proximate to thanking is silence. The highest silence is the one which, as answer [*Antwort*] to the address [An*wort*] of the claim, is supposed to take to speech, could do so, and yet does not, i.e., does not sound out in public but, instead, holds back.

Silence at first as the ceasing of ordinary speech ("being still"). This cessation can be determined and disposed in various ways.

*

Remaining within a secret patience.
Keeping silent not primarily about beings, but inceptually about beyng.

The *mildness* which has prevented all disagreeableness; the *directive* which thanking already bears and which in turn bears the thanking. *Contentment.*

*

Thanking—χάρις.
χάριτος σχέσις· μνήμη μετ' εὐεργεσίας. Pseudoplatonic Ὅροι 412e, 12s. The attitude of thanking; remembrance with beneficence? Pliant allocation.

358. Thinking and thanking

Thanking—as a remembering [*Ge-denken*] which is a thinking ahead [*Vor-denken*].
Ingratitude—as the essential inability to thank.
Gratitude is the essential ground of thinking.
Gratitude as belongingness to beyng.
Ingratitude not a consequence of disrespect but, rather, its ground.

359. Thanking and beyng

Thanking as gift and specifically as counter-gift.
The countering and reciprocating are essential.
Reciprocation as the echo of the appropriation.

Or even
thanking as the "beginning" of the reciprocation.
The "beginning" here as acceptance of the appropriation.
Thanking here not as subsequent *expression* of thanks.
The word as answer.
The thoughtful word is essentially an answer to the claim, an answer to the favor in the appropriating event. Donation, relegation, but at the same time restrained return to oneself—concealment in the concealedness of indigence.
Thanking—
Thanking in advance—admission
Thanking: self-donation into the belongingness to beyng and therein precisely steadfastness in Da-sein—to take possession of the essence.
Bestowal *and* preservation—steadfastness in the truth of beyng.

360. Appropriating event and thanking

are favor, enchantment. They place the magic, the magical, into the "between" that opens; the "between" possesses, altogether inceptually, this basic character.

361. Thinking

Learn to thank and you can think.
The essence of thinking is never thought of by means of "logic." For, "logic," even if we take it originally as a hermeneutics of saying and asserting, has already abandoned a relation to being; more precisely, it could never, in accord with its origination out of an interpretation of being as ἰδέα, have a relation to being.

The essence of thinking lies in the thinking in advance that remembers, toward which the inceptuality of the beginning (being as event) disposes and thus remains determinative for all relations to beings.

The essence of thinking is revealed only when thinking is determined by the voice of beyng as event, and the dignity of beyng is illuminative for the inceptual respectfulness which has its essence in the thanking of gratitude. Thinking, thanking, poetizing are the same in the inceptuality of the essence proper to the history of beyng. Thanking is a founding.

The ones who thank would have to come to be out of the calculative ones. Yet precisely that is impossible. The calculative ones take even their own and others' "thanks" as something with which they calculate, something they manage to take calculatively as payment and reward.

It is not merely that the "world" pays us only with ingratitude; for this world, even "gratitude" is at most merely a form of payment.

Thanking and keeping in mind.
Thanking and remembering; thinking toward . . .
a "thankful" heart—capable of thanks
a "thankful" enduring—productive of thanks.

Thanking and stillness.
Stillness as the essence of time-space.
Stillness is closer to beyng than is rest, even if the latter essentially occurs as the inceptual gathering of motion.

362. Thinking and cognition

Thinking means heeding the relation of saying to beings and, for that, above all heeding beyng itself in its truth as such. Thinking is something essential only when it is appropriated by beyng.

Precisely for that reason, and inasmuch as it is projected from the projection of beyng, thinking follows a multidirectional course and is in each case an inventive thinking which alone corresponds to the appropriation. The multidirectionality means that the essence of beyng can always be thought in one respect, such that the other respects are co-thought without this multiplicity damaging the uniqueness of beyng or, accordingly, the univocity of thinking. The univocity of essential thinking does not consist in the empty uniformity of a fixed and universally water-tight "definition." That sort of "thinking" is already a "calculating" which stands in service to cognition.

To be sure, *cognition* is always univocal in its own specific domain. The univocity stems from the restriction to beings; they of themselves demand univocity.

Only thinking, as the thinking of beyng, gives to all cognition the possible "strictness" of the concept, whereby the seriousness of the multidirectionality is concealed to cognition.

Calculating and planning are only apparently "thinking"; in truth they remain inferential cognition. Despite all the apparent novelty of its surprises, transformations, and transpositions, as these might be required, such cognition lacks every essential kind of imagination.

The suffocation of the imaginative powers, which receive their impulses only from the dignity of beyng itself, levels "thinking" down to calculation and dissolves everything into values and transvaluations. What can be expected from the arrangements and calculations is merely the managing and solving of various sorts of "tasks."

Cognition	and	thinking
Grounding	—	determination
Ground	—	abyss
Cause	—	beginning

(cf. Leibniz)

Cognition aims at beings, explains beings by falling back on other beings, is satisfied with beings, and therefore strives to establish a highest being, as the clearest being, out of which then everything can be explained, even being. In the determination of being as "Idea," the way is paved to this explainability.

But thinking is the maintaining of the relation to beyng, i.e., the relation of beyng to truth, the truth in which thinking is steadfast.

363. Thinking

is the thinking of beyng, is the cessation of the decamping of beings into the abandonment by being.

The cessation, however, does not effect anything, does not take hold. The cessation eventuates such that within the leaving and passing on there appears a resting which does *not* somehow present a pause in the progression of beings; the resting arises and intervenes. Whence? Out of beyng. And proximally out of what is concealed and is not at all paid attention.

Only *the fact that* a gathering eventuates, and otherwise nothing further, suffices for all decamping to be transposed into an other; whether this other is perceived immediately or if it is perceived at all is not essential. Only this "that it is"—of a *cessation.*

Yet this cessation has now the property of seeking nothing of its own and of thrusting up against something. Instead, the pure coming allows something to come and thus alone is disposed in the releasing toward the proper domain of the event. Cessation—a dispositional saying of beyng.

*

Not a decree of the (conditional or unconditional) subjectivity of the thinker with regard to beings, not a subjugation of the thinker to the absolute being—reason—faith, but instead the *demand of beyng into the graciousness of thinking. Temperament.*

*

Thinking as human pursuit and endeavor—as *reflexion*!

Thinking as demand of being.
Thinking as the enduring of a truth of being.
Thinking as the celebration of the dignity.
Thinking as cessation of beings out of the releasing of being.
Thinking as disposing.
How in the foregoing the various moments of thinking are gathered up.

*

What always hinders a co-thinking is the inability to enter into the unique and into its uniqueness, to persevere therein without the fatal assistance of familiar notions, and to unfold the unique into its proper inceptuality.

Cognition, on the other hand, "works" precisely with this appeal to results and to the arts of explanation—digressing in all directions.

"Cognition" spoils us for thinking and distracts us from it. And especially if cognition has become calculation.

*

Thinking is steadfastness in inceptual knowledge.

Because the beginning, by its very essence, never results in—or delivers itself up into—propositions but, rather, is elusive and mired in concealment, thinking is therefore without result (on account of this incapacity of the beginning to produce results).

The saying is not a proposition; instead, it is a sounding that fades into the departure.

*

Besides the strictness and the track of the work of cognition, there is carefulness in sincerity of thinking.

Here the determinateness of the grasp into the riches of the saying. Here the artificial and rote fixity of following rules is never enough.

Here only the *determination* is sufficient.

*

Philosophy and thinking: the expectation that here something would be explained and made understandable, whereas in fact thinking leaves the things understood to their own devices.

*

The distinction between thinking and cognition is not only broader but is also more inceptual than the one between philosophy and the sciences. For, philosophy only *one* kind of thinking of beyng; the sciences only *one* mode of the cognition of beings (praxis—technique). Cf. Poetizing and thinking.

*

Thinking, as differentiated from cognition, seems to be mere thinking and to be already in the realm of what is merely thought up and contrived.

This "opinion" *even* something cogent—something true, more than it might like to admit.

*

Philosophy—thinking
The barrier in the way of most people who seek entrance into "philosophy" lies in the notion that this thinking is a "working" which, drawn by a goal and simply following a line, is undertaken persistently and in various way in order to achieve a result.

But "thinking"! is appropriation into the beginning.

*

Differentiation—to point immediately into the inceptuality.
Its *squandering.*
The beginning—as abyss; no whence and why.
Determination and grounding.
Beyng determines—takes away into the beginning;
beings ground, provide a ground.

E. Poetizing and thinking

Cf. Cognition and thinking
Cf. Poetizing and thinking
Poetizing and thinking
On the beginning {GA70}
Cf. *Überlegungen* {in GA94–96}

"Mythology" and "philosophy"
Cf. s. s. 42, p. 37, concerning Ἑστία
{GA53, p. 141ff.}

364. Poetizing and thinking

out of *that to which* they are "related," whence they are determined in their essential descent; how what is determinative disposes and thereby on the one hand discloses itself and at the same time ordains thinking and poetizing and, in addition, ordains the type of grounding proper to them.

Poetizing and thinking cannot simply be taken as "creation" and "creative activity"; that is of many kinds. Furthermore, the relation to language is insufficient, if language remains undetermined in its essence and no consideration is given to how this essence ordains itself in thinking and poetizing.

What is decisive for the characterization of language in the sense of the founding of being is precisely the relation to being. And! "being" is meant here as what is worthy of question (cf. *Grundbegriffe,* s. s. 41 {GA51}).

Poetizing and thinking—their "relationship" cannot be established through a "timelessly" valid rule; since they themselves fundamentally ground the historicity of the history of the human being, *they* are historical in the original sense (sending a destiny; ordaining as dispensing).

Thus it can *happen* that whereas poetizing used to determine thinking (how? as it called thinking something equiprimordial), yet now thinking must think *in advance* of poetizing. This thinking in advance, however, must liberate historicality out of the ground of being into its essential occurrence, and for that what is necessary is an inceptuality of thinking itself.

Poetizing and thinking as *grounding* the truth of beyng; grounding as *founding;* grounding as *heedfulness.*

Then what about language? better, the word? Both poetizing and thinking precisely in the differentiation out of the unity—of what? (Beyng and humans).

365. Thinking and poetizing

Must thinking dwell only in apprehending, representing, and considering, or indeed can it still transport? This transporting is then the projection: the opening up of the truth of beyng. This transporting is carried out in the word. And so thinking is found in the word along with poetizing. Poetry transports, by way of saying, as a captivation.

Thinking is the imageless opening up of the abyss. The rigor of the thoughtful word does not know the law of the play of the poetizing word.

Yet thinking and poetizing are also conceived here historically as ways to accomplish the grounding of the truth of beyng in the beginning; not as a general "theory" of "poetry" and "philosophy."

*

"*Thinking*"—to maintain oneself *in the relation* to being (*as*—).
"Poetizing."

*

The counter-essence of poetry is planning.
Humans dwell poetically—
even when they merely plan; then they "dwell" *unpoetically,* which is to say: poetically *in a distorted way.*

*

Thinking — not "mere cogitating," deliberating, calculating.
Poetizing — not "empty delight" (sentimentality—wallowing in images).

*

Poetizing — inventing—founding: "image."
Thinking — imageless experience.
Poetizing — a giving of thanks } thanking
thinking — a thanking
basic disposition
Da-sein.
Not to be simply read off from actual poets and thinkers;
only *examples*— Heraclitus —Parmenides—λεῦσσε
Kant (freedom)
Sophocles—Pindar
Goethe.
Whence ποίησις— (τέχνη) "making" that which *is not yet;* what is "made" is not the poetized—for the inceptuality, only truth procures a *making one's way* to and for. . .

*

Simile [*Gleichnis*]— (imaging) does not compare [*vergleichen*] but, instead, has twisted free of comparison.
gives—appropriates the equal [*das Gleiche*]
in the equal the same.
And also to traverse the simile and no longer interrogate similes.

F. The poet and the thinker

366. Poetizing and thinking

Hölderlin's poetry and the thinking of the history of beyng
(fire) and (water)
Are not the poet and the thinker separated in the manner of fire and water? Therefore when they encounter each other, the encountering might very well demand attention. Either fire is extinguished by water, or water is vaporized in fire, depending on which is stronger. Thus the one must disappear in the face of the other.

But what if both are equally strong, equiprimordial in essence, and separately two different beginnings?

And what if poetizing is not the mere blazing of fire, and thinking not the mere wateriness of water?

Furthermore, what if the poetizing of this poet is at the same time a thinking, and the thinking that encounters it at the same time a poetizing?

Then the poetizing and thinking of this historical moment will not disappear in the face of each other, nor will they blend in an unclarity of essence; on the contrary, in the encounter this most separate essence is in each case liberated to its own, so that in the sharpness of the extreme separation there appears the unique unity of that poetizing and thinking.

If poetizing and this thinking belong together at this historical moment in their most separate essence, then it no longer seems that "the lived experience of feeling" has jurisdiction over the dialogue with the poetizing word. But then there also arises the possibility that thinking in its original essence is indeed "cold and sober," although the mere calculating in "concepts" is otherwise.

Hearing only in heeding, heeding only in dialogue, dialogue only in the same language; therefore saying: the same word; the word essentially the same. Only original thinking is a saying and brings us back into the word. Only thinking is in the sameness of the essential beginning with poetizing, i.e., in the word.

*

Thinking, in the sense of thoughtfulness, is a *thanking* and thereby at the same time *a* thanking.

All thinking sacrifices. The sacrifice is the word. Therefore poetizing also thinks, namely, in the word.

Because poetizing and thinking possess in the word the same thing for their own, they then are properly distinct on the basis of the word, i.e., according to and through the mode of saying. (Cf. Thinking and the word. The preeminent relation of the word to beyng.)

*

To think *properly:* *to experience the essence of the true*
to preserve the essence of truth.
How a thanking?

367. The truth of Hölderlin's poetry

So circumspect is the essence of the poet of this poetry that this essence dwells only in the poetizing of itself. The "truth" of this poetry is determined only out of this poetizing circumspection in the face of its poetic fate, insofar as we think here, in the modern vein, of "validity" and "bindingness." We cannot confront this poetry with a groundless claim which would demand of it the understandability of the propositions of calculative thought or the sentimental impressiveness of "lived experiences."

This poetry also cannot be arranged in a literary-historiological way within the series of familiar poets, whereby the series itself stands within a mere domain of historiological presentification. In that way, poetry is torn out from its truth and degraded to a historiological object. And, thus deformed, it is haled into the court of law which demands of it a "bindingness" "for us." As if "we" could thrust "ourselves" forward so groundlessly as the measure. As if who we are is established and already decided in a "binding" way. As if we surmised something of the essential type of truth proper to this poetry.

368. The first and most extreme separation of thinking and poetizing

The propensity to deduce all things, to explain them, and thereby at the same time to calculate them and mix them together could easily lead to the supposition that these comments on Hölderlin and the "allusions" to his poetry derive from an intention to deliver up thinking to poetry and even to seek refuge in poetry. This would agree well with the supposed condemnation of "logic" in "What is Metaphysics" {in GA9} and likewise with the "preference" for the "dispositions" and especially with the "unscientific" character of Heideggerian thought.

In truth, however, the beginning of thinking requires the inceptual separation of that which is most separated in essence, and only thus is there clarity. Yet, for that, the things which are most separate must first of all be thought and experienced as "near" to each other—not "systematically" but, rather, historically according to the destiny of poetizing and according to the event of the thinking of beyng. To the thinker, the poet becomes a fate. And for a while it seems as if the thinking of the history of beyng must first of all and long into the future remain a self-denying allusion to the poet, so that the domain of confrontation would appear as one that not only is set free in thinking but also is freed from the concealment in which it essentially occurs in fuller riches.

369. Thinking and poetizing

Seen in terms of poetry, thinking plays on the soundless strings of empty concepts, and "concepts" count as general representations. They can then be dispensed with in favor of what is actual, and the meagerness and impotence of thinking are proved. Strange how the appeal to poetry and art so eagerly sets out to prove, without asking whether something provable is here at all. As if we did not first need to be shown into the domain which alone makes room for a distinction between poetizing and thinking. As if this domain on its own presented itself to everyone.

370. Poetizing and thinking

Insofar as what is to be poetized and what is to be thought are *the same,* the truth of this that is the same must unfold at any time out of poetizing and out of thinking. If we name what is to be poetized the holy, and if we call what is to be thought the beginning, then the sameness is at any time an equality, insofar as it is an indication of the time-space of the history in which even nature first comes to its truth.

The disparity in the extreme equality is nevertheless manifest in the fact that the poetical is grounded in becoming at home, whereas the thoughtful leads away into the un-homelike of question-worthiness. What is the same cannot be expounded in the manner of the identity of an object or in general of a being, since this sameness, thoughtfully said, is the truth of beyng; poetically, however, it rules over gods and humans and brings them into their open realm.

Here, in the openness of the open realm, lies the extreme separation of both in the most intimate belongingness, whereby nevertheless this openness must always be experienced poetically or thoughtfully, never indeterminately.

Nor are there stages here in the manner of the metaphysics which, calculating from the standpoint of an absolute, equates the science of philosophy with metaphysics and postulates art as an unconditional preliminary stage.

*

The different relation of humans to the poet and to the thinker.

The immediate, easier, fruitful, attractive relation to the poet.

The merely mediate, difficult, deprivational, repelling relation to the thinker.

The thinker, in the form of the annotating of his annotations to the poetry of the poet, a form necessary in terms of the history of beyng.

The poetical consonance of the discussion of the poet with the poet.

The thoughtful discordance of the dialogue of the thinker with the poet.

371. Poetizing and thinking

Their essence, and that also means their relation and their difference, can never be determined either by poetic science or by philosophical scholarship. As if poetizing and thinking were two plants the botanist has lying before him in order to determine them as objects in an indeterminate sphere of an objectivity of apparently timeless consideration.

Only historically do poetizing and thinking decide their essence as well as their encounter, out of their respective destiny and out of the event of their meeting and separating.

Only the poet poetically determines poetry and its relation to thinking and this latter itself.

Only the thinker thoughtfully determines thinking and its relation to poetizing and this latter itself.

The poet and the thinker separate historically in their encounter, which, as historical, in each case has its unique fate.

Now is occurring the history of the passing by of the most extreme abandonment by being and the history of the preparation of the other beginning. The afternoon of the evening of the West.

*

Poetizing is remembrance [*An-denken,* lit., "thinking toward"].
Thinking is poetizing away from [*Weg-dichten*], *de-founding.*
Thus the two are separated in the *extreme,* but both are also appropriated out of the history of beyng.

Poetizing away from? Through thinking, to bring into the abyss of the departure.
Not simply non-founding,
not simply counter-founding,
but rather away from and outside the domain of founding, but in that manner still related (the mountains)—otherwise in the submissiveness to the inceptuality.

*

Thoughtful thinking—not to reject, but to find sufficiency in the surplus of the questioning of what is question-worthy; therein, however, also a renunciation of the "image" and of being *immediately* heard.

372. The thanking of the renunciation is thoughtful thanking

The renunciation of the holy out of the necessity of the appreciation of what is question-worthy. The renunciation stems from the experience of the proper domain of the fullness of this dignity.

This thanking is not a sheer rejection; it has its "yes" and its determination out of the voice of the dignity of beyng itself and of the event of the twisting free of beyng.

To thank is to pass by ungrounded being and to pass by the power of beings.

*

Thanking is thinking:
1. thanking as poetic thinking.

2. thanking as thoughtful poetizing.

In 1, the thanking is a poetizing—greeting.

In 2, the thanking is a thinking—as a questioning of that which is *worthy of question.*

*

The differentiation of poetizing and thinking is above all a segregative separation of what is purely and simply distinct.

But this differentiation separates because it distinguishes something original such that the separated things are determined to an essence out of which, in a respectively different way, each thinks, and poetizes, over to the other.

The thinking of beyng is by way of poetizing.

The poetizing of the holy is a thinking.

The danger and the appearance of commingling is here, where what rules to the greatest extent and most tenaciously is the most separated of that which is original.

*

Poetizing and thinking not explainable out of "poetry" and "philosophy," as if these latter were fixed domains in themselves, as if the issue were to explain them.

At most, poetry and philosophy are grounded in poetizing and thinking. But how so and whence experienceable? The realm of agreement in the respectively different grounds and levels, according to the poetic or thoughtful experience; a third is excluded.

Experience and *experience*—the *plight*—history.

373. With respect to the history of beyng, the future essence of the poet and the thinker[6]

The poet	*The thinker*
founds the remaining of that which remains, the dwelling of beings in the home-like, through the saying of the holy.	grounds the abyss of beyng in the twisting free of the latter toward the downgoing of the beginning; grounds the steadfastness in the un-homelike of beyng.
Is preparation for the advent of the gods.	Is the venture of experienced godlessness.

6. Cf. above on (event) and beginning.

Poetizing is the hallowing of the holy.	Thinking is appreciation of what is question-worthy.
Poetizing is the finding of what is questionless—"knowing."	Thinking is the seeking for what is without holiness.
Poetizing is a straying between the holy and the unholy.	Thinking is the straying course between the inceptuality (that which is uniquely question-worthy) and beings (as what is "actual—objective"), beings which, in a way that is not question-worthy, disallow all questioning.
Poetizing is, in finding, the naming word (the naming).	Thinking is, in seeking, the questioning word (the saying).
Poetizing is the *thanking* of the becoming at home in the homelike, i.e., in beings.	Thinking is the thanking of the renunciatory not-being-at-home in the un-homelike, i.e., in beyng

In thanking
resides the intimacy of the most extreme discrepancy
between poetizing and thinking.
The *expression of thanks* the thanking

Poetizing is the communicating of the homelike in the imagistic word of the nearness of the holy.	Thinking is the departure into the un-homelike in the imageless word of the conjuncture of beyng.
Poetizing is the founding of the history of a humanity in relation to the homeplace of the gods.	Thinking is the grounding of the historicality of beyng into the abyss of what is without holiness.
Poetizing is called by the holy to the festival.	Thinking is appropriated by the beginning and into Da-sein.
The poet is greeted in order to reply to the greeting and, as greeted, to be saved. The poet greets.	The thinker is addressed in order to venture experientially into the claim of freedom. The thinker "questions," i.e., endures the departure.
The poet becomes the partaker of the festival of the hallowed guests of the gods.	The thinker leaps into the freedom of the abyss of truth toward the confrontation of the appropriative event of the beginning.
Poetizing is a becoming at home out of what is un-homelike.	Thinking is a becoming at home in the un-homelike. (in the inhabited place of the departure) Enduring of the difference.

If the poet and the thinker are essentially differentiated in this way, then the question still remains as to whence this differentiation is carried out and in respect to what essential belongingness of the things differentiated it can be ventured. Inasmuch as a "question" remains here and a venture appears, we already betray that this differentiating is ventured by thinking. Thus we do not stand over and against poetizing and thinking such that they would be two objects which could be considered from a standpoint outside of themselves.

Poetizing is interrogated and conceived here from the standpoint of thinking. What does that signify for the differentiation and for its truth? Is not poetizing thereby envisioned from its "most separated mountain," and is not this determination in thinking precisely a transformational thinking into the domain of the truth of thinking? Or does a concealed unity of poetizing and thinking come to light here, a unity that must be allowed its concealedness? And is not this allowing possible only in the venture of thinking?

Is not the experience (again only in thinking) of the concealment of this concealedness of the belongingness between poetizing and thinking and, in a still more concealed way, between the holy and the beginning, is not this experience, as extreme freedom, the liberation of this concealment into its pure essential occurrence, an essential occurrence that is without effect, without need of effectivity and causality, and without knowledge of all such things? How are we supposed to name it and say it?—Essential occurrence? Here is the pure interrogation of the unity of the ordinance of destiny and of the event of the beginning. Here is illuminated the homelike—un-homelike inhabited place of historical humanity in the "between" between being and beings. Here is revealed the concealed "essence" of that which thinking calls (extrinsically and thus only as a matter of empty "logic") "the differentiation" of being and beings and, in its questioning, questions again and again and to the exclusion of all else as the most question-worthy.

But if the history of beyng enters into this moment of thinking, then must not poetry now also poetize thinking and the thinker? Have this thinking and its thinker already been poetized? Is Hölderlin's "Empedocles-poetry" already this poetry? Or is what is poetized here still a transitional "between" and indeed a manifold "between"? The "between" between poetizing and thinking and thinking itself again as the unity between the previous and the forthcoming, and this historical "between" itself still in the form of the proper history of this poet in his transition from "Hyperion" to the hymnal poetry.

Is this poetry of the thinker and of thinking already outside the purview of metaphysical thought? If so, in what way? Does the differentiation of the essence of poetizing and thinking come to light poetically? Or does this differentiation disappear in a still-unexperienced and -unsayable concealed-articulated unity?

What do the various "stages" of the Empedocles-poetry say in this regard? Is poetically in motion here a poetic thinking?

Must not thinking also be a thoughtful poetizing at this transitional time of the history of the West? And is this then an effacing of the limits of poetizing and thinking, or is it in each case an essentially different, concealed passage through the domain of the concealed "unity" of the holy and beyng? And whence again this "unity"? Does everything again press out toward differentiations of formal differences?

Is not the foregoing differentiation of the essence (with respect to the history of beyng) of poetizing and thinking a mere antithetics and the temptation toward the "dialectics" of the relation of both? Or must we prescind from all such "thetics"? Have we not already prescinded, because here thinking derives from historical experience and itself stands in a confrontation—thus is in itself a matter of the history of beyng? Indeed.

Seen from the outside, however, there remains the appearance and possibility of a merely representational and intentional apprehension and thus of a "dialectical" sublation and arrangement. If it comes to that, and if only that is the aim, then the experience of thinking is absent and so is the obedience to poetry. Then everything is in advance detached from the concealment of the unity of both and from the destiny and event of this concealment as the appropriated ordinance of a consigned destiny, one we can experience in questioning the beginning and in being able to hear the naming of the holy. As long as we remain tempted to sidestep into dialectics and to amuse ourselves in the empty play of oppositions, we have still forgotten that a destiny is already ordained and that the event is already consigned. On account of this forgetting, we persist in the technology and historiology of the actual, and we know and sense history only as incidents. We are not familiar with the evening of historiality, and we do not surmise our assignment to the land of the evening. We are still European and still possess the European aspiration to the planetary. We still take poetizing and thinking as modes of "creativity" and as flashes of "brilliance" on the part of the "genius." We continue in representations of creativity and of the self-absorption of modern humanity in the age of the abandonment of beings by being. We persist in the anthropological outlook, and we concern ourselves with "culture" and with the saving of the "spiritual." We drag that which is of another origin into the arrangements of the contemporary technology of the world and of the subject; we do not hear the questioning and do not listen to the naming.

374. Poetizing and thinking in their relation to the word

The word belongs neither to poetizing nor to thinking; nor do they "possess" the word simply as a means to a fiefdom, as might be supposed in view of the identification of language and word. Language first arises from the word. But the word does not arise from poetry, or from thinking.

The difference between poetry and thinking is also not that the former is granted the imagistic word and the latter is compelled to imagelessness; or that the poetic word is sensuous and intuitional, the word of thinking conceptual. These are distinctions deriving from metaphysics and therefore are essentially unsuited for clarifying the essence of the word and the essence of the relation of poetizing and thinking to the word.

375. One thinker and another

The thinker already thinks in beyng the history of beyng. The scholar researches the historiology of (the opinions about) philosophy.

Only the thinker is able to think along with another thinker so as to find in the other the original thinking even of the already constituted thoughts which historiology can prove to have been "in" that other one (bestow, think in advance).

The thinker never desires to understand another thinker by way of confrontation, for the understanding of the other is thereby compelled instead of being allowed to remain question-worthy in order for that which is understood to open itself. Such a desire would lead the thinker astray into a mistaking of himself and of the other thinker and would keep barred the domain of thinking. Therefore the thoughtful confrontation with another thinker necessarily leads to an original emergence of what is thought in the other's thinking. Thereby the confrontation makes itself superfluous, in case it might subsequently be conceived as a "critique." A "critique" can aim only at the one who is thinking along with the other and can show thereby that the limits of the domain of thinking are maintained in a differentiated way.

The scholar in historiology proceeds differently. Such a one understands and desires to understand. And such a one does understand only when the other's thoughts can be explained on the basis of what has already been thought and what is understandable to the scholar and when everything can thereby be resolved into influences and dependencies. Here nothing remains left of a thinker but an opinion, and one must try and find a balance among the many historiologically acquired opinions or else have recourse to other makeshifts, such as the concepts of development and "relativity."

G. "Commentary" and "interpretation"

a. Thinking with respect to Hölderlin "Interpretation"

376. Hölderlin

Should all interpretation cease? Should the word of this poetry wait to be heard purely out of itself? But what does "out of itself" mean here?

And is the interpretationless apprehension and non-apprehension not interpretation?

Ability to hear and obedience. Poetry.

Heedfulness and submissiveness. Carefulness of thinking.

377. The interpretation of Hölderlin

Poetry—only from word to word and each word more essential than the other.

But certainly "informative"; on this path, however, we are never "finished"; how then are we to master all the other poets? Should we do so?

Or must we decide not to restrict ourselves only to that poet who requires such a procedure but, rather, to remove limits regarding what is unique?

378. "Interpretations" of "Hölderlin"

are immediately communicated as "explications" of poems and seem to be contributions to literary-historiological research. Because they stem from "philosophy," they might give the impression of being arbitrary, "constructive," unprofessional, and therefore also incompetent. Thus these "interpretations" are made to compete with "research," although such a competition is foreign to their sense.

They have unexpectedly fallen into ambiguity, from which they can be liberated only with difficulty.

For these interpretations are neither literary-historiological "explications" nor even "philosophical interpretations." Instead, they seek in Hölderlin's poetry a historical foothold which could occasion a preparation for an inventive thinking of the beginning. To be sure, therein is manifest a historical determination of Hölderlin's poetry, a determination of which we still know nothing, since the essence of this history is still concealed to us. In truth, Hölderlin serves for the interpretation of an attempt to think the inceptuality of the beginning. In this way is not poetry made subservient to thinking and "philosophically" abused?

*

Interpretation alienates and demands the renunciation of understandability.

"Explication" explains, makes understandable, and provides the reassurance of something acquired.

Whoever appraises interpretation according to the standards of explication lapses into nonsense and must dismiss all interpretation as madness. Yet such a judgment is always more genuine than the presumptuous one which concedes that an interpretation might contain a few valid observations. (Cf. transcribed excerpts from the "deliberations" on Hölderlin {in GA94–96}.)

379. Thinking about Hölderlin

The "interpretation," if calculated according to what ordinarily is supposed to be graspable "content," is not an interpretation [*Auslegung,* "laying out"]; but by the same token it is also not a swindle [*Hineinlegen,* "laying in," "taking in"]; for the swindle is here only the "erroneous" interpretation, which deserves renunciation. Such renunciation is superfluous, because this thinking about Hölderlin is in an *essential* sense "not" an interpretation. Instead it is a confrontation—this, however, taken again in the sense of the history of beyng and not as a squabble over correctness and incorrectness. Confrontation of historical exigencies in their historicality; therefore, confrontation [*Auseinander-setzung,* "setting in opposition"] also not merely a "setting" ["*Setzen*"] arranged by us. Instead, it is the obedience of a listening to the voice of beyng.

Confrontation as insertion [*Einsetzung*] into a dialogue.

380. The interpretation of Hölderlin within the other thinking

The "interpretation" is not a "historiological explication" claiming correctness and objectivity. Nor is it a timely revitalization of poetry.

If an easily misjudged comparison is allowed, the relation of the interpretative word to the poetic word may perhaps be set into an analogy with the relation of Hölderlin's word to the fragments of Pindar.

A proper word, i.e., a necessary word in what is coming, is here in dialogue with a proper word. Neither can be assimilated to the other. But in dialogue is expressed what neither the one poet nor the other could say. Both speak out of a saying which is not an asserting.

Therefore those who want to maintain "their own Hölderlin" and claim to possess perfectly the "correct" Hölderlin may remain tranquil. Likewise, those who merely "open" Hölderlin to our century as one poet among others should do so in their own way and should "concern" themselves further with the historiological objectification. Indeed one can even lament that here, in the thoughtful confrontation with Hölderlin's poetry, this poetry is misused and is made to conform to the aims of "a philosophy." Even this lament may be in its rights.

Besides all this, there nevertheless exists the possibility of a questioning which concerns neither the historiologically discussed poetry nor a currently pursued "philosophy," but which instead arises out of beyng itself and out of the history of beyng and which has its own necessity. In view of this necessity, there are no "considerations." Here an age can either neglect everything or else reconcile itself to an inceptual obedience. To this obedience, everything is exclusively a plight.

b. "Commentary" and "interpretation"

381. "Commentary"

can never amount to an interpretation. The latter follows the enduring in which the truth of the poetry opens up its own domain in order to harmonize with its essence within the structure of this domain. Only a poet or, on a separate path, a thinker can follow the enduring of poetry. Each must follow differently. The poet's interpretation is the poet's utterance of the enduring. The thinker's interpretation converses with the enduring and brings the enduring to language in a way proper to the interpretation.

Comments are merely appended. They can perhaps prepare the necessity of an interpretation. Yet they can never substitute for an interpretation and can never effect one. The comments are entirely dependent on the poem. What they themselves furnish is an expedient.

The interpretation is conferred only on those who dwell close to the poet on the most separated mountains. They are the "darlings" who bring themselves reciprocally into their essence and who remain in proximity only on account of such separation. The interpreters can follow.

Comments merely call attention to the opinions we ourselves have concerning the poetry. They can awaken heedfulness to the possibility that interpretations are necessary. What is otherwise called "explication" and "interpretation" is a commentary, provided the "explication" and "interpretation" succeed; if they fail, they care for the errant begging of mendicants.

382. Commentary and interpretation

Because comments are merely appended to the poem, they offer this advantage: they can easily be omitted at any time, to the singular credit of the poem itself.

The interpretation, on the contrary, is of another claim and remains possible and essential only as confrontation. The latter alone would accord thoughtfully with the poetical.

The thoughtful confrontation with the poet is of such a unique sort, however, that we face the risk of hastening on and forgetting what is needful. For, thinking, from which the confrontation originates and which it at the same time consummates, belongs to an experience foreign to our time.

A comment on these comments is necessary, so necessary that it even must be stressed despite the fact that it runs counter to the attitude of commenting and utterly counter to the opportunity for this basic distinction in essential knowledge. But it can all the more be separated from the poem. It is misunderstood if it diverts meditation from what is noted in the commentary and if it degrades the "poem" of the poet to an occasion for discussing "questions of method."

The comments on the poem have the single aim of arousing obedience to the poem and preparation for hearing the poem poetically from its own word.

If the impression arises that the comments foist a "philosophy" onto the poem or even "pull" a "philosophy" out of it, then the reader should leave them alone. One should adhere to the poem itself—indeed to the poem and not to one's opinions about it. Precisely because these are the reader's own opinions, they have no more justification than the presumed and feared philosophy of someone else. One should therefore let them both go and then attend to the perplexity which might arise.

383. Comments

Does it still need to be established at length that comments (ones which not only unpoetically but also a-poetically comment on every word of the poem separately) do not think to disturb the single consonance of the poem? Nor does the consonance, where it is perceived, allow itself to be disturbed. But the consonance could become even more perceptible in the dismissive forgetting of what has been commented, to which a precedent thinking through of the comments admittedly belongs. The self-sufficient ingathering of the poem could come more readily into a resounding in the incontestable consonance of its verses.

384. The comments

are appended to the poem from the outside. Therefore we can also take them away again with ease. Then the poem stands for itself alone in its own "space." We merely need to set aside, along with the comments, also our usual opinions about the poem, ones which have in the meantime perhaps become clearer. The comments can more readily call attention to these opinions than they can serve the poem itself. The comments seem to descend from unbridled arbitrariness. Indeed they have had in view one single thing out of all else that the poet says. To be sure, what is determinative for the comments, for their execution and for their "content," one that can never be grounded in the poetry, is a thinking which endeavors to remain obedient only to the voice of the concealed history of Western thought and its plight. If the comments were supposed to have the property of becoming immediately superfluous, then this would perhaps be a first sign of their possible "truth."

The *interpretation* is different in kind from such commentary. The path to the interpretation is broad. The law of the interpretation is determined by what is to be interpreted itself. The interpretation stems either from the poetizing dialogue or else originates in, and belongs to, the thoughtful confrontation with Hölderlin's poetry. Such a confrontation and its conditionality are even scarcer than that dialogue. But both would occur, if ever one of them occurs, only out of, and in a respectively different way out of, a proximity to the poetizing word. The proximity would be conferred only on those who, in relation to the poet, "dwell close by, on the most separated mountains" (Hölderlin, "Patmos").

385. Comments

The straightforward verses are laden with a content which may perhaps fill up a system of philosophy but which is nevertheless not supposed to deform the simplicity of these poetic words. Nor are the comments supposed to do so. But they might serve as an impetus for a return to the simple. Yet is it not simpler to take in a simple way that which is simple? Certainly; it is a basic delusion of the age of self-glorification, however, to believe that the simple has been conferred on it in a simple way. Nothing depends on the commentary, everything on the poem.

The comments on the poem "Remembrance" [*"Andenken"*] allow us to heed the thinking [*Denken*] which is poetized in this poem and which is itself a poetic thinking.

The question presses as to what then thinking is besides, and what thoughtful thinking is, and how the latter relates to poetizing. To consider these matters is necessary for us; the truth of the poem does not require it. Such a consideration, if attempted here, could attract attention away from the poem. And that must not be. It appears nevertheless that here poetizing and thinking draw near to each other, not to say even mix together. Yet this appearance could also be the impetus to interrogate the abyssal distinction between poetic thinking and purely thoughtful thinking, because with this question the entire foregoing meditation would gain a foothold allowing an approach to the domain in which poetizing and thinking must transpire in order to be essentially separate from each other.

386. The interpretation

is thoughtful confrontation. The confrontational interpretation of poetry requires violence and must overtake the word. But if the interpretation succeeds, then it makes concessions to the poetizing word. The interpretation says something else, something the sayer of the word has not experienced. Of course, it is erroneous to maintain that the sayers are thereby better understood than they understood themselves. For, "better" and "worse" are standards of scholarship. An interpretation, strictly taken, is a matter of "research." (We are using this word in a lax sense for any sort of gloss on poetry, including commentary. Interpretation, "strictly taken," is itself possible only as poetry.) Only a poet can interpret poetry, out of the same—i.e., poetic—vocation, which therefore is not the identical vocation. A thinker can also "interpret" poetry, out of an incomparably other vocation, one which is always compelled into extreme opposition with the poet and which therefore, however, indeed remains destined to the same out of the same.

Editor's Afterword

This is the sixth in the series of seven great treatises on the history of being to appear out of the literary remains of Martin Heidegger. The series was inaugurated by *Contributions to Philosophy (Of the Event)* (GA65). The current text bears the title *The Event* and appears as volume 71 of Heidegger's *Gesamtausgabe* ["Complete Edition"]. Between volumes 65 and 71 stand the already published treatises, *Besinnung* [*Meditation*] (GA66), *Die Überwindung der Metaphysik* [*The Overcoming of Metaphysics*] (GA67), *Die Geschichte des Seyns* [*The History of Beyng*] (GA69), and *Über den Anfang* [*On the Beginning*] (GA70). The seventh treatise, *Die Stege des Anfangs* [*The Paths of the Beginning*] (GA72), is the only one in the series not yet published.

All the treatises on the history of being, understood as the history of the event, do of course deal with the event. Yet only the herewith-published sixth treatise explicitly bears the title *The Event.* Its special rank is thereby indicated. As regards its inner structure, the text breaks down into eleven parts, or chapters, and 386 sections.

To prepare the text for publication, I had available Heidegger's manuscript of 682 handwritten pages, dated 1941–42, as well as two copies of the typewritten transcription produced by Fritz Heidegger. The handwritten sheets, as a rule in DIN A 5 [6×8-inch] format, bear in the upper right corner the internal pagination for those sections which comprise more than one sheet. The pagination is in arabic numbers or lowercase letters. Fritz Heidegger numbered his typescript by hand in the upper left corner. This numbering begins anew with each chapter. The entire typescript of 259 leaves also bears a running pagination in the upper right.

The handwritten table of contents specifies "The first beginning" as the initial chapter, after the "Forewords." Yet the folder that was supposed to hold the handwritten sheets of this chapter, and that is labeled as such, contains only a slip in Heidegger's writing: "the manuscript in Marburg for the lecture course w. s. 42/43. 'Parmenides and Heraclitus.' 24. Oct. 42." (The reference is to the lecture course published under the title *Parmenides* as GA54). Since the sheaf of the first chapter had not been replaced by the time the typed transcribing began, the typescript omits the first chapter and starts with the second, "The resonating," but does include the title of the first chapter in the table of contents. The manuscript of chapters 2–11 is stored in the Marbach files labeled B 14 and B 15, and the manuscript of the first chapter was eventually discovered and identified in slipcase C 25.

I had to begin by transcribing the 187 manuscript pages of the rediscovered first chapter, "The first beginning." Then I compared, word for word, Fritz Heidegger's typescript of chapters 2–11 with the manuscript. In so doing, I repaired a few omissions, silently corrected a number of misreadings, retained the stylistic peculiarities, resolved unusual abbreviations (especially ones relating to Heidegger's own manuscripts and writings), incorporated into the text Heidegger's handwritten supplements from the typescript, expanded the punctuation here and there, changed into italics the underlinings and interspacings (in the typescript), made the paragraphs correspond strictly to those in the manuscript, placed in footnotes Heidegger's references to his other manuscripts and writings, and expanded these references by indicating the relevant volumes of the *Gesamtausgabe*. At times, certain conceptual terms stand near the title of a section; these are Heidegger's brief indications of the content. A number of footnotes reproduce Heidegger's marginalia in the second copy of Fritz Heidegger's typescript and are marked as such. Heidegger's handwritten emendations of the wording of this second copy were directly incorporated into the final text.

I furnished the eleven chapters of the treatise with roman numerals and the 386 sections with arabic. Some chapters include subchapters, numbered with capitals A, B, C. In a few cases, these subchapters are further articulated into subdivisions a, b. In the manuscript, all the divisions and subdivisions are indicated by Heidegger's own inscriptions on the corresponding folders, so that his plan for the articulation of the entire treatise could be instituted with certainty.

On the basis of my transcription of the first chapter and Fritz Heidegger's typescript, supplemented and revised in the ways mentioned, I prepared a clean copy for printing.

The eleven chapters of the treatise *The Event* bear the following titles: I. "The first beginning," II. "The resonating," III. "The difference," IV. "The twisting free," V. "The event. The vocabulary of its essence," VI. "The event," VII. "The event and the human being," VIII. "Da-seyn," IX. "The other beginning," X. "Directives to the event," and XI. "The thinking of the history of beyng. Thinking and poetizing." The last of the six "Forewords," under the heading "In regard to *Contributions to Philosophy (Of the Event)*," names, from the temporally later standpoint of the present treatise, six respects according to which the approach of

Contributions seemed insufficient and which are taken into consideration in *The Event.* This "Foreword" shows that even now the further development of the thinking of the history of being is oriented toward *Contributions.* This corresponds to the preliminary remark in *Contributions,* according to which that treatise is supposed to serve "as the straightedge of a configuration" (p. 1). The textual center of the eleven chapters is chapter V, which unfolds the vocabulary for the eleven modes of the essential occurrence of the event in their relations and contexts: event, appropriation, expropriation, consignment, arrogation, adoption, properness, eventuation, appropriateness, dispropriation, and domain of what is proper. The manuscript of this prominent chapter consists of 25 numbered DIN A 4 [8×12-inch] sheets in landscape orientation. The running text is on the left, while the respective right side is employed for textual amplifications. In the course of his thinking in *The Event,* Heidegger also refers, repeatedly, to the other five treatises that stand temporally between *Contributions* and the text published herewith. As a result, readers and interpreters are invited to think through *The Event* out of its thematic connection with the preceding treatises and thereby also to observe the not unessential shifts in the meaning of numerous basic words.

*

I offer heartfelt thanks to the executor of his father's literary remains, Dr. Hermann Heidegger, and to his wife, Jutta Heidegger, for checking the prepared text against the manuscript and against Fritz Heidegger's typescript and, in addition, for the considerable role they played in the correction of the galleys and page proofs. A great help to me in the very extensive work of correction was Dr. Klaus Neugebauer, philosopher and Germanist, who already as a student in the 1970s was a proofreader for volumes 1, 2, 5, 9, 20, 25, and 39. I thank him cordially for his conscientious, precise, and expert collaboration. I owe deep gratitude to headmaster Detlev Heidegger for valuable help in resolving very difficult problems of deciphering. I sincerely thank the director of the manuscript division of the German literature archive at Marbach, Dr. Ulrich von Bülow, for making available excellent copies of Heidegger's handwritten text. I conclude my acknowledgments with special thanks to Dr. Paola-Ludovika Coriando (U. of Innsbruck) for dialogical accompaniment in the editorial labors of the present volume, 71, *The Event,* after she had edited the preceding volume, 70, *On the Beginning.*

F.-W. v. Herrmann
Freiburg
September 2009

German–English Glossary

das Abendland	West
der Abgrund	abyss
der Ab-grund	abyssal ground
die Ab-sage	gainsaying
der Abschied	departure
das Abständige	rigidity
die Ahnung	presentiment
die An-eignung	adoption
der Anfang	beginning
anfanghaft	inaugural
anfängerhaft	incipient
anfänglich	inceptual
die Angst	anxiety
das Anheben	commencement
der Anklang	resonance
die Anmerkung	comment
der Anspruch	claim
anstimmen	attune
die Anwesenheit	presence
die Anwesung	presencing
die Armut	indigence
der Aufgang	emergence
die Auseinandersetzung	confrontation
die Auslegung	interpretation
das Aussehen	outward look
der Ausspruch	adage
der Austrag	endurance
die Befindlichkeit	situatedness
der Beginn	start
die Bergung	sheltering
die Berückung	captivation

die Besinnung	meditation
das Bewahren	preservation
das Bleiben	continuance
das Danken	thanking
das Dasein	Dasein
das Daß	the "that it is"
die Differenz	difference
die Eigentlichkeit	properness
das Eigentum	domain of what is proper
die Eignung	eventuation
der Einfall	incursion
ein-genommen	intrigued
der Einklang	consonance
die Empfängnis	reception
die Entbergung	disconcealment
enteignen	dispropriate
das Ent-gründen	de-grounding
die Entrückung	transporting
die Entschwerung	disburdening
die Entwindung	disentanglement
das Er-denken	inventive thinking
das Ereignen	appropriation
das Ereignis	event
das Er-eignis	appropriating event
ereignishaft	event-related
die Er-eignung	appropriating eventuation
die Erfügung	structuration
das Erlebnis	lived experience
das Er-sagen	inventive saying
das Erschrecken	shock
die Er-stimmung	predisposition
die Existenz	existence
existenziell	existentiell
die Folgsamkeit	submissiveness
der Fortgang	advancement
der Fug	junction
die Fuge	conjuncture
das Fügen	ordaining
sich fügend	compliant
fügsam	pliant
die Fügung	dispensation
die Geeignetheit	appropriateness
das Gefüge	structure

das Gefügnis	articulation
die Gegenwendigkeit	counter-turning
der Geist	spirit
die Gelassenheit	detachment
das Geschehen	happenstance
das Geschicht	historiality
die Geschichte	history
geschichthaft	historial
geschichtlich	historical
die Geschichtlichkeit	historicality
das Geschick	destiny
das Geviert	fourfold
die Gewährung	bestowal
die Gewirktheit	effectivity
der Grund	ground
die Grund-erfahrnis	basic faring
die Grundfrage	basic question
die Grundstimmung	basic disposition
heimisch	homelike
die Historie	historiology
der Holzweg	timber trail
die Innigkeit	intimacy
inständig	steadfast
die Interpretation	explication
das Inzwischen	the in-between
die Irre	errancy
die Kehre	the turning
die Langmut	forbearance
die Leitfrage	guiding question
die Lenkung	steering
der letzte Gott	the last god
die Lichtung	the clearing
die Loslassung	releasement
die Machenschaft	machination
die Nähe	nearness
die Negativität	negativity
das Nichten	negation
die Nichtigkeit	nullity
das Nichts	nothingness
die Nichtung	denial
das Nicht-wesen	non-essence
die Not	plight
die Notlosigkeit	lack of a sense of plight

German	English
das Occidentale	Occidental
das Offene	open realm
die Ortschaft	inhabited place
das Planetarische	the planetary
die Reflexion	reflexion
die Rührung	compassion
der Schein	semblance
die Scheue	diffidence
das Schicken	sending
die Schickung	ordinance
der Schrecken	horror
der Schmerz	pain
das Sein	being
das Seiende	beings
ein Seiendes	a being
die Seiendheit	beingness
das Seiendste	the highest being
die Seinlosigkeit	beinglessness
die Seinsgeschichte	history of being
die Seinsvergessenheit	forgottenness of being
die Seinsverlassenheit	abandonment by being
die Seinsverlassenheit des Seienden	abandonment of beings by being
das Seyn	beyng
das Seyn (crossed out)	beyng (crossed out)
das Sich-einfügen	insertion
das Sich-fügen	integration
das Sich-nicht-fügen	non-compliance
die Sorge	care
der Spruch	dictum
die Spruchweisheit	maxim
der Sprung	leap
die Stiftung	founding
die Stimmung	disposition
der Streit	strife
die Subjektität	subjectity
die Technik	technology
die Temporalität	primordial temporality
die Übereignung	consignment
der Übergang	transition
die Überwindung	overcoming
die Umwendung	overturning
der Unfug	disjunction

das Ungeheure	uncanny
der Untergang	downgoing
die Unterscheidung	differentiation
der Unterschied	difference
die Unverbergung	unconcealment
die Unverborgenheit	unconcealedness
das Unwesen	distorted essence
das Verbringen	tarrying
die Ver-eignung	expropriation
die Verendung	demise
die Verfügung	disposal
das Vergehen	passing away
die Verneinung	negation
das Vernichten	nihilation
die Versagung	withholding
die Verschweigung	reticence
verstellen	dissemble
die Verwehrung	repudiation
die Verweigerung	refusal
die Verwindung	twisting free
die Verwüstung	devastation
der Verzicht	renunciation
der Vorbeigang	passing by
vorhanden	objectively present; present at hand
die Vorstellung	representation
die Wahrheit	truth
die Wahr-heit	trueness
das Welt-Gebirg	global mountain range
das Weltspiel	world-play
der Wille zum Willen	will to willing
der Wink	intimation
das Wesen	essence
die Wesung	essential occurrence
die Wonne	bliss
Worte	words
Wörter	vocables
die Zeitlichkeit	temporality
der Zeit-Spiel-Raum	temporal-spatial playing field
die Zu-eignung	arrogation
das Zurückgehen	going back
die Zuweisung	assignment
der Zwischenfall	episode

English–German Glossary

abandonment by being	die Seinsverlassenheit
abandonment of beings by being	die Seinsverlassenheit des Seienden
abyss	der Abgrund
abyssal ground	der Ab-grund
adage	der Ausspruch
adoption	die An-eignung
advancement	der Fortgang
anxiety	die Angst
appropriateness	die Geeignetheit
appropriating event	das Er-eignis
appropriating eventuation	die Er-eignung
appropriation	das Ereignen
arrogation	die Zu-eignung
articulation	das Gefügnis
assignment	die Zuweisung
attune	anstimmen
basic disposition	die Grundstimmung
basic question	die Grundfrage
basic faring	die Grund-erfahrnis
beginning	der Anfang
being	das Sein
a being	ein Seiendes
beinglessness	die Seinlosigkeit
beingness	die Seiendheit
beings	das Seiende
bestowal	die Gewährung
beyng	das Seyn
~~beyng~~	das ~~Seyn~~
bliss	die Wonne
captivation	die Berückung

care	die Sorge
claim	der Anspruch
the clearing	die Lichtung
commencement	das Anheben
comment	die Anmerkung
compassion	die Rührung
compliant	sich fügend
confrontation	die Auseinandersetzung
conjuncture	die Fuge
consignment	die Übereignung
consonance	der Einklang
continuance	das Bleiben
counter-turning	die Gegenwendigkeit
Dasein	das Dasein
de-grounding	das Ent-gründen
demise	die Verendung
denial	die Nichtung
departure	der Abschied
destiny	das Geschick
detachment	die Gelassenheit
devastation	die Verwüstung
dictum	der Spruch
difference	die Differenz; der Unterschied
differentiation	die Unterscheidung
diffidence	die Scheue
disburdening	die Entschwerung
disconcealment	die Entbergung
disentanglement	die Entwindung
disjunction	der Unfug
dispensation	die Fügung
disposal	die Verfügung
disposition	die Stimmung
dispropriate	enteignen
dissemble	verstellen
distorted essence	das Unwesen
domain of what is proper	das Eigentum
downgoing	der Untergang
effectivity	die Gewirktheit
emergence	der Aufgang
endurance	der Austrag
episode	der Zwischenfall
errancy	die Irre
essence	das Wesen

essential occurrence	die Wesung
event	das Ereignis
event-related	ereignishaft
eventuation	die Eignung
existence	die Existenz
existentiell	existenziell
explication	die Interpretation
expropriation	die Ver-eignung
forbearance	die Langmut
forgottenness of being	die Seinsvergessenheit
founding	die Stiftung
fourfold	das Geviert
gainsaying	die Ab-sage
global mountain range	das Welt-Gebirg
going back	das Zurückgehen
ground	der Grund
guiding question	die Leitfrage
happenstance	das Geschehen
the highest being	das Seiendste
historial	geschichthaft
historiality	das Geschicht
historical	geschichtlich
historicality	die Geschichtlichkeit
historiology	die Historie
history	die Geschichte
history of being	die Seinsgeschichte
homelike	heimisch
horror	der Schrecken
inaugural	anfanghaft
the in-between	das Inzwischen
inceptual	anfänglich
incipient	anfängerhaft
incursion	der Einfall
indigence	die Armut
inhabited place	die Ortschaft
insertion	das Sich-einfügen
integration	das Sich-fügen
interpretation	die Auslegung
intimacy	die Innigkeit
intimation	der Wink
intrigued	ein-genommen
inventive saying	das Er-sagen
inventive thinking	das Er-denken

junction	der Fug
lack of a sense of plight	die Notlosigkeit
the last god	der letzte Gott
leap	der Sprung
lived experience	das Erlebnis
machination	die Machenschaft
maxim	die Spruchweisheit
meditation	die Besinnung
nearness	die Nähe
negation	die Verneinung; das Nichten
negativity	die Negativität
nihilation	das Vernichten
non-compliance	das Sich-nicht-fügen
non-essence	das Nicht-wesen
nothingness	das Nichts
nullity	die Nichtigkeit
objectively present	vorhanden
Occidental	das Occidentale
open realm	das Offene
ordaining	das Fügen
ordinance	die Schickung
outward look	das Aussehen
overcoming	die Überwindung
overturning	die Umwendung
pain	der Schmerz
passing away	das Vergehen
passing by	der Vorbeigang
the planetary	das Planetarische
pliant	fügsam
plight	die Not
predisposition	die Er-stimmung
presence	die Anwesenheit
presencing	die Anwesung
present at hand	vorhanden
presentiment	die Ahnung
preservation	das Bewahren
properness	die Eigentlichkeit
reception	die Empfängnis
reflexion	die Reflexion
refusal	die Verweigerung
releasement	die Loslassung
renunciation	der Verzicht
representation	die Vorstellung

repudiation	die Verwehrung
resonance	der Anklang
reticence	die Verschweigung
rigidity	das Abständige
semblance	der Schein
sending	das Schicken
sheltering	die Bergung
shock	das Erschrecken
situatedness	die Befindlichkeit
spirit	der Geist
start	der Beginn
steadfast	inständig
steering	die Lenkung
strife	der Streit
structuration	die Erfügung
structure	das Gefüge
subjectity	die Subjektität
submissiveness	die Folgsamkeit
tarrying	das Verbringen
technology	die Technik
temporality	die Zeitlichkeit
temporality, primordial	die Temporalität
temporal-spatial playing field	der Zeit-Spiel-Raum
thanking	das Danken
the "that it is"	das Daß
timber trail	der Holzweg
transition	der Übergang
transporting	die Entrückung
trueness	die Wahr-heit
truth	die Wahrheit
the turning	die Kehre
twisting free	die Verwindung
uncanny	das Ungeheure
unconcealedness	die Unverborgenheit
unconcealment	die Unverbergung
vocables	Wörter
West	das Abendland
will to willing	der Wille zum Willen
withholding	die Versagung
words	Worte
world-play	das Weltspiel